# Reclaiming The City
## Mixed Use Development

Edited by
Andy Couplan
University of Westminst

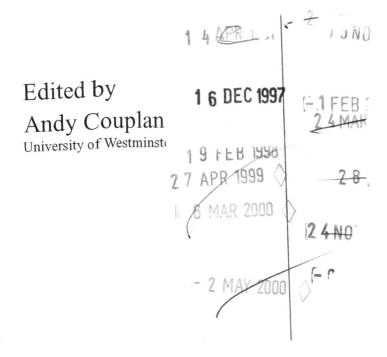

**E & FN SPON**
An Imprint of Chapman & Hall

London · Weinheim · New York · Tokyo · Melbourne · Madras

**Published by E & FN Spon, an imprint of Chapman & Hall, 2–6 Boundary Row, London SE1 8HN, UK**

Chapman & Hall, 2–6 Boundary Row, London SE1 8HN, UK

Chapman & Hall GmbH, Pappelallee 3, 69469 Weinheim, Germany

Chapman & Hall USA, 115 Fifth Avenue, New York, NY 10003, USA

Chapman & Hall Japan, ITP-Japan, Kyowa Building, 3F, 2-2-1 Hirakawacho, Chiyoda-ku, Tokyo 102, Japan

Chapman & Hall Australia, 102 Dodds Street, South Melbourne, Victoria 3205, Australia

Chapman & Hall India, R. Seshadri, 32 Second Main Road, CIT East, Madras 600 035, India

First edition 1997

Printed in Great Britain by the Alden Press, Osney Mead, Oxford

ISBN 0 419 21360 0

A catalogue record for this book is available from the British Library

Library of Congress Catalog Card Number: 96-70576

# Contents

# Contributors

The authors of *Reclaiming The City* are all involved in teaching and researching in the School of Urban Development and Planning in the University of Westminster, where the idea of research into mixed use development was first initiated in 1993.

**Andy Coupland** is a Senior Research Associate with the University of Westminster. He has worked as a planner, community researcher, journalist, consultant, and lecturer in London since qualifying as a town planner and teacher.

**Tony Lloyd-Jones** is a Senior Lecturer and researcher in the Urban Design Unit at the University of Westminster. He has a number of years' experience as a consultant architect, urban designer and urban planner both internationally and in the UK. He writes on a broad range of urban design issues.

**Robert Maitland** is a Principal Lecturer in Tourism and Planning, qualified in Environmental Planning and Economics as well as holding an MBA. He is course leader of the University's Tourism and Planning undergraduate programme, and wrote *Tourism and the Inner City* (HMSO, 1990). He has just completed writing a book, (with Rob Davidson), on planning and managing tourism destinations.

**Chris Marsh** is a Principal Lecturer at the University of Westminster. He is a member of both the RTPI and the RICS, and teaches both planning and estate management. He is completing a PhD on the topic of Planning Gain, an area of policy that he has specialised in for a number of years. His publications include the *Planning Gain Manual* (Planning Aid for London) and co-authoring *Public Art in Private Places*.

**Peter Newman** is a Senior Lecturer in Urban Planning. He has published extensively on urban politics and planning, and is joint author, (with Andy Thornley), of *Urban Planning in Europe* (Routledge, 1996). He is currently researching approaches to urban regeneration in London and the Ile-de-France.

**Geraldine Pettersson** has many years' first-hand experience of problem-solving crime and safety issues through involvement in research and implementation of targeted solutions, especially in inner city areas and town and city centres. She is an Associate Consultant with Crime Concern, the Home Office initiated national crime prevention agency.

**Marion Roberts** is a Senior Lecturer in Urban Design, and Course Leader on the BA in Urban Design. She qualified as an architect, completed a doctorate in 1986, and has published book chapters and journal articles. Her book, *Living in a Man-Made World* (Routledge) was published in 1991. She is on the Editorial Boards of the *Urban Design Quarterly* and the *Journal of Urban Design*. She is co-editing *Introducing Urban Design* with Clara Greed, to be published shortly by Longmans.

**Helen Walker** is a Principal Lecturer and Course Leader of the BA in Environmental Analysis and Policy. She is Director of the Environment Resource and Information Centre of the University, and has wide experience in local government, most recently working on green and environmental policy issues. She was awarded a doctorate in 1988, and her publications include a contribution to *Consumption, Identity and Style* (Routledge, 1990).

# Acknowledgements

Many people have helped in the preparation of the text of this book, and the research that backs it up. All of them are gratefully thanked, and without wishing to exclude any by identifying only a few, we should particularly like to thank the following:

Local authority planning department staff, notably Andy Haigh in Bradford, Bob Hawkes in Islington, Iain Painting at Westminster, Jo Ley at Hammersmith, Valerie Ruddlesden in Camden, Sue Taylor in Bristol, and Patrick Willcox in Tower Hamlets. Housing association staff, including Peter Hibbert at Network HA, Simon Sellens at Soho HA, and Brendan O'Sullivan at Peabody Housing Trust. Architects including Stephen Barnett, Charles Everard, David Levitt, and Richard McCormac. We must also thank Iain Tuckett of Coin Street Community Builders, Roland Stross at St James Securities, Alan Chatham at Argent (Brindleyplace), Stephen Mallen at Knight, Frank Rutley, Stuart Morley at Grimley J R Eve and Andrew Wilson and his colleagues at the Howard deWalden Estate. We gratefully acknowledge the cooperation of Michael Bach and Robert Chubb at the Department of the Environment, Meike von Zimmermann in Hanover, John Owen, Ben Frerichs, Dennis Meier and Nathan Tortelson in Seattle, Gillian Anabel and Claire Morse in Oxford, Alison Ewart and Jo Hillier from CHiCL for the hard work on the resident's surveys, and Geraldine Pettersson for the analysis of the findings. Many thanks to colleagues at the University, especially Robin Crompton for work on Berlin and Frances Reed for proof reading. Finally, thanks go to our long-suffering families, and to the publishers at Spon, who have put up with the slow gestation of this manuscript.

# Illustrations

All photographs are by Andy Coupland except those of Amsterdam (Tim Edmundson), Berlin (Robin Crompton), Glasgow (Nick Bailey), Hanover (Harald Koch), Oslo (Simon Coupland), Lille (Peter Newman), and Toronto (Alan Jago). All line drawings are by Tony Lloyd-Jones, except those supplied by the architects, which are individually credited in the appropriate caption. Many thanks to all concerned.

# Preface

For over twenty years, I have shopped at the Berwick Street market, in Soho. I don't consider myself particularly unobservant, but throughout this period I have never looked up to notice the block of flats that towers over the market stalls. We tend to view the street in relationship to the ground floor uses: its vitality, and the interaction with people in the street, affects how we feel there. But behind and above the streetfronts are a wide variety of other uses.

In much of London, and in many other towns and cities, there is a rich mix of uses. Commerce, industry, shopping and housing are located together as they have been for centuries. It is those places where there is an absence of this mix which are notable, and these are a relatively recent phenomenon. Concern to retain and enrich this mix of land uses is strong, and comes from a variety of sources.

On the property side, businesses are shrinking, fragmenting and modernising. While a few companies are growing, many more are now losing employees, although not necessarily business. Just as manufacturing industry has contracted, leaving thousands of unwanted factories, so too are white collar office companies. The stock of office property, much of it coming to the end of the second 25-year institutional lease cycle, is often older, larger, and increasingly unwanted. Owners and investors are therefore reviewing their property portfolio, seeking new uses and in turn changing the nature of areas of our cities which have become wholly commercial.

At the same time environmental concerns are crystalising into policies to encourage sustainable development and limit damage from the use of private transport. Increasing household creation [despite little population growth] is creating further pressure for new housing. It is generally accepted that this cannot all go into greenfield sites and new towns; much must go back into the cities, often in areas previously used for commerce or industry.

Equally, we now wish to prevent any further damage to the vitality and viability of our cities due to shopping and leisure uses going to car-dependent sites out-of-town. Policies now favour locating these back in the town and city centres, along with a new mix of uses to increase the opportunities for city centre residential development. For the first time in over a century reality has caught up with the game of Monopoly; there are hotels in Fleet Street and the Strand and houses in Park Lane.

(overleaf)
Berwick Street Market, Soho, London. A traditional street market, with a mix of uses, and a residential community.

# Chapter 1

# An Introduction to Mixed Use Development

*Reclaiming The City* is a book about mixed use development, and is mostly concerned with property development in cities. Mixed use development is a term that might at first sight seem obvious, but that is sometimes used in ways which are more confusing than helpful. Increasingly, mixing different land uses in the same geographical area is seen as a positive contribution to planning policy. It is hoped that by increasing the mix of land uses, and especially residential uses, residents will lead more 'sustainable' lifestyles, using their cars less. In addition, town and cities will become more attractive, viable and safer to live and work in. In effect, government policy is encouraging greater urbanization, and higher density cities.

The book examines some of the evidence to see whether this re-occupation of cities will have the desired effect. It introduces some new evidence that suggests that mixed use development may make a difference, and examines some of the wider factors that may nevertheless limit mixed use developments and so fail to deliver the significant changes that may be necessary to create more sustainable cities. This introductory chapter examines the background to the discussion about mixed use development and sets out the main points contained in the chapters that follow.

## The Mixed Use Jigsaw Puzzle

As we have already stated, this book is concerned with the mixing of different uses, including residential uses, in city centres. Mixed use development has become increasingly important in recent years. There are a number of reasons for this, some of them interrelated. Each explanation for the interest in creating more mixed use development is like a piece in a jigsaw puzzle. This book attempts to describe each of the pieces, and show how they fit together to create a complete picture of the mixed use debate.

In recent years development pressures have continued to concern politicians and the wider public. Although the population of the UK is hardly growing, for various reasons the number of households continues to increase, creating a need for housing in addition to the necessity to replace worn-out buildings. Concerns about sustainability and the need to reduce car use – or at least to stop it increasing – have led to calls to stop the expansion of urban areas. Development pressures on rural landscapes or areas of particular scientific importance have become increasingly contentious. These pressures have led to new proposals to increase urban densities and create new ways of getting more people living in existing centres. This debate has tended to focus on the concept of the 'compact city'. There are sharp disagreements between commentators about the value of this idea to UK planning practice, and Michael Breheny (Jenks *et al.*, 1996) has questioned the relevance of the debate at all, given the degree of continuing urban decentralization. There are further heated debates about the nature of the evidence on the value of higher density cities.

At the same time the shake-out in employment, which once decimated manufacturing industry, has started to affect service employment. The introduction and use of new technologies requires new types of office building, and perhaps in the future less space (with fewer staff). New technologies also allow businesses to relocate anywhere in the UK or even beyond. London Electricity, for example, are establishing their customer services department in Sunderland. The Prudential are establishing a new telephone-based bank, which will be located in Dudley in the West Midlands. In most cities older, 'secondary' office space is no longer needed; and may never be needed again. Other uses have to be found, as the economics of redevelopment (and the lack of demand for the space that would be created if redevelopment were to occur) means

*Figure 1.1*
60 Sloane Avenue, London. Conversion of the former Harrods depository into a mix of offices and retail uses in a predominantly residential part of Kensington.

that demolition is not a serious option. So throughout London, and in cities across the UK, former office buildings are considered for conversion to apartments, hotels or student halls of residence. And former industrial premises, and those once used for services supporting relocated industries, are also re-used in imaginative ways.

A further piece in the mixed use puzzle is the wish to sutain and improve town and city centres. Partly driven by the concern about increasing car use, government has acted to prevent many new proposals for out-of-town shopping (rather too late, in the view of some commentators). Instead, efforts are being concentrated on improving the vitality and viability of town and city centres. Similarly there are concerns about the quality of the places that are being created: the liveliness; the level of activity throughout the day; the design of individual buildings and the urban design context in which they exist. Mixed uses offer an opportunity to change aspects of this liveliness and design. A linked worry is about safety and crime levels; again, by mixing uses and having greater activity and therefore observation within an area it is thought that crime – or the likelihood of certain crimes taking place – can be limited.

The government has recently explained the basis on which they increasingly support mixed use development in planning policy statements. This is illustrated by the diagram below (DoE, 1995a):

```
        Concentration and diversity of activities
                 |                        |
            Vitality              Less need to travel
                 |                        |
   A more secure environment    Less reliance on the car
                 |                        |
        More attractive and      More use of and opportunity
   better quality town centres      for public transport
                 |                        |
        Economic, social and environmental benefits
```

The Secretary of State for the Environment, John Gummer, has outlined this approach in a number of speeches. It has developed throughout 1995, and is reflected in the changing Government policy statements. One of the more detailed explanations was made at a conference in Manchester in July 1995 (DoE, 1995b):

> The emerging consensus is that development is more sustainable if it produces a mixture of uses. Segregation of land uses, encouraged in the past, is not relevant now. The trend back to mixed usage brings a number of potential benefits. It ensures vitality through activity and diversity. It makes areas safer. It also reduces the need to travel, making people less reliant on cars, bringing welcome environmental benefits.

Diversity of uses adds to the vitality and interest of town centres. Different, but complementary uses, during the day and in the evening, can reinforce each other, making town centres more attractive to residents, businesses, shoppers and visitors. That is why my draft revised PPG6 promotes mixed use development.

Mixed use development should increasingly become the norm rather than the exception. It will be a gradual process of raising awareness amongst developers and investors of the benefits which can be realised.

We will be expecting developers to think imaginatively in future as to how proposals can incorporate mixed land uses, to produce lively and successful developments over both the short and long term, and provide a positive contribution to the quality of our towns and cities.

This book examines many of these claims. While the overall views put forward by the Secretary of State seem persuasive, there are indications that some parts of the argument may be based more on hope than reality. The discussions about the topic can be summarized in the diagram below.

## Why Mixed Uses?

| ADVANTAGES | DISADVANTAGES |
|---|---|
| **Definite** | **Definite** |
| Attractiveness and vitality – diversity; up to 24 hour city | Harder to dispose of property asset quickly |
| Uses unwanted or obsolete property, including listed buildings | Requires active management of property |
| Range of uses means greater likelihood of some parts letting | Therefore harder to raise finance and may put some possible tenants off |
| **Possible** | **Possible** |
| Reduction in travel (shorter trips, more multi-function) so reduced emissions; | Lower rents achieved |
| sustainability | Problems of separate access needed for each use |
| Reduction in crime; more activity; greater uses; observation of street | Conflict between activities; noise, traffic etc (e.g. housing over wine bar) |

While some of the advantages of mixed use can be accepted as absolute, others may or may not be true in certain circumstances. And there are undoubtedly certain perceived disadvantages of mixed use development that are overlooked by the government's statements, and which may well be the deciding factors in the decisions taken by development companies or investors. Some of these are illustrated in the case studies and examples that are included in the following chapters.

Clearly there are very good reasons that can be advanced for the development of mixed use schemes and areas, and these are examined in the book. It is also worth noting that there are distinct advantages for the government in adopting this approach as the basis for policy. The policy has no financial consequences for the government; no additional public expenditure is needed. However, the property industry may well incur greater development costs in building mixed use schemes.

In addition, by attacking obsolete local authority zoning (which is almost non-existent, and reflects an approach abandoned by local authorities since the late 1960s) there is a perception of pushing down barriers that many in the property market believe still to exist. 'Planner bashing' has been a favoured approach to excuse failures of the market for many years: for example, Michael Heseltine made a statement in 1979 about jobs being locked away in planners' filing cabinets to justify speeding up the development control system. This might be seen as merely a development of that approach (Thornley, 1991).

## Definitions: Mixed Use and Mixing Uses

The terms 'mixed use' or 'mixed use development' are widely used, but seldom defined. Without definition, considerable confusion can be generated, mainly because the issue of scale can be crucial. Recent debates over planning policies designed to create a greater mix of uses show why this can be important.

Some planning authorities have adopted policies that have a size threshold; schemes over (for example) 300 m² must include a mix of uses. Others have been less prescriptive, concentrating on encouraging a mix of uses within an area. For the potential developer these differences of definition can be crucial; do they have to provide a couple of retail units on the ground floor of an office building? Would a development of flats on an adjacent site next to an office development meet the planners' requirements?

These are therefore more than merely academic questions, and it is possible to illustrate the range of ways that 'mixed use development' can be interpreted. In some parts of the USA for example, mixed use implies a mix of commercial and residential. Offices over shops would not fit the bill; they are both commercial uses.

Again, in the USA, the Urban Land Institute takes an even harder line; mixed use developments (MXDs) must have three or more significant revenue-producing uses, with significant physical and functional integration (including uninterrupted pedestrian connections), and be developed in conformance with a coherent plan. Everything else that has a mix of uses is downgraded to a 'multiuse project' (Urban Land Institute, 1987). Yet even with this apparently limiting definition, hundreds of large-scale planned mixed use development projects exist in city centres across North America.

Confusions can arise over the use of the term 'mixed development'. In the context of housing, the term 'mixed development' often turns out to refer to a mix of houses and flats. In another housing context the same term is used to refer to a mix of private for sale and rented accommodation. In other contexts it has been used in relation to a mix of public and private development. None of these necessarily involves any mix of uses.

Confusion also clearly exists in the minds of some chartered surveyors. A recent journal article on mixed use development included a photograph of Milton Keynes, captioned 'Milton Keynes demonstrates the advantages of well-planned mixed-use development' (Mills, 1994). Yet according to the planning department in Milton Keynes there are no mixed use policies for the city, and almost no mixed use developments. This confusion illustrates the importance of establishing terms and definitions; putting housing and industry side by side is not the same as mixing uses in an integrated and symbiotic manner.

The scale of development is also an issue of some importance. How much of a mix of uses is necessary before a scheme is truly 'mixed

*Figure 1.2*
'Byzantium', Amsterdam, The Netherlands.
An unusual example of a mixed use building designed by Rem Koolhaas in the late 1980s with offices and flats in adjacent sections of the same building, with retailing and restaurants underneath.

use'? The US definition requires 'significant revenue-producing uses'; in Berlin at least 20% of the gross space should be devoted to residential use in a commercial scheme; in the UK the situation is often far less clear cut. A recent book listing development projects includes (among many others) Canary Wharf as a mixed use development, owing to its retail element (Powell, 1993). The total area of non-office space is much less than 10%, and the retail space is ancillary to the office use, needed to provide services for the office staff. How valid therefore is the description of this project as 'mixed use'? In another context reference is often made to 'mixed use' business parks where the development envelope may be 100 ha and may feature a range of uses. These uses can be entirely unrelated, and on discrete areas of a landscaped campus. Effectively they are a number of separate developments which happen to be being pursued by one developer (Mills, 1994). A book published in 1993 titled 'The best in mixed-use development design' is in practice purely concerned with business parks, some of which have no uses other than commercial space (Phillips, 1993).

Throughout this book we shall be concerned both with buildings with a mix of uses within them, and with schemes, sites or continuous street frontages with different uses. Generally (unless we make it clear) we shall not be referring to very large developments, nor those where there is one particularly significant use and a token volume of another use.

## The Geography of Cities

The size and spacial arrangements of most British cities are different from those in either Western Europe or North America. London must be excluded from the picture; it is vastly bigger than any other UK city with around seven million residents. With the singular exception of the City of London, which has a tiny residential population (c.5 000) and a vast area of commercial office space, the rest of Central London has a very mixed character; residential accommodation can be found throughout the whole of the area, both owner occupied and rented; privately owned or managed by housing associations and local authorities.

Outside London the population of the largest English city is in the order of a million (Birmingham) and then the size falls to around 500 000 or less in Sheffield, Liverpool, Leeds and Manchester. In Scotland, Glasgow has a population of around 700 000. Below this Bristol has a population of around 400 000, Coventry 320 000 and then Leicester, Bradford, Nottingham, Hull, Stoke on Trent and Wolverhampton have population figures that descend from 280 000 to 250 000.

The spacial arrangement of all these cities, Birmingham included, is for there to be a central business district, with a shopping centre of regional significance and commercial space occupied by a variety of local and national companies (some as regional headquarters with a few as national centres). In addition there are a range of artistic, cultural and leisure facilities as well as local, regional and some national government offices. This core area will be mixed in character; but this mix comprises the uses listed above; almost without exception it excludes residential uses. These can be found close to the city centres, in areas that are predominantly housing. Other uses will exist in conjunction with the housing: local shopping, churches, schools etc. Many of the cities have a significant area of industrial buildings between the city centre and the residential areas, and there may be some industrial premises within the older, more traditional turn-of-the-century residential areas that pre-date the more rigid segregation that was to follow. Many of these industrial areas are no longer in industrial use; these are the areas where significant regeneration has been undertaken in the 1980s and 1990s, and in these areas a much greater mix of activities is being provided, with a mix of new-build and re-use of important parts of the industrial heritage. This has led to thousands of new residents in the former warehousing area of Glasgow's city centre Merchant City area for example.

It is interesting that the residential density of cities does not seem to relate to the spacial arrangement. Birmingham, (4 444 people per km$^2$) has a similar overall density to London (4 182) and Munich (4 125). Paris, however, has a dramatically higher density (20 848) (Kivell, 1993).

During the 1960s different countries showed significant variation in the expansion in size of urban areas taken by a 1% increase in population, with France showing a 1% increase, the UK a 2.09% increase, the USA only 0.77%, and the Netherlands 0.69%.

*Figure 1.3*
Ihme Centrum, Hanover, Germany.
An early 1970s development near the city centre, of housing, offices and shops. Mixed used developments do not necessarily generate good architecture, wherever they are built. See the case study in Chapter 10.

In many ways US and Canadian cities follow a very similar pattern to UK cities (other than London). However, in some cities the residential area around the city 'downtown' has been significantly abandoned (e.g. Detroit). In other cities there have been more concerted attempts to introduce a residential component, often in the former industrial areas close to the city centre (Seattle, Toronto). These areas include significant residential elements. Other cities have seen no major loss of earlier residential areas (eg. Boston), and in New York residential conversion of office space is taking place in a similar way to London.

The pattern in many Western European cities is somewhat different. Many cities have populations in the millions. Germany's federal structure means that state capitals have significant government functions as well as local finance organizations of national significance. While in the UK all significant national functions are found in London (newspaper publishing, finance, national government), in Germany individual centres have particular characteristics. Hamburg, population c.2m, is the base for several national newspapers; Munich, which is a similar size, is the home to Porsche and BMW; Frankfurt, with a population under 700 000, has all the largest financial headquarters, while Bonn, which is smaller still, is the heart of government as well as being an important university city. The largest city is Berlin, with over 4 million people.

In these German cities, as in the Netherlands and France, the same functions of regional government, commerce, retailing and artistic and leisure functions can be identified that are found in UK cities. But the residential population is interspersed throughout the city in a similar way to London. Even the central areas of these cities have significant residential populations. These are 'real' long-term residents, not merely second home owners or company lettings which can be found in London. As a consequence, the basic facilities that these populations need are also still found in much greater concentrations than can be found in many UK cities.

In the UK, developers have often fought against the idea of mixing residential and commercial space. Issues arise about the need for separate access, the financial costs of a separate service core, the potential nuisance or noise problems. For example, a property adviser to the Cadogan Estate in Chelsea, while claiming that he supported the idea of mixed uses, wrote in the following terms;

> Mixed uses should *not* be contained within the same structure where this can be avoided and valuable investment resources used in a more profitable way. Particularly, residential accommodation on top of offices should be replaced by sensible financial negotiations locating the housing in an adjoining area (Sim, 1994)

While it is possible to identify a few large-scale mixed use British developments – the Barbican in the City of London, the Brindleyplace development in Birmingham – they are relatively few and far between. Yet things are seen as very different in other parts of Europe. In Berlin, significant developments are being undertaken by a range of developers. The plans require around 20% of the space in most city centre developments to be residential, and most of these projects allocate the residential space to the upper floors, over offices, which in turn are above retail and restaurant uses. This pattern of development is now the norm, and raises few questions from developers or apparent difficulties with potential funders. The case study on Berlin in Chapter 10 goes into greater detail.

While German practice is somewhat different from that in the UK, other European countries have a similar approach to the UK. In the Netherlands, for example, there are very few mixed use buildings, and where they do exist uses are segregated within the building structure. Planning policy there is much more concerned with accessibility of development for those who will need to use it, and with ensuring that sufficient facilities exist in new developments to avoid the need to travel to obtain basic services. The resulting developments are not so different from those large-scale schemes of redevelopment in the UK such as Brindleyplace in Birmingham or the regeneration undertaken in Leeds or Manchester.

## What Lies Behind the Concern for Mixed Uses?

As has already been noted, the effect of promoting mixed used development and higher density urban development would, if successful, put greater numbers of people in the cities. The European Community Green

*Figure 1.4*
Queen's Quay Terminal, Toronto, Canada.
A conversion and reconstruction by Olympia and York of the 1920s warehouse to offices with retailing below and apartments on the top storeys. See case study 1.1.

Paper explicitly supports this approach by promoting the concept of the 'compact city' (CEC, 1990). This is examined in greater depth in chapter 3 on sustainability. However, encouraging more urban residential occupation, whether in mixed used schemes or in mixed use areas, may not be straightforward.

The British often give confusing messages about their attitudes to cities. On the one hand, cities are still seen by many as the place where fortunes are made, and there continues to be an exodus from the countryside by those seeking to gain a wider range of experiences or opportunities for employment and leisure. On the other hand, most people aspire to live in the countryside – or, failing that, the suburbs. This is not in any way a recent phenomenon. Raymond Williams examined the way in which cities have continually been seen in literature as places of dirt, ugliness and evil compared with the positive pastoral description of the countryside. Here too attitudes are generally negative – the countryside is consistently recorded in literature as being a worse place to live than it had been years, decades or centuries earlier (Williams, 1973).

People in the UK state a preference in overwhelming numbers for living in the countryside. A survey carried out by the Henley Centre for Forecasting shows that only 3% of the population identified city or large town centres as their preferred residential location. On the other hand, 45% expressed a preference for a country village (Henley Centre, 1994). And a substantial proportion state a preference for owning their own property rather than renting – 75% or more, depending on the survey (at least, that was the proportion before the advent of significant 'negative equity'; evidence suggests that owner-occupation is a slightly less attractive option in the mid-1990s).

This apparent hostility – or at least ambivalence – to cities is not reflected in the views of residents of many other Western European countries. There is a much greater acceptance of and expectation of living in the great cities: Paris, Amsterdam, Prague, Berlin or Barcelona. Many who live in these cities happily occupy rented accommodation, either social housing with a degree of state support or subsidy, or from a private landlord. However, there is an increasing proportion of owner occupation in these cities too, as well as a steady flow of population to the suburbs.

In North America the flight from the cities to the suburbs has been even greater. Despite the attempts of planners to sustain them, the central areas of many cities have become almost deserted. Lewis Mumford described the suburbs as 'a collective attempt to lead a private life' (Mumford, 1938). Edmund Fowler (1992) explains how suburban development reflects the low-density aspirations of Americans and Canadians. Peter Hall offers a similar analysis; because population densities are low, the possibilities for fruitful human interaction are much reduced. Even the quality of material life, in the range of shopping goods and entertainments available, is impoverished and standardized (Hall, 1975).

Some views on the preference for suburban living are even more extreme. The architect Christopher Alexander cites a study in Vienna in

1956 (Alexander, 1972). The city planning department sampled 4000 people to find their housing preferences. Most preferred apartments to single-family houses because they wanted to be near the centre, where everything was happening. (These were of course Viennnese residents, who had already opted to be in Vienna, not the countryside.) A Viennese psychiatrist then gave the questionnaire to 100 neurotic patients in his clinic. A much higher proportion wanted to live in one-family houses; they sought, in Alexander's words, 'the suburban dream'. His main hypothesis is that:

> It is inevitable that urban concentrations create stress. Our first reaction to this urban stress is to move away from it; to turn our backs on it; to try to escape it. This is very natural. Yet the remedy is worse than the disease. The ills of urban life which are commonly attributed to density and stress, are in fact not produced by the original stress itself, but by our own actions in turning away from that stress. If urban society is to survive, we must overcome this over-reaction. If people do not expose themselves, if they do not dare to make themselves vulnerable, life will become more and more intolerable, and we shall see more and more of the signs of dissociation which are already far too evident.

These attitudes to housing affect an individual's willingness to live and work in a city. However, cities change over time, as do attitudes to living in cities that appear to have been changing in the past few decades. Some North American cities have been increasing their inner city residential population in the same way that British policy would hope to achieve. In Toronto a former warehouse was redeveloped (by the same developer who created Canary Wharf in London) into a mix of retailing, offices and apartments. In Seattle there are several successful inner city residential projects, particularly in the areas no longer required for industry. A similar situation can be found in the rapidly expanding city centre population in Vancouver, while in Manhattan millions of square feet of unwanted offices are being converted to apartments. This reflects a trend that can also be observed in the UK: there are changes in the way that property developers and funders view the value of development sites.

Recent changes to our cities and towns have been driven predominantly by technological development. The twin engines of this change are continuing economic growth and technical developments that ensure that new technologies continue to be developed. Those technologies – once considered sophisticated and expensive – become cheaper and more widely available. Continued growth also leads to greater choice; more people can choose where they work, where they shop, what they want to eat, where they live. They can also afford technology that influences these choices and their lifestyles: freezers, video players, caravans and ,most crucially, cars.

The continued increase in car ownership allows many more choices for car users in meeting their needs and preferences. The technologies and the car combine to allow people to choose to eat interesting (frozen

*Figure 1.5 (opposite)*
Waterfront Place, Seattle, Washington, USA.
Part of an early 1980s complex of offices, apartments and shops on the edge of the downtown office district. A typical US city centre mix of uses, with residential towers over commercial uses and garage parking. See case study 1.1.

or restaurant prepared) foreign food, with minimum preparation; to col-
lect a recent film release, then watch it at home; to phone for a freshly
prepared pizza to eat at home; to travel to see friends on the other side of
town, the next town, or 100 miles away without significant inconvenience. Yet this increased choice has had a negative impact on non-car
users (and on car users once they are out of their vehicle).

At one time – and not so long ago – a particular, but probably typical
village in rural Norfolk had a baker, a butcher, two grocers, a post office,
banks, a choice of pubs, a secondary school, a cinema and even a drapers.
Yet in size and population it was about the same as it is today. Cars were
relatively scarce, and the links to the two nearest towns, each about 6
miles away, were by bus. One of the towns was served until the mid
1960s by a railway.

Now there are three general shops, the post office, a bank open two
days a week, and just two pubs. The junior school remains, but the
secondary school has gone; all the specialist shops and services have
gradually closed as villagers transact more business elsewhere. They
travel there by car. Those without access to a car have much more limited
choices. The railway has gone. There are three buses a day to one town,
none to the other (except the school bus). There are no cinemas either in
the village or in either town; the nearest is 25 miles away, a 12-screen
multiplex on an edge-of-town retail park outside the nearest city. This
model holds true throughout the country. Indeed, it is true in much of
Western Europe, and can be found in an even more extreme form in
North America.

The response of the planning system to these developments, which
have taken place over the past few decades, is understandable but not
necessarily wholly beneficial. Cars were accommodated, with more and
wider roads and with bigger parking areas. New estates were designed,
which required the residents to use a car to obtain almost any service.
New settlements were designed, which were predicated on high car
ownership. Entire US cities developed wholly dependent on car use, in
such a way that alternatives (public transport, cycle or walking) were
almost impossible. At the same time the planning system was also trying
to tidy up and simplify patterns of land use. 'Inappropriate' uses were
removed; new areas of development were 'zoned' for single uses; the
development industry developed with distinct specialisms in building
just one type of structure. Housing developers built housing estates. Other
development companies built shopping centres, industrial estates or office
blocks. Single-use areas started to replace the confused mix of the
nineteenth-century industrial city.

Only very recently has it been realized that this is not necessarily all
good – how 'unsustainable' this could be. Now many city authorities
are trying to improve public transport, to encourage shared car pooling
or park-and-ride schemes, and to reduce or even remove city centre traffic.
As we shall see, policies are being developed to mix uses back together
so that residents can meet their needs and preferences without necessarily
having to rely on using the car.

## Attitudes to Mixed Use Developments

DeNeufville, (1981), points out that land policy defines the land use patterns that a society may seek; sprawling or compact; mixed or homogeneous; short or long distances between home and work; protection of ecologically fragile lands or unique scenic areas. However, in and of themselves these patterns have little meaning; they are means to other ends. This must be relevant to this study; mixed use in itself has little intrinsic significance – its importance is what it represents. This can be likened to the use of the term 'urban village'. Probably first used by Herbert J. Gans to describe community neighbourhoods within cities (Gans, 1968), and later by Tony Aldous in a similar vein in London (Aldous, 1980), it has now been taken up and used in a subtly different way for the purposes of promoting new development: in the USA to increase densities of existing urban communities, and in the UK to justify wholly new higher density settlements. Yet as David Sucher points out there is an apparent contradiction between the concepts of 'urban' and 'village'. It may be that the term is being used (almost subconsciously) to create the feeling of the perceived attractions of the rural village and the advantages of the city (Sucher, 1995).

There is a link to a related aspect of mixed use development that needs to be considered: the basic question of attitudes to and preferences for living in cities. In many ways this too is a contradiction; rural (or at least suburban) owner-occupied single-family dwellings are understood to be the preferred housing choice for most of the population (in the UK and the USA at least). The advantage of cities is the ease of access to a wide choice of employment, shopping, leisure and other facilities. However, cities have not been widely perceived as a good place to live.

Clearly, there are exceptions to this; there has been a steady and continuing shift of population from rural areas to cities, which then reversed for several decades as population moved back to suburban areas. The new housing recently sold in UK cities has proved popular. And some inner parts of many cities have always been very attractive and sought-after residential areas. London's inner city residential communities in Mayfair, Belgravia or the Barbican do not generally experience hardships usually understood as 'inner city' problems. In practice the areas of cities with the greatest concentration of problems are often on the outer fringes, not in the centre at all. The housing estates that are considered the worst are almost without exception the largest mono-use developments. One of the most frequent complaints about such housing areas (whether located in the city centres or in the outer parts of cities) is the lack of social, shopping or employment opportunities.

A further aspect of the attitudes to mixed use development relates to the nature of the residential accommodation that may be included in some schemes. These will usually be flats; although if they are in the private sector they will be called apartments, lofts, penthouses or condominiums. But in the USA – and probably in the UK too – 'single family housing is thought to be more conducive than apartments to attracting residents who will be responsible members of the community' (deNeufville, 1981).

However, changing patterns of household development and lifestyle choices may be playing a part in changing the potential for developing successful mixed use schemes. More single-person and single-parent households; greater numbers of students; more couples choosing to remain childless; earlier retirement ages and higher disposable incomes – all alter the pattern of housing occupation and the potential interest in occupying property in higher-density and mixed use locations.

## Changing Cities

Our research suggests that cities can attract significant numbers of residents. However, these will not be 'normal' communities; they will consist of specific groups of people. They will include students, single young professionals, childless couples, and those whose children have left home. They may well include significant numbers of 'part-time' residents. These may be individuals whose work requires them to move between several different places. They may be professional people whose family lives elsewhere in the country, in the suburbs, or in another country entirely. Many of these people will contribute significantly to the local economy, as they use local restaurants, leisure facilities and entertainment more than the average. However, their attachment to the area, their social networks and involvement will clearly be far less than in other areas. How much of a 'community' these areas represent is debatable.

For residents to consider long-term occupation of these areas would clearly take significant policy initiatives in areas other than town planning. Surveys suggest that crime is perceived to be a greater problem than is actually experienced. Government policy is currently evolving, with a range of initiatives including much greater use of CCTV, which may have an effect on the perceived safety of city centres. Education is clearly a significant issue, and the quality of schools which are located near higher-density mixed use areas must be improved sufficiently to alter attitudes to the appropriateness of such areas as places to raise a family. Planning policies on provision of public open space and general environmental quality would need more attention and resources.

Some residents of UK cities have little option but to stay in the centre. There are still housing areas in the inner city with serious housing problems. These have been addressed by various policy initiatives, most recently 'City Challenge' and the 'Single Regeneration Budget'. Some commentators have argued that these have had little effect to date. There are other policy initiatives aimed at improving towns and cities throughout Britain. The government is encouraging developers and councils to revitalize the centres of cities, limiting development of edge-of-town and out-of-town facilities, including shopping centres, leisure facilities (including multi-screen cinemas) and public facilities like hospitals. City centres are seen as having a future, and part of that future is widening the range of uses and mixing the types of development. The remainder of the book examines this process in greater detail.

# The Chapters:

## A History of Mixed Uses

This chapter examines the history of the development of British cities, and the way in which areas of mixed use have altered over time. Initially, it has been argued, cities came to exist, and grew, because of the benefits for communication (Berry, 1973). The scale of the city was limited by the technology available at the time – initially, walking.

Mixed uses were the order of the day, with the same living space used as a home, as a base for business (both manufacturing and/or retailing), and for many other uses too. Specialist buildings existed, but these were (for the most part) located cheek by jowl with the everyday activities that carried on continuously.

The rise in trade and commerce led to the creation of purpose-built office buildings, often among areas of housing. In the larger cities, as these areas grew rapidly, they displaced residential areas and became commercial business districts, mixed with a range of shops, pubs and other related services. In London though, as elsewhere, remarkably, throughout these centuries of sustained growth little change occurred to the city's boundaries. Instead, population density increased steadily until the mid nineteenth century.

The development of the railways led to a dramatic expansion of the city centres (Mumford, 1961). Before this the cities were limited by the need to move around on foot or by horse-drawn bus. The development of public health legislation in the nineteenth century and newly introduced town planning laws changed the way in which housing and industry was mixed. Across Europe and in the USA 'zoning' was developed –

*Figure 1.6*
Herbal Hill Gardens, Farringdon, London. The redevelopment of a site intended for offices, completed to framework level before the receivership of the developer. Now developed as flats over shops.

albeit less consciously in Britain. Here the removal of non-conforming uses (whether housing in industrial areas or industries from residential areas) led to single, or much simpler, patterns of land use.

The changes in manufacturing industry, which saw increasing specialization, led to greater travel between towns and a greater reliance on the private car, which, once purchased, also came to be relied on for shopping and leisure trips. By the 1950s, 1960s and into the 1970s 'slum' clearance continued, prompting the clearance of huge areas of Victorian housing and the creation of massive new areas of housing. These often omitted other uses, were isolated from industrial areas, and were frequently built with system-construction techniques with high-rise blocks as part of the development. Some of the cleared areas were used to increase industrial development, but many of the city centre sites

*Figure 1.7*
St John Street, Clerkenwell, London.
Conversion of industrial premises to residential uses on the city fringe.

were developed as huge enclosed shopping malls, often with multi-storey parking.

The commercial centres of cities, which were still expanding, also continued to spill into and displace surrounding residential areas. This was the era of 'comprehensive development areas' (CDAs) – both in the USA and in the UK. There were questions raised about the nature of these developments – particularly about their effect on vitality, safety and traditional community networks (Jacobs, 1961). More recent changes in attitude and policy are based on the realization of the environmental problems caused by car use, and the need to revitalize towns and cities. This has led to a new set of policies and advice to encourage mixed use development.

## Mixed Use Development as an agent of Sustainability

This new planning advice follows a series of important reports from the late 1980s. Helen Walker identifies these, and draws out the relevant material that relates to mixed use development. In practice, the debate on sustainability is one that has been based on limited evidence or research. Moreover, where that research has been carried out it has not always shown the results that policymakers would like.

More recent policy changes have been based on the increasing environmental concerns that arose in the 1970s, together with the issues of revitalizing the inner cities, which had experienced particular problems. The adoption of council planning policies and government statements (and even possible legislation) on mixed use development can be seen as a result of all these developments. The hope is that more mixed use areas and more residential development in cities will reduce the need for car use. Shorter journeys and more multipurpose trips would reduce car use, and so emissions. More city centre residents with access to good public transport would be willing to use this method of going to work or out in the evening, rather than using their car.

Work has been undertaken which shows that these hopes have only a small chance of being met. Increasing the density of existing centres may make these areas less attractive and therefore may increase commuting, often from greater distances (Breheny, 1992).

Mixed use development is thought to reduce the demand for car use. This is based on studies of density and transport use, which show a clear relationship in that people living in higher-density residential areas have a lower use of private cars.

However, studies show that, in general, car use (in terms of both journey length and frequency) is increasing (DoT, 1995). New research has been undertaken that for the first time looks at the car use associated with mixed use and centrally located residential development. This shows that city centre residents do use public transport more and their car less than the national average, or in comparison with residents in more suburban locations. However, it also shows that many of the new city centre developments are not occupied full time, with a significant proportion being for short-term rental, company homes or weekday *pieds à terre*.

## Cities, Tourism and Mixed Uses

Robert Maitland examines the way in which increasing tourism, art and cultural activity and conferences are changing cities, and how these changes relate to mixed use developments. The increased leisure activities of the population are creating a demand for facilities that are being located in cities. In many cases these are being included in mixed use schemes. And new city centre leisure uses may well include other uses within their developments. New planning policies (DoE, 1996) are increasingly encouraging these leisure projects to be located (as with retailing) in the centre of existing towns and cities.

The chapter examines the changing city economy and the role that cultural and leisure activities play in this change. It examines the various different types of tourist and leisure facilities and the buildings they occupy, and assesses how these types of development relate to area regeneration strategies and policies that seek to increase mixed use development.

Importantly, the chapter also examines the potential and actual problems that these new developments may bring. The future planning policies for mixed use will have to understand and build on the experience of developing more vibrant city centres. The chapter looks at a number of detailed examples of these attempts.

## Mixed Use Development and the Property Market

Chris Marsh examines the attitudes of property developers and funding agencies to mixed use development. While there remain significant parts of our towns and cities that are mixed in character, the property industry has for many years avoided creating buildings or even whole developments with more than one use. The chapter examines this traditional antipathy of investment institutions, looking at the reasons for these attitudes and explaining the structure of the property development industry, which reinforces these views.

The chapter includes a detailed look at the current state of the property development industry, and the current attitudes of agents, developers and funding institutions to mixed use development and to government and local authority policies designed to encourage a greater mix of uses. It looks at the prevailing circumstances that are leading to a greater diversity of land uses in areas where up to now a mono-culture has existed, and looks forward to possible future models of mixed use property development.

*Figure 1.8 (opposite)*
The Victoria Quarter, Leeds. A successful attempt to transform the heart of the shopping centre by glazing over a street to create comfortable year-round shopping facilities.

## Mixed Uses and Urban Design

Marion Roberts and Tony Lloyd-Jones examine the design issues that relate to mixed use development. There is no automatic relationship between mixed use development and a well-designed environment. The chapter examines the design issues that have to be addressed to create successful mixed use areas and good design.

It examines issues of scale and the crucial importance of accessibility, both within a development and through transport links within an area. The chapter examines many of the ideas presented by Jane Jacobs, and their continuing relevance to the current debate on mixed uses. It puts forward the critical importance of ground floor uses, and examines MacCormac's notion of internal and external transactions, helpful in assessing vitality of uses.

Through presenting a number of examples the chapter also assesses problems that can arise, including potential conflict between users, and the ways in which good design can address these successfully.

## Crime and Mixed Use Development

Geraldine Pettersson examines the link between built form and crime. She surveys the research and literature on the subject, and examines how mixed uses affect perceptions of safety as well as the actual level of crime. Other crime prevention policies are reviewed, including CCTV, and the relationship between these policies and attempts to revitalise city centres is explored.

She examines the crucial difference between actual levels of crime and perceptions of how safe an area is. She too examines the views of Jane Jacobs and their continuing relevance to the debate about making cities safer and more attractive places to live.

In addition to this the chapter examines the direct evidence from research into the experience of city centre residents in mixed use schemes. This research also examines perceptions of safe environments, and what initiatives could or should be taken to make cities safer places to live in, including the role of mixed use developments in meeting this aim.

## Local Policy and Mixed Uses

In this, and the following chapter, Andy Coupland outlines the changing government policy on mixed use development and the ways in which local authority planning departments are responding to these policy initiatives. Through examining a series of case studies and examples the chapters identify attempts to create a greater mix of uses in different towns and cities, and the problems which have been found in trying to implement policies to encourage such a mix.

The chapter also identifies examples of where mixed use developments have been unsuccessful; either because certain uses have failed to be developed in accordance with their original plans, or because different uses have not attracted occupants and have subsequently changed.

## Why Developers Build Mixed Use Schemes

This chapter links closely to the earlier one concerned with the views of the property market. It examines the motivation of different types of developer who have, despite the prevailing attitudes, created mixed use developments. It looks at the progress of a number of development projects in London and Glasgow, where mixed use schemes have been undertaken by commercial development companies. These have particularly featured older buildings in conservation areas, or where the buildings themselves are listed.

The chapter also examines London's Coin Street development, where a community-based development organization has undertaken a mixed use project on a prominent site in the centre of the Capital.

## Mixed Use and Exclusion in the International City

Peter Newman examines the larger-scale proposals and projects that have come forward in different European cities. In particular, he looks at the politics that are embedded in the decision-making process. The chapter identifies the particular nature of major new development projects and in particular the way in which these are segregated from the remainder of the city and the ways in which the mix of uses within such schemes relates to their surroundings.

*Figure 1.9*
Ilkley, West Yorkshire.
A development of flats over shops in a small market town; mixed uses are viewed favourably by some developers.

# References

Aldous, T. (1980) *The Illustrated London News Book of London Villages,* Secker & Warburg, London.

Alexander, C. (1972) The city as a mechanism for sustaining human contact, in *People and Buildings,* (ed. R. Gutman), Basic Books, New York.

Berry, B.J.L. (1973) *The Human Consequences of Urbanization,* St Martins Press, New York.

Breheny, M. (1992) *Sustainable Development and Urban Form,* Pion, London.

Commission of the European Communities (1990) *Green Paper on the Urban Environment,* European Community, Brussels.

deNeufville, J.I. (1981) *The Land Use Policy Debate in the United States,* Plenum Press, New York.

Department of the Environment (1995a) *PPG13: A Guide To Better Practice,* HMSO, London.

Department of the Environment (1995b) Putting quality back into town and city centres, (press release, 24 July) DoE, London.

Department of the Environment (1996) *PPG6,* HMSO, London.

Department of Transport (1995) *Transport Statistics Report; National Travel Survey 1992/94,* HMSO, London.

Fowler, E. (1992) *Building Cities That Work,* McGill Queens University Press, Toronto.

Gans, H.J. (1968) *People and Plans,* Basic Books, New York.

Hall, P. (1974) *Urban and Regional Planning,* Penguin Books, Harmondsworth.

Jacobs, J. (1961) *The Death and Life of Great American Cities,* Random House, New York.

Jenks, M., Burton, E, and Williams, K. (1996) *The Compact City,* E. & F.N. Spon, London.

Henley Centre for Forecasting (1994) *Local Futures 94: prospects for local markets after the rececession,* Henley Centre, London.

Kivell, P. (1993) *Land and The City*, Routledge, London.

McCue, G.M. and Ewald, W. (1970) *Creating The Human Environment,* University of Illinois Press, Chicago.

Mills, L. (1994) A mixed outlook, *Estates Gazette,* 19 November, 124-125.

Mumford, L. (1938) *The Culture of Cities,* Harcourt Brace Jovanovitch, Orlando, FL, (1970 edn).

Mumford, L. (1961) *The City in History,* Martin Secker and Warburg, London.

Powell, K. (1993) *World Cities; London,* Academy Editions, London

Sim, P. (1994) Mixed Use Development. *Journal of Planning & Environmental Law; Occasional Papers; Planning Icons: Myth and Practice,* pp. 53-60. Sweet and Maxwell, London.

Sucher, D. (1995) *City Comforts,* City Comforts Press, Seattle, WA.

Thornley, A. (1991) *Urban Planning under Thatcherism,* Routledge, London.

Urban Land Institute (1987) *Mixed-Use Development Handbook*, ULI, Washington DC.

Williams, R. (1973) *The Country and The City*, Chatto & Windus, London.

# Case Study 1.1

# Seattle and Toronto

This case study offers examples of mixed use developments in two North American cities, Seattle and Toronto.

### Waterfront Place, Seattle

Waterfront Place in Seattle (Washington, USA) illustrates many features of North American mixed use developments. It is on a scale almost never seen in the UK, and where that scale is found in a similar location (the equivalent might be the city centre of Birmingham or Leeds), then the mix of uses would never arise.

Seattle is a modern city, founded only in 1851, located on the western shoreline utilizing a natural deep-water harbour. The city centre downtown business district follows the steep hillside contour rising from the waterfront, with tiers of typical tower buildings on streets running northwest – south-east. Waterfront Place occupies six city blocks, and consists of a mix of 'historic' buildings and new construction (bearing in mind that Seattle has a relatively short history!) There are 194 apartments occupying 255 000 ft$^2$ on three of the six blocks, and in total some 500 000 ft$^2$ of offices. There is also 165 000ft$^2$ of retailing, a luxury hotel, and extensive parking for over 800 vehicles. The scheme commenced in 1979, and was completed in 1986.

The historic buildings on the site dated back to the turn of the century when the city grew rapidly, rebuilding after a devastating fire and benefiting from the gold rush of 1897. One of the buildings remained in use as a warehouse, although the waterfront had gradually moved further away (through landfill) by nearly 100 yards. Built in 1904, the National Building was cleaned and repaired and re-used as retailing with five floors of offices. The Arlington Building had been constructed in 1901 (originally as two structures) originally used as offices and as a hotel. This now houses 43 apartments. The Globe Building, also of 1901, was built as offices, but around 1920 was converted into a parking garage. Following restoration it is now a 54-bed hotel.

Among the new structures is the Watermark Tower (see Figure 1.5). This 20-storey structure includes 94 luxury condominiums on the upper floors with offices on five floors below and retailing on the ground floor. One of the two office towers (both of which include integral parking garages and ground floor retailing) includes three storeys of housing on the top floors. The developer hoped that some of the housing in the scheme would receive Urban Development Action Grant, a Federal financing scheme that allows expensive housing to be offered for rent at moderate levels. This was not approved, so all the housing had to be at market prices.

This required an additional eight floors on the Watermark Tower to make the scheme financially viable.

The fact that different uses were mixed in the same structure added costs; the 20 townhouses on the top of the Waterfront Place One office tower needed a separate lobby and elevator. However, this still proved both viable and successful. Other mixes of uses have also proved complementary; hotel services (which have to operate for 24 hours a day) can be offered to office tenants during non-business hours.

## Belltown, Seattle

The city's planning authority have been trying for a number of years to ensure that Seattle has a mix of uses throughout the city. The zoning ordinances that control development are very sophisticated documents with complex rules about permitted mixes of uses, designed to encourage residential uses throughout the city without becoming the sole use anywhere. As with many UK cities, industrial uses close to the city centre have been in decline, and plans encourage developers to create alternative uses on these sites. To the north-west of the downtown office district an area known as Belltown (or the Denny Re-grade) has seen a dramatic change from fishing-related industry to a highly desirable residential location. While

*Figure 1.10*
Belltown, Seattle, USA.
An example of a multi-storey structure of the 1980s, with 18 floors of flats above offices (and a roof garden) with ground floor retailing.

parts of the waterfront continue to operate as working wharves, inland sites are being developed like the downtown Waterfront Centre with residential towers over office blocks with retail and restaurant uses on the ground floors.

## Broadway Market, Seattle

Outside the city centre other areas are also seeing mixed use developments. Some are re-using historic buildings (such as schools) for retail,

*Figure 1.11*
Broadway Market, Seattle, USA.
The shopping centre and cinema on the main street.

residential and office use. Others are being encouraged into improving neighbourhoods like Broadway Market. Here, developers have created a lively three-storey shopping mall on the main street of a popular area just north of the University district. The lower floor is a large store, while the ground and first floors offer a variety of shops and food outlets. On top is a multi-screen cinema. The remainder of the development block has been completed as single-aspect housing constructed over a parking garage, which serves both the retailing and the apartments. The design and feel of the two faces of the same building could hardly be more different, yet each supports the other by creating a successful mix of uses, which do not interfere with each other in any way.

## Queens Quay Terminal, Toronto

First used as a warehouse in the mid 1920s, the building now known as Queen Quay Terminal was converted in the early 1980s. Developers Olympia and York took a building originally linked to a rail-head and partly used as a freezer store. Over a million square feet of space was utilized in Canada's first poured-concrete structure, recognized by the equivalent of listed building status. The terminal became redundant with the development of containerization in the 1960s, and became part of the 1970s revitalization

*Figure 1.12*
Broadway Market, Seattle, USA.
The housing at the back of the Broadway Market shopping centre,

of the lake-front area.

The development consists of 100 stores and cafes in 100 000 ft$^2$ of space on two levels. Six floors of offices were created over this of nearly 400 000 ft$^2$. Four new floors were built on top of that, to create 72 luxury apartments behind green-tinted glazed walls. These are arranged around a central courtyard with a 22 ft waterfall. Public facilities include a landscaped waterfront terrace and a 450-seat theatre for the Premiere Dance Company, partly funded by the developers.

*Figure 1.13*
Queen's Quay Terminal,
Toronto, Canada.
The 1920s warehouse
conversion seen from the
waterfront plaza.

# Chapter 2

# A History of Mixed Uses

## Andy Coupland

## Introduction

This chapter looks at the historical development of land uses, attempting to trace the changes in towns and cities: the ways they developed from having small-scale diverse and mixed land uses in the pre-industrial era to increasingly mono-functional and planned areas in the industrial period. It ends by setting the scene for the changes of policy in the post-industrial phase of urban development.

Towns and later cities developed in ways that saw a considerable mix of uses throughout the urban area. With certain exceptions, mixed uses were the norm, but from the later part of the nineteenth century onwards more land use specialization and segregation of uses developed. The reasons for this were complex and often interlinked. Some were related to concerns about the negative effect of industrial developments on the health of residents. Some of the reasons were concerned with the developing industrial technologies, while other explanations can be found in the greater scale of development needed by the expanding industries, and the greater specializations developing in different areas, and by different companies.

Until the 1960s the concerns of planners were often about zoning areas into single uses, removing non-conforming uses, and creating 'tidier' and more ordered patterns of land use. Questions about the effect of some of these policies on the vitality of areas, about the complexity of the different inter related aspects of social, economic and land use planning only started having any effect on policy from the 1970s. And only today are those concerns leading to policies that explicitly seek a greater mix of uses, as other chapters in this book explore.

## Roman Roots

Early people may well have occupied more organized settlements in Britain than was generally appreciated until a few years ago. The scale of bronze age mine workings in Wales, and the vast wooden lake platform in East Anglia, both dating back to 2000 BC, imply a highly organized society: a fact already suggested by the existence of monuments like

Stonehenge. However, little archaeological evidence exists to support the existence of towns or cities.

The Roman period almost certainly saw the introduction of the ideas of town planning to Britain; the Roman towns and cities were, like their transport network, highly efficient and far in advance of anything seen before in the country. The Romans brought a distinctive and developed style of town building. Initially, military concerns determined the design of the settlements. By AD50 they were establishing new settlements of a more permanent nature, founding London in the process. At the heart of the Roman town was the forum, a civic square, surrounded by colonnaded buildings used as shops, offices and meeting rooms. Public buildings included bath houses and, in larger towns, amphitheatres. Although streets were organized and planned, buildings of different scale and importance were mixed together with little sign of planning (Lloyd, 1984).

With the departure of the Roman presence the archaeological record suggests that the population abandoned most of the Roman infrastructure and continued to occupy a large number of smaller agriculturally based settlements. With the increasing Saxon influence, and elsewhere Viking conquests, defensible sites again became important. The evidence shows Roman walled cities like Winchester being re-occupied in the Saxon period, but with a completely new network of streets overlying the Roman grid (Platt, 1976). Many had a religious and administrative role, but trade between towns seems not to have been common, and most continued to have strong agricultural connections with the surrounding countryside. A similar pattern existed in other European countries during the ninth century (Pirenne, 1925).

## The Middle Ages

The physical arrangement of most towns and cities in the Middle Ages can be found in pre-industrial cities throughout the world. Defensibility was important, so a wall or rampart was built around the urban area. Within the town a central building or buildings was almost always found, reflecting the controlling power in the city: either a castle, a cathedral or both. As their influence lessened, other municipal buildings may have become important, particularly market buildings, often, as Sjoberg (1960) notes, next to or nearby the dominant religious structure.

During the twelfth and thirteenth centuries there was a dramatic increase in the number of towns, possibly encouraged by the newly arrived Norman lords. New towns were deliberately created, some having distinct planned grids of streets. Others grew from existing smaller settlements. While defence was an important consideration in the eleventh century, by the thirteenth century most newly established towns developed without the protection of a castle. Instead, location (particularly in relation to trade) became crucial; both crossroads of major roads and good port locations were important. Markets became a vital defining element of a town. In Suffolk 12 markets or fairs existed prior to 1100. Between 1100 and 1350 74 further markets were registered. Only another six were registered after 1350 (Platt, 1976). Many English market towns developed differently from Continental towns in that the market place was not necessarily a central 'plaza' or piazza. The markets were often along the street, which was sometimes wider to reflect this use (Lloyd, 1984).

As towns developed, so too did specialized activities, which the higher densities permitted. The archaeological evidence shows that, in Southampton, the twelfth century residents almost certainly kept animals and butchered them at home. By the thirteenth century they were eating a much wider range of different types of meat, suggesting the creation of a specialist trade of butcher. By this time they were also eating imported grapes, figs and walnuts.

Despite the dramatic increase in the number of towns, 95% of the population were rural, and this percentage was not to change for a further two centuries. The subsidy returns of 1520 show that an average country town in southern or central England had a population of 500 – 600. York had under 8 000 inhabitants; only London compared to the great continental cities with a population of 50 000 – and then only just; Paris had approaching 240 000 inhabitants by the end of the thirteenth century, while in 1339 Florence had around 90 000 (Mumford, 1938).

Residents of urban centres faced a greater threat to their health than did their rural counterparts. The concentration of population led to severe effects from the outbreaks of Black Death, which commenced in 1348, as well as the endemic diseases like tuberculosis and smallpox.

## Early Suburbs

Many larger towns developed suburbs, which, in general, seem to have been populous, but poor. The exact numbers are hard to determine, as the very poor paid no taxes, and so went unrecorded. Seventeen percent of Leicester taxpayers lived in the suburbs around 1270, but by 1524 45% lived there. However, none of the wealthy citizens lived there. This may not be universally true; in Warwick, the popularity of the extensive borough-owned suburban field system led the wealthiest residents to live in the suburbs during the fourteenth century, but by 1543 the nine wealthiest men in the town all lived in the centre, none in the suburbs (Platt, 1984).

From the late twelfth century, and probably before then, wealthier town residents were acquiring land in the countryside, joining the gentry. Throughout western Europe the gentry were country residents.

> The knights who were settled in the town or in the burg no longer had any reason for living there after the military importance of these old fortresses disappeared. There was a distinct tendency, at least in the north of Europe, to retire to the country and to leave the towns. Only in Italy and in the south of France did the nobles continue to have their residences in the town (Pirenne, 1925, p.163).

Wealthy families sought to become country gentry, and by the fourteenth century many had succeeded. Throughout the sixteenth century more and more town-related wealth was spent on acquiring country land and property (Clark, 1981). A similar practice (in reverse) can be observed for the rural gentry. By the mid sixteenth century the luxury trades that had developed in the towns attracted wealthy country gentlemen to buy town houses. Here they came to buy luxury goods, to patronize tailors or to get business correspondence written (Platt, 1976). Thus the wealthy – whether from town or country – often ended up with a home in each location,

In the towns themselves small specialized markets grew up where individual trades developed. Some were related to the need for resources; dyers occupied the area near the river in Winchester; fullers occupied riverside sites, for example, in Stratford, Kings Lynn and Alnwick.

## Mixed Use Buildings

The buildings reflected the mix of trade and home. In merchants' houses the ground floor 'shop' may have served as both sales space and production area (depending on the trade), with underground storage where necessary or appropriate and a kitchen at the back of the building, a large hall over the shop for communal family use, and various sleeping chambers arranged behind it. In some houses the arrangement stretched further back, and was built only two storeys high. In Coventry there are reconstructed fourteenth century weavers houses with a two-storey frontage, a hall the full height of the building behind this and then single-storey kitchen and workshops behind this again.

> Functions tended to be separated vertically, with retailing and craft activities on the ground floor, masters and their families living on the first and second storeys, and higher floors and attics being used to house apprentices and servants and to provide storage space that could be reached by hauling up goods on ropes and pulleys (Clout and Wood, 1986, p.20).

While individual properties contained a mixture of uses, similar crafts or activities often clustered together to form a 'generalized pattern of zoning by occupation'. Sjoberg explains why this arrangement developed:

> This localization of particular crafts and merchant activities in segregated quarters or streets is intimately linked to the society's technological base. The rudimentary transport and communications media demand some concentration if the market is to operate: in this way producers, middlemen retailers and customers alike can more readily interact (Sjoberg, 1960, p.101).

The way that land uses were mixed together can be seen very clearly at London Bridge. Building commenced in 1176, and the completed structure was over 900 ft, with 19 arches crossing the river. A chapel was constructed on top of the bridge. By 1358 there were 138 shops as well, most with living accommodation; the rent helping to support the upkeep of the bridge (Schofield, 1984).

## Early Zoning

By the end of the fifteenth century a re-arrangement was taking place. Butchers, fishmongers and tanners, all 'notorious offenders in matters of public hygiene' (Platt, 1976), were assigned to localities where their trade did least harm. Potters too were excluded (because of the fire risk associated with their craft – especially in towns with wooden and/or thatched buildings). Towns had a wide range of tradesmen, which made them self-sufficient in most necessary items, although trade took place between towns, in some cases over large distances. Trade also took place on an international basis; British woollen cloth was, for example, highly valued in Europe.

By 1600, in a growing economy, greater specialisms and larger industrial processes can be found. Some of this production took place in towns and cities, creating larger zones of industrial activity. Others, such as the development of the brick fields and furnaces, took place outside the towns but had a significant impact on the rebuilding of the towns themselves.

There was a 'new taste for privacy', which led partly to the rebuilding of much of the medieval structure, and to the subdivision of that which remained. Mumford argues that the withdrawal from the common eating hall started with the lords and ladies retiring to eat privately, noting that this was commented on by Langland in *Piers Plowman* in 1362 (Mumford, 1938).

Bricks were imported from Flanders in the fourteenth century, leading to a revival in brick-making, which had lapsed after the Roman withdrawal. By the sixteenth century brick chimneys and coal became more widely available, allowing heating in bedrooms, so the hall became less important. Brick and tile making were trades that were also kept out of the city centre; but as the cities expanded these facilities

*Figure 2.1*
Staple Inn, Holborn, London. Built in 1586, although much restored in 1866 and again in 1937. The only remaining sixteenth century domestic architecture in London of typical half-timbered construction.

remained in the centres of the new residential population. Forshaw and Bergstrom (1990) note that brick kilns were established in Smithfield, using the clay in the valley of the river Fleet. A brick kiln continued to stand beside St John's Gate in St John's Lane until 1829.

Professions started to separate their homes and work premises, although some – like lawyers and accountants – could continue to occupy a single building without any serious conflict.

## Changing Fortunes

Through the late sixteenth and early seventeenth centuries the fortunes of towns varied considerably. Some expanded; partly because of internal growth, but also because of immigration. Others declined, particularly those reliant on weaving, which was rapidly expanding as an activity (and in the quality of output) in outlying rural areas. A factor that affected the town population was the steady enclosure of the countryside, driving smallholders and labourers out, who headed for the nearest town.

London, however, saw exceptional growth. In part this was due to Royal support, which tended to favour the capital, with investment in docks leading to most of the foreign shipping trade using the city. Ports like Kings Lynn and Gloucester abandoned Continental trade and concentrated on coastal traffic. London was also the centre of fashion; trades based in London grew at the expense of regional centres. Luxury goods were imported through London and were bought by the wealthy few who controlled the other urban centres. But little of this wealth benefited the growth of those other centres directly, other than through house building.

Although disrupted by the effects of the Civil War, many towns developed in both size and prosperity during the seventeenth century. Some ports developed and thrived; others had either physical problems (e.g. silting up) or were located badly for the growing industrial production and trade. Many towns saw growing population, but no commensurate growth in employment, so faced mounting poverty and distress (as in Winchester, which by 1630 had been 'brought ... to its knees' (Clark, 1981). Other cities suffered too. The thriving economy of Coventry collapsed, the population in the early 16th century falling by perhaps 50%. Some towns grew in Elizabeth's reign through patronage and the development of education; particularly Oxford and Cambridge.

Smaller market towns seemed to prosper, many closely linked to increasing rural prosperity following agricultural reforms (which did little to benefit the rural poor, but much to increase the wealth of farmers, who then invested in neighbouring towns). The Reformation, and the loss of monasteries and hospitals, resulted in a disruption of many towns. Throughout the first half of the seventeenth century the whole of England faced a series of epidemics, plagues, famines and economic crises; not helped by factors such as the Thirty Years War, which reduced demand for cloth dramatically. The plagues affected the suburbs more than the wealthier (and healthier) central parts of cities (Clark, 1981).

The structure and physical arrangement of towns appears to have changed very little during these years, although many towns saw physical changes as a result of the Reformation and the Civil War. The town of Ashby-de-la-Zouch, for example, was severely damaged, as were many other towns in the centre of the country.

Most land uses in the towns were still as mixed as they had been in medieval times. Lloyd gives us a good idea in his description of the maltsters who lived in Ware in Hertfordshire, who processed barley to supply the London breweries. Their houses were between the High Street and the river:

> The merchants and maltsters would live on the upper floors of the houses fronting the street; the ground floors and attached outbuildings would be used as shops, offices and stores. Wheat or barley was brought through the passageways from the street; the barley might be processed in maltings behind; the grain or malt would be loaded into barges at the ends of the plots. To add domestic touches, there were, beside many of the loading places, gazebos or summer houses overlooking the river, where the merchants and their families could enjoy a little relaxation – since the rest of the plots were given over to business (Lloyd, 1984, pp.64–65).

From the mid seventeenth century onwards living conditions generally started to improve. Population growth slowed, and agricultural output picked up, in part thanks to the ending of the Civil War. Trade restarted, so certain ports grew dramatically (Bristol for example grew from 20 000 in the 1670s to 45 000 in the 1730s) (Clark, 1981). Populations continued to be affected by the plague, which killed tens of thousands in London, and many more in other towns and cities during the 1660s. The Great Fire of 1666 saw a restructuring of the City of London and a dramatic growth in the West End, which became a temporary refuge for many of those affected by the fire, and a permanent new home for some (Martin, 1961).

## New Industries

The highest growth continued to be associated with new industrial growth, as technological developments started to increase output. The centres that were to benefit from the Industrial Revolution actually started their phenomenal growth somewhat earlier; both Birmingham and Leeds grew from insignificant market towns of a few hundred population at the turn of the sixteenth century to between 7 000 and 8 000 people by 1700 (Clark and Slack, 1972).

Specializations developed in manufacturing processes. Northampton shoes, Witney woven blankets, Stockport hats, Coventry ribbons: all developed using improved or more intensive technology. These developing industries had a direct effect on the structures within the town.

Cooperation between town and countryside developed, replacing the previous rivalry. Leicester was a centre for stocking making, but an attempt by some freemen of the town to limit production to the town itself led to a petition signed by 2 000 poor people who worked in the trade both in town and in surrounding villages, opposing the idea. While much of the increased production was for home consumption, more was going abroad, especially to the colonies. In return a wide variety of overseas products and materials were coming in, creating growth of regional centres as shopping and distribution centres. Roads and waterways were improved as goods and people travelled further.

## Leisure and Towns

With the rising economic fortunes of the country, new towns were developed and existing centres expanded to meet the new demands for leisure. In particular, spa towns, (Cheltenham, Buxton, Tunbridge Wells and Bath for example), became popular for holidays and rest cures for the wealthy. The whole economy of some of these places rested on the new development. Bath grew from a town of 2 000 people before 1700 to over 30 000 by 1800. Martin (1961) notes that in the seventeenth century in both Bath and Buxton, while the resorts were known for the restorative powers of their water, other amusements were provided for the patients, 'including plays by London companies, and walking-galleries, the origin of the seaside promenade, at Buxton'.

Shopping became a way of spending leisure time, leading to areas of towns devoted to the pursuit of fashion. Every town had developed a shopping area based on the market place, but new towns developed specialist centres like the Pantiles in Tunbridge Wells. Goods were delivered to permanent shops rather than travelling round the country with their salesmen to markets and fairs. Main streets in towns and cities therefore tended to have a mix of both uses and building styles. Older properties, some dating back to the medieval period, might still exist, interspersed with more contemporary buildings, or at the very least more modern facades. Where commercial uses, shops or professional services, had developed in scale, they might replace all residential uses in particular buildings, while others might remain wholly as houses.

Throughout the eighteenth century 'Improvement Acts' saw provincial towns and cities clearing their worst areas and creating new civic centres. Street lighting was introduced. Public festivals and cultural spectacles were developed. These in turn led to a demand for public buildings; a civic core was developed in many towns and cities, with theatres, assembly rooms and libraries joining the coaching inns. These acted as a meeting place, the location for many collective activities like cock-fights and auctions, as well as providing accommodation for visitors.

Successful towns were extensively redeveloped. Where facilities were being built to attract the gentry (as in Newcastle and Litchfield), then new quarters of fine housing were created. However, not every town grew. Stafford, for example, stagnated in the late seventeenth century, unable to develop a specialist role. The number of market centres in England and Wales declined by as much as a fifth between 1640 and 1720, with some towns declining to the status of village (Clark, 1981).

## Eighteenth Century Growth

From the early eighteenth century the population of England and Wales rose steadily: from 5 million or so in 1700 (of whom 80% were still rural inhabitants) to around 7 million in the 1770s. Population growth then started to accelerate, and the highest birth rates occurred where buoyant industrial activity was found. As this tended to be more and more an urban phenomenon, a significant shift occurred, so that by the middle of the nineteenth century 54% of the population were urban dwellers, and the population had risen to around 18 million (Walvin, 1984). Part of the reason for the rapidly rising population was the improvements in farming; by 1795 the average weight of carcases sold at Smithfield market in London was double that in 1710 (Forshaw and Bergstrom, 1990).

This huge growth in the urban population took place almost entirely within the confines of existing development. Even in London, with a population by 1851 of 2.3 million, it was easy and quick to walk to the surrounding countryside. While there was a clear physical division between town and country, the proximity meant that there were continuing complex interrelationships between them.

Throughout this era of growth, the differences between towns became more important than ever. In the early eighteenth century most towns – about 500 or so – still had a population under 2 000. A few regional

*Figure 2.2*
Market place, Devizes, Wiltshire.
Early nineteenth century buildings in a medieval market place.

centres were larger: Norwich, Bristol, York, Exeter and Newcastle in particular. London was by now relatively vast in population terms – 20 times bigger than any other centre. By 1801 a dramatic change had occurred. Only Bristol and Norwich remained in the list of the ten largest towns; industrial towns and ports had blossomed, albeit from much smaller but well-established locations.

This change came from two directions: new technologies and growing demand in some towns and decline in traditional production in more traditional centres. The weaving industry illustrates this well, expanding in the new locations in Lancashire (the county population doubling between 1751 and 1801, and trebling between 1751 and 1821 to a million) and declining in traditional areas of rural production like East Anglia. The expanding industry meant that the city at the centre – in Lancashire, Manchester (and in connection with Yorkshire woollen production, Leeds) – developed as centres of finance and specialized trades to service the growth. Once improved communications networks – particularly the waterways – had been developed, the goods produced in these expanding cities were shipped through the rapidly growing ports: Liverpool and Hull for example, as well, of course, as London.

The 'gentry' – now expanded to include the increasingly wealthy middle classes – were still keen on the medical benefits associated with the spa towns. In addition they were persuaded of the medical benefits of sea water, so Brighton grew from 7 300 population in 1801 to 24 400 in 1821 (Walvin, 1984).

## The Growth of The Factory System

The main addition, in physical terms, to the mix of land uses found in the cities was the factory. However, it is important to note that its existence remained unusual, except in certain very particular industries and regions. These were, for the most part, the cities where the greatest population growth can be observed. The greatest growth was in textiles, especially in cotton cloth manufacturing. The importance of this trade cannot be understated; by 1830 50% of the nation's exports were cotton products; by 1841 83% of cotton workers were in factories; by 1851 more than 500 000 were employed in the industry (Walvin, 1984). The industry obviously involved the exploitation of the colonies and the use of the slaves and plantations to supply the raw materials. The technology to utilize the cotton developed rapidly, first using water power and then steam. In 1813 there were 2 400 power looms in England; by 1850 there were 224 000. These were spread throughout a huge number of small and medium-sized buildings. The average spinning firm employed 100 workers; weaving firms were slightly larger with a 108. The huge mills we still see today – New Lanark (where 1 500 were employed) or Saltaire – were exceptions.

Most key industries followed the transformation to larger-scale factory production: potteries, breweries, ship-building, metalworks, glass-making and chemical plants were developed. Other industries grew in size but stayed small in scale; the Midlands metalworkers continued to occupy small workshops, but there were more people producing locks, jewellery and screws. By the early nineteenth century the growth of industry was starting to replace residential activity. In Smithfield,

> smarter residential streets, such as Britton Street or Charterhouse Square, were no longer the height of fashion. Industry and commerce began to occupy many of the houses. Printing, publishing, clothing and meat processing all flourished in Smithfield; so did the precision and precious metal craft industries centred on Clerkenwell and Hatton Garden – watches and clocks, scientific instruments, jewellery, gilding and plating (Forshaw and Bergstrom, 1990, pp.71-73).

Not every industry followed this pattern. Lloyd notes how Coventry virtually missed the Industrial Revolution because the two major industries, silk ribbon-making and watch making were not easily mechanised. New equipment using steam power for ribbon weaving was developed in the 1850s, but weavers were reluctant to move from their independent workshops and into factories.

> The opposition was so strong that in the early 1860s rows of houses were built, with upper weaving lofts in the old tradition, but with machinery in each loft connected to a crankshaft driven by a steam engine at the end of the row (Lloyd, 1984, p.216).

## Industrial Growth

The industrial revolution and the use of water, steam and later electrical power created a change in the health and nuisance experienced in the cities. Industry started to require much more space, and to create dangerous conditions for the resident population living among the factories and mills.

The processes that allowed firstly iron smelting and later the refining of the metal date back to the eighteenth century. The development, by Cort in 1784, of a cheap and simple refining method allowed a vast increase in the amount of wrought iron, which in turn allowed iron to be used both in engineering and in construction, creating far bigger building complexes. These housed the equipment that was developed to produce goods far more efficiently and on a much greater scale.

Many industries, particularly those associated with cloth making, (spinning, weaving, and dyeing) had already developed to require huge buildings, well beyond the domestic scale. So too had breweries and other processes where economies of scale could be applied. Now these were able to expand further, using the new construction materials, and were joined by other industrial processes.

The rise in trade and commerce led to the creation of purpose-built office buildings, often among areas of housing. In the larger cities, as these areas grew rapidly, they displaced residential populations and ultimately became commercial business districts, in part mixed with a range of shops, pubs and other related services.

Here though, as elsewhere, remarkably, throughout these centuries of sustained growth little change occurred to the city's boundaries. Instead densities of population increased steadily until the mid nineteenth century, especially as the developing commerce removed large numbers of residents from the central parts of the cities, particularly London.

During the early nineteenth century the Prince Regent was carrying out his master-planning of large areas of what we know now as the West End. Nash designed Regent Street, with fashionable housing over colonnaded shops. (Lloyd, 1984).

| | City of London | Rest of London* | Total |
|---|---|---|---|
| 1700 | 208,000 | 367,000 | 575,000 |
| 1801 | 128,000 | 831,000 | 959,000 |
| 1851 | 128,000 | 2,235,000 | 2,363,000 |
| 1901 | 27,000 | 4,398,000 | 4,425,000 |

*Table 2.1*
London: Changing Population (London County Council boundary )
source: Clout and Wood 1986, p.17.

## New Transport

The development of the railways led to a dramatic expansion of the city centres. Before this the cities were limited by the need to move around on foot or by horse-drawn bus. Early photographs show the immense congestion of city centres that resulted.

> Early cities did not grow beyond walking distance or hearing distance. In the early Middle Ages to be within the sound of Bow Bells defined the limits of the City of London; and until other systems of mass communications were invented in the nineteenth century, these were among the effective limits to urban growth (Mumford, 1960).

Contemporary diaries record how thousands of residents welcomed Queen Victoria to the Mansion House to visit the Lord Mayor. In 50 years nearly all those residents' homes had gone. The railways allowed city workers to live much further away and 'commute' to work. Thousands of homes were cleared to allow the construction of the new engineering of the railways; 4 000 were lost for the construction of Holborn Viaduct in the mid 1850s (Forshaw and Bergstrom, 1990). In London, as in many other large cities, huge Victorian office complexes were erected.

Additionally, new bridges over the Thames allowed growth south of the river. Up to then a 3 mile – or one hour's walk – limit existed on the size of London. The railways, the creation of season tickets, and the development of the underground railway (1863) and rival omnibus and tram routes all saw an explosion of housing, along the railway lines and out into the countryside. The urbanization of Britain took place at a phenomenal rate. In 1801 the urban population of England and Wales was around 3 million; by 1911 it had reached over 36 million (Ward, 1994).

The greatest growth outside London took place in those towns – and groups of towns (or conurbations) – where industrial processes were developing. The scale of the change was vast. The *Manchester Guardian* of 17 November 1832 stated that 'the manufacturing system as it exists in Great Britain, and the inconceivably rapid increase of immense towns under it, are without previous parallel in the history of the world'.

The growth of the railways, themselves a product of the Industrial Revolution, as well as permitting people to move around the city more easily, also allowed goods to be moved around the country. The use of steel allowed bridges to carry the railways pretty much anywhere.

The growth associated with the railways was not even, or predictable. Towns like Shrewsbury and Durham stayed relatively unaltered; others, like Sheffield, Bradford and Luton, expanded dramatically (Lloyd, 1984). Bradford grew from around 21 000 in 1831 to 103 000 in 1851. In 1800 there were no towns outside London with a population over 100 000; by 1891 there were 23 (Briggs, 1963).

## City Centres

The creation of the sort of city centre we find today occurred in Victorian times. With the growth in population, and the move of population (along the rail routes), came the reconstruction of the city centres.

> By the end of the century the centres of large British cities were predominantly devoted to commerce, entertainment, local – and sometimes national – government and other activities we now associate with central areas (Lloyd, 1984 p.217).

In 1860 Birmingham Council decided to levy a penny rate to establish a central reference library, a museum and an art gallery (Briggs, 1963). In some parts of the cities new developments were removing the previous residential population. In the east end of London a 25 acre site with 1 500 houses, warehouses and a church was cleared in the 1820s to allow construction of the St Katharine Docks, close by the Tower of London (Greeves, 1980). In Leeds, during the Victorian era, the traditional main street, Briggait, became the shopping centre.

> The older buildings, usually both commercial and domestic, were replaced piecemeal by shops and other business premises, many of which extended also over the sites of slums which had accumulated in the courts behind (Lloyd, 1984, p.222).

Chadwick describes the Piccadilly area of Manchester in 1849, noting that it was at that time not the central location it was to become:

North of Piccadilly at this time is a great mixture: industry (including the very large Newton Street Cotton Mills near Stevenson Square), livery stables, chapels, public-houses, horse and carriage repositories and private dwellings. Most buildings are rather domestic in scale, save for the cotton mills, and many hotels line Piccadilly itself. South of here, towards Oxford Street, is another multiplicity of buildings in what is to become the predominantly warehouse area of Portland Street – great Renaissance palaces to replace the mixture of back-to-back and terraced housing, courtyards, public houses, schools, timber yards and mills.

The changes in this area of Manchester, north and south of Portland Street, are to be of great significance for the city: functionally, in the displacement of mixed uses, including manufacture, by warehouses and commerce; visually in that many of the city's finest nineteenth century buildings ... are to arise here. Over a century later, however, some domestic structures still remain (now used as offices), and the basic street pattern is unaltered (Chadwick, in Dyos and Wolff, 1973).

Also in Manchester, Love and Barton's Handbook of 1842 notes that:

within the last few years Moseley Street contained only private dwelling houses; it is now a street of warehouses. The increasing business of the town is rapidly converting all the principle dwelling houses, centrally situated, into mercantile establishments, and is driving most of the respectable inhabitants into the suburbs (Briggs, 1963, p.107).

Manchester had been the source of much survey and comment. Engels also described the structure of the city centre in the 1840s:

Manchester contains, at its heart, a rather extended commercial district, perhaps half a mile long and about as broad, and consisting almost wholly of offices and warehouses. Nearly the whole district is abandoned by dwellers, and is lonely and deserted at night; only watchmen and policemen traverse its narrow lanes with their dark lanterns. This district is cut through by certain main thoroughfares upon which the vast traffic concentrates, and in which the ground level is lined with brilliant shops. In these streets the upper floors are occupied, here and there, and there is a good deal of life upon them until late at night (Engels, 1845 in Carter and Lewis, 1990, p.21).

Areas wholly devoted to housing also grew up. Mumford notes that this was the period when the 'private house' came into existence: private from business. As Thompson points out, this suburban development and new found exclusivity had a specific gender aspect:

In a male-dominated society this was an essentially male view of the attractions of suburbia since it was the man who went out to work and then sought daily relief from the strains of business and the demands of relations with colleagues and strangers by escaping to the supposedly undemanding comforts of the family home, while his wife was left to make what she could out of day-long isolation in the cherished privacy and seclusion. The creation of an environment in which this division of middle-class male lives between a public world of work contracts and a private world of family life was what the rise of suburbia was all about (Thompson, 1982, p.9).

## Victorian Suburbs

Suburban development mostly consisted of housing. Thompson notes that the builders preferred to create larger homes for the middle classes, but cheaper terraced housing also grew up:

> in general ... on sites which developers and builders did not think sufficiently attractive to be eligible for anything of a better or more expensive grade, and those sites tended to be those nestling against some undesirable existing feature – a factory or workshop, a railway line or a previous piece of lower class development (Thompson, 1982, p.21).

David Thorns suggests that while the growth of industrial and warehousing buildings displaced population from the centres of Birmingham and Manchester, the railway was less influential in the creation of residential suburbs. Only one suburban line was opened in Manchester, in the 1840s, to Altringham (Thorns, 1973). Instead, the horse omnibus was the important form of public transport linking the new suburbs to the centre. In the northern suburbs of Leeds, Treen notes, the range of uses permitted and subsequently developed was very diverse. In the 1840s ironworks and worsted factories grew up, surrounded by housing, mostly back to back. Houses were built a few at a time: often for sale, sometimes as investments for rent (Treen, in Thompson, 1982).

## Slums

Frederick Engels surveyed the 'great towns' in 1845, and described the conditions of London, Dublin, Edinburgh, Liverpool and Manchester. His summary was that

> The dwellings of the workers are everywhere badly planned, badly built, and kept in the worst condition, badly ventilated, damp and unwholesome. The inhabitants are confined to the smallest possible space, and at least one family usually sleeps in each room. The interior arrangement of the dwellings is poverty-stricken in various degrees, down to the utter absence of even the most necessary furniture (Cherry, 1988, p.31).

In the poorer parts of cities, industry and housing developed side by side, often with appalling consequences for the residents. The rapid growth of the industrial areas led to conditions that would have been familiar to residents of early medieval towns. A Leeds doctor detailed evidence of overcrowding, and joined in demands for proper drainage, sewage disposal and street paving. Briggs notes that the cottage that paid the highest return was in Boot and Shoe yard, right in the heart of the city in Kirkgate, from where 75 cartloads of manure were removed in the days of the cholera (Briggs, 1963). Other commentators identified similar conditions throughout the country, notably Henry Mayhew and Charles Dickens, both as a journalist and as a novelist. All industrial cities, but notably Leeds, Bradford and Sheffield, were prone to smoke pollution:

> Factories were permitted to exist wherever the owner happened to have bought enough land to build on: 'free competition' alone determined location, without thought of the possibility of functional planning; and the jumbling together of industrial, commercial, and domestic functions went on steadily in industrial cities (Mumford, 1938, p.163).

Francis Jones, in a study of industrial towns in the nineteenth century, describes the mix of uses in the new areas of housing:

> The image of terraced streets as a uniform series of dwellings only, withdrawn from the main roads which provided shops and public buildings, does not conform to the reality. The block pattern of such housing shows a variety of other uses, particularly shops and public-houses at the corners, and chapels often placed in the run of the terrace (Jones, in Dyos, 1968).

## Health Legislation

The creation of local councils saw new developments to counter the worst health problems. The water supply companies were taken over by the local councils during the 1850s in Leeds and Bradford, among other cities. Building regulations were introduced during the same decade in Bradford. In Birmingham, despite a sharp increase in the death rate in preceding years, there was no agreement on running the water company until 1875, but it then coincided with the creation of the Council's Health Committee. The death rate dropped from 25.2 per thousand in 1871–75 to 20.7 per thousand for 1880–85.

The development of public health legislation led to significant clearance and redevelopment of the centre of cities. In 1875 the Artisans Dwellings Act allowed the compulsory purchase of insanitary areas, which once cleared could be replaced by new housing. In Birmingham the legislation was used comprehensively to buy 43 acres at a cost of over £1.3 million. Eight acres were used to create new streets to relieve central traffic problems, and Corporation Street was created between 1878 and 1882. Rather than create artisans' dwellings as the Act intended, commercial space of shops, offices and hotels was allowed to be built. The industrial areas of the cities continued to be a tightly developed mix of houses and factories. Lady Florence Bell, writing about Middlesbrough in 1907, notes how the necessity of living near the steel works meant that workers had to rent cottages in unattractive rows of little brown streets. 'It is a side issue for the workman whether he and his family are going to live under healthy conditions; the one absolute necessity is to be at work' (Briggs, 1963).

These observations were not only true for the inner parts of the cities; the suburbs too were developing similar problems. Michael Jahn notes that in Acton, developed from the mid 1850s onwards, there were serious problems in the area by the 1880s, caused by the laundries and slaughterhouses in an otherwise densely populated residential area:

> By 1881 it was reported to the council that nearly 1,200 pigs were being kept in the area. Numerous objections had been received over the maintenance of manure heaps and the boiling and crushing of bones (Jahl, in Thompson, 1982, p.108).

## Charles Booth

By the turn of the twentieth century the processes of industrialization and suburbanization had transformed many towns and cities. The concerns of those who were studying and working in urban areas were not just with the physical arrangements that resulted, but the effects of this on the people who lived there. Charles Booth, a businessman rather than an academic, nevertheless produced the most comprehensive study of poverty in Britain to that date. It is of particular value in considering mixed use, because he was as concerned with spatial structure as he was with social status. His studies principally concerned themselves with London.

His 17 volumes of work show how different functions had become identified with specific localities. He notes, for example, that the manufacture of silk hats concentrated in the Blackfriars Road, with 17 factories – half the total in London – in that district. He notes that particular trades grew up surrounding other manufacturing plants for reasons of efficiency. The detail in which he recorded activity gives a clear picture of the spread of economic activity, and throws up some surprises. The packing case industry, for example, was located in the City of London, close to the trade in the docks, but increasingly out of place as the banking and finance sectors developed.

Booth's report was published in 1902, but the research covered many years of study. He was therefore able to describe both the pattern of development and the change that was taking place. With specific exceptions in the West End, the centre of the city was by now occupied by the poorest people. Much of the new housing was in the areas served by the new tube and commuter rail services, in places like Walthamstow, Leyton, Hammersmith and Tooting. Booth observed this vast building activity as being due to increasing pressure on housing in the centre. This, he said, was due to four factors: the natural increase in the population; the excess of migration from rural areas and abroad; the demand for space other than for residential purposes; and the requirement for higher personal and official standards of living.

Booth documented all these different factors, as well as demand for other land uses. Massive engineering operations were under way in this period to bring the services up to date, particularly in terms of transport links. At the same time public health concerns were removing the worst areas of housing, often replacing them with the 'model dwellings', many built by philanthropic organizations. He describes this in relation to the east and west central areas of the city:

> the greatest change during the last ten years has been the displacement of dwelling houses by warehouses, the last to leave the more central parts being the poor or the inhabitants of the model dwellings ... the poor, displaced by demolition, having first tried to crowd the neighbouring streets and only partially succeeding, have been forced to go further afield (Booth, in Pfautz, 1967, p.97).

The spread of trade and industry into residential districts also affected the wealthier population.

> The rich and fashionable, who once dwelt in Soho and Bloomsbury, have left ... their places having been taken by business houses, offices, hotels and boarding houses ... Generally speaking, the poor have been driven out by demolition and by rebuilding for the middle classes, and the middle classes by the encroachment of business houses and the multiplication of boarding houses and hotels (Booth, in Pfautz, 1967, p.97).

Booth also studied the reasons why some of this movement was taking place voluntarily. The type of housing and the reputation of the area were mentioned, but the main reason to move to the suburbs:

> depends not so much on class or on amount of income – over a certain minimum – as on the constitution of the family. The father of young children finds it best to establish their home as far from the crowded parts of London as he can afford to travel to and from his work ... but later on, when employment is sought by the younger generation, or better opportunities of education for them, or of pleasure for all, the balance may turn in favour of more central quarters (Booth, in Pfautz, 1967, p.99).

Many areas of suburban growth were outside the contemporary boundary of London; Booth notes how this would have to change as London grew. He also notes the trend, even at this early date, for factories to move from the centre to the suburbs, where much more ground at much lower rents was available.

Booth's detailed descriptions of streets and their occupiers give us a very detailed account of the activity of the resident population. It also tells us how mixed many of the activities still were: in many ways indistinguishable from the medieval pattern of work. For example, in the 'Poverty Series' Booth describes the residents of Ginger Street, near Billingsgate. This is an area that now has no resident population, or industrial activity. In 1902, however, things were very different:

> No. 18. Rorke, smoker and hawker of haddocks, lives here. He smokes his fish at the back here as well as at No 16. He has a wife, and one

infant. The home, which might be comfortable, is miserable through drink...

No. 30 is occupied by David, a coal porter at docks. During the summer he was at night work. For some weeks past has been out of work. He has a wife and six children. The oldest girl has been in service, but is out of place. All the others are of school age, or under. The wife would be glad to do 'cleaning', if she could get to do it. They are very poor...

No. 32 is occupied by a blind man, a basket maker. He had a blind wife, who used to sing in the streets, taking one of the children with her. She was, not long since, run over by a cab and killed. The man succeeded in placing all his children in schools, and married again – another blind woman. His earnings are pretty good and he seems comfortable.

These detailed descriptions give a very clear idea of the mix of people and activities that could be found throughout London. Other descriptions are of streets with a mixture of shops, public houses, industrial premises and saw mills, all with resident families on the upper floors. Some of those people worked in the adjacent trades; others worked some distance away.

## New Ideas

A range of different initiatives can be identified that were developed as a response to these conditions. Along with the new municipal authorities' initiatives to improve public health, philanthropists like the American merchant Peabody started to build model housing developments to replace the slums. But, as Mumford records, they were forced to build higher buildings of up to six storeys in order to create sufficient space to make the projects viable and affordable to poorer workers. By the turn of the century the London County Council had decided to use their powers to build on a large scale on vacant land. Others sought even more radical alternative new forms of development.

Probably the most important was Ebenezer Howard. He based the form of his proposal on the company town, which created housing and social facilities around new employment. However, he saw advantages in having no single controlling employer. He also recognized the continued de-population of the countryside created an opportunity to offer an alternative location for work to the existing cities.

Town and country must be married, and out of this union will spring a new hope, a new life, a new civilization (Howard, 1898).

As Hall (1988), points out, it is important to separate Howard's ideas for cities of up to hundreds of thousands from the realized country towns at Letchworth and Welwyn. He was almost certainly influenced by the period when he was living in Chicago, when the first park suburbs were being developed. He must also have been impressed by Kropotkin's *Fields, Factories and Workshops*, also published in 1898.

The physical arrangement of Howard's ideal garden city was reliant on a comprehensive rail network. A circular rail loop enclosed a 1 000 acre city, with a population of around 32 000 living in houses arranged around a central park, with public and community services along a 420 ft wide 'Grand Avenue'. Industry was arranged alongside the outer rail loop. Around the loop was a permanent reserve of countryside: a green wall to protect the city and to allow local production of food.

In reality, Letchworth and later Welwyn were developed only partly in accord with these ideas. Areas were identified for housing, industry and a town centre with shops and other services. Although these were planned to be self-sustaining (indeed, 'sustainable') places, the garden cities were too conveniently located to London to avoid having a high proportion of workers commuting to the city. The changes in manufacturing industry, which saw increasing specialization and a tendency to more monopolistic production, led to greater travel between towns and a greater reliance on the private car, which, once purchased, also came to be relied on for shopping and leisure trips.

Howard's ideas were, as we shall see, hugely influential. They offered a planned vision of an alternative to the existing cities, and one which had been actually tried on the ground rather than merely written about. It offered a vision for some to try to emulate, and for others to reject. However, most development continued along the same lines for several decades.

The growth of city government with the development of both new authorities and new powers, led to greater intervention and the development of planning. By 1909 a new Act of Parliament allowed British local authorities to establish special areas called Town Planning Schemes. Plans were created for new areas of expansion such as Edgbaston outside Birmingham. Commerce had moved into residential areas near the city centre, causing the wealthier merchants to move to the new low-density suburb created by the Calthorpe family. By 1890 a villa suburb existed, but further pressure for new development led the Local Government Board to draw up plans for over 2 000 acres between the existing areas of Edgbaston, Harbourne and Quinton.

Peter Hall records an even larger project in London, between Ruislip and Northwood. Here 6 000 acres were planned, with areas of housing at densities of 12 per acre or less, roads, areas of open space, shops and factories (Hall, 1988). So cities were spreading into the surrounding countryside, encouraged to do so in a planned manner, but only really in terms of new residential areas. The centres of the cities continued to have a mix of uses, with commerce and industry expanding into the residential areas abandoned by the new suburban residents.

## Zoning

In the USA the first comprehensive zoning came to be created in New York in 1916, although as Hall notes it had been used (much as in

*Figure 2.3*
Peabody Trust Housing,
Mayfair, London.
An example of philanthropic
housing (with mixed uses) in
the West End of London,
built in the early 1900s.

medieval Britain) to control unwanted activities, such as Chinese
laundries in California from the 1880s. Los Angeles had land-use zoning
from 1909 (Hall, 1988). The relationship between planning and zoning
was, Hall notes, tortuous. The point of zoning was to protect investments
and sustain values; it kept the poor in their tenements and out of the
desirable new suburbs built along the new subway lines (Hall, 1988).
The earliest application of the new power was when it was used to relieve
congestion of traffic and land uses within the garment district of New
York (Kivell, 1993). It spread rapidly to be in use in all 48 states by
1946, and by 1968 every major city except Houston had adopted it.

## Between the Wars

After the First World War, development in Britain was slow to build up. Demobilization led to huge demand from new families, but little was built until 1924. By 1918, influenced by the ideas of Raymond Unwin, (who had published the pamphlet *Nothing Gained by Overcrowding!* in 1912) a Committee of Housing recommended that local authorities should build 500 000 houses in five years, mainly on the outskirts of cities at densities of no more than 12 to the acre (Hall, 1988). These were dormitories; the housing was related to basic local services, but the employment opportunities were in traditional locations reached by public transport. The housing was for sale, many in the popular new style of semi-detached houses, and for rent on large estates, both on the edge of the city and in the centre of the city in blocks of flats, usually four and five storeys high.

Between 1924 and 1929 over a million homes were completed. Mass production developed, as housebuilders became major businesses and as new construction techniques were developed, and the resulting housing estates (whether public or private) were single-use and increasingly large in scale.

It was argued that London's subsoil would not support high buildings, 'so the metropolis spread outwards into rows of neat little houses' (Montgomery, 1970, p.44). The residents of these houses often worked in office jobs in the city centres, while the residents in the centre found the new factories moving out to new locations. Tim Pharaoh points out that in London some of these newly developed suburbs were designed in a way we would accept as sustainable; 'Metroland' was designed around the newly expanded suburban rail network, and especially the surface-run parts of the Underground system. Local trips were taken on foot, or possibly by bus (Pharaoh, 1991).

> In the Birmingham 'outer ring' comparable development was going on at Longbridge, Solihull and other suburban districts. The council estates were being built almost entirely on the outskirts, and 70 percent of council tenants travelled over two miles to their work (Branson and Heinemann, 1973, p.83).

The major employers in the heavy industries, which had dominated the economy, were slow to pick up once the war was over. By 1930, when unemployment in Britain was over 2 million, over a half were in Lancashire, Yorkshire, Staffordshire and Durham. Instead of the older heavy industries new science-based manufacturing was developing. Electrical goods, radios, aluminium, cars and other forms of road transport all expanded. These often occupied new buildings designed in art deco forms along the newly expanded orbital routes on the edges of cities. Industrial estates were developed in new locations like Slough; massive new manufacturing plants were established to meet the demand for goods such as the Dagenham Ford factory, constructed in 1930.

Unwin was in many ways more influential than Howard; while Howard's theories and ideas sparked interest in town planning, Unwin was the one who (working with Barry Parker) started to make things happen. His attitudes were, according to his biographer Miller (1992), related to wider concerns of social welfare, and the problems that others had already noted in relation to the expanding urban population. His solutions, as designed and executed, were predominantly influenced by rural ideas; the new estates and industrial villages were almost all of cottages around a green, with some appropriate community buildings. By the 1930s their designs had changed to include more cul-de-sacs and fewer through routes, a design theme that became widely adopted. But throughout the work on new settlements the concerns were with segregating residential and employment uses, providing a lower-density alternative to the city (his ideal was 12 dwellings to the acre). It is interesting to note that the early designs for some of the towns (like Letchworth) show much more grandiose and urban centres than were eventually realized.

In the USA important design developments created initially the 'Radburn' layout, which would remain a feature of much suburban (and some urban) housing design for decades, and soon after, in the 1930s, the Forest Hills Gardens layout of Clarence Perry. This sought to create residential neighbourhoods that would have between 3 000 and 10 000 residents, with schools and institutional buildings within the area. Each neighbourhood was divided by major roads, forming boundaries preventing through traffic. Shopping was located on the periphery of the neighbourhood at the junction with other neighbourhoods. This design, Perry believed, would nurture face-to-face, and therefore intimate, relationships (OU, 1973).

More and more both residents of new houses and operators of businesses relied on road transport. In 1911 there were just 47 000 private cars in Britain. In response to price cuts, sales in 1921 doubled from the previous year to a quarter of a million. Public transport developed too, with expansion of the trolley bus network beyond where the trams had gone at the turn of the century, and the steady increase in the number of motor buses. Private car ownership rose from a million in 1931 to nearly 2 million in 1938 (Branson and Heinemann, 1973).

So by the 1930s, patterns of new development saw major investment in new development that was increasingly of only one use (whether housing, offices or industrial), and almost completely without any reference to any other use, or to any overall plan. Commentators argue that this was the period when the traditional social patterns finally broke down. Workers became more mobile, and less attached to the place they lived or worked in. The population were becoming more mobile, and the effects were obvious both in the physical development that resulted and in the social patterns that were developing: 'the sense of belonging to a community was particularly lacking in the new housing estates on the outer rings' (Branson and Heinemann, 1973).

The unplanned development of industry caused problems, and early attempts to place a Green Belt around some cities resulted. But housing could be built almost anywhere; the 1932 Town Planning Act allowed local authorities to control the location of houses, but the compensation provisions, if a scheme was refused, made the Act ineffective.

> All over everywhere little brick houses were erupting like pimples, chaotically thrown up, often without adequate transport, without shops, pubs or any of the amenities that make life worth living. Nearly always far from the offices or workplaces of the new occupiers, they sprawled out along the approach road to every big town (Branson and Heinemann, 1973 p.206).

By the 1930s it was apparent that the developing cities, and their rapidly expanding suburbs, had problems. While the war obviously limited the opportunity for any new building, the town planners were trying to define a better way of controlling and promoting development. The devastation of many city centres allowed comprehensive planning, and the unified feeling in the country allowed a new socialist government to introduce legislation to advance town planning in ways never seen before in Britain.

Thomas Sharp, in his 1940 book *Town Planning,* had identified the processes of change that had led to the decline of the compact city: new means of transport, communications and power, which created the opportunity for 'widely scattered factories manned by labour drawn from widely scattered houses' (Sharp, 1940). Writing in 1938, Anthony Bertram offered a similar vision:

> The present chaotic state of affairs has led to the indiscriminate sprawling of our towns through ring after ring of shoddy suburb, to ribbon development and the commercial exploitation of the countryside (Bertram, 1938, p.21).

But the greatest problem, according to Sharp, was that cities had been undermined as civilized places by a revival of the romantic view of the countryside, coupled with a century of 'architectural and social degradation'.

> And now, instead of pride and triumphant certainty in the town, we have only shame and hatred and an impelling desire to escape (Sharp, 1940, p.33).

Sharp looked back at what he called 'Neither Town nor Country' – the Garden Cities of Howard and Unwin – and questioned their value if so much time and effort was going into travel (as they were already clearly not self-sufficient, but increasingly dormitories). Many of the comments and much of the analysis of problems that Sharp identifies could be cited as a 1990 text. The problems are very much the same; the debate about restricting personal freedom against despoiling countryside is still with us, and remarkably unchanged.

Sharp was in favour of greater density in cities, pointing to the application of health legislation in a comprehensive way as one reason for the lower (more sprawling) densities being achieved at the time. He wanted the 12 dwelling per acre standard to be raised to 20 or 30, in the context of some form of overall density control for discreet areas of cities. At no point did Sharp address the issue of proximity of different uses, or the need to obtain a mix of uses. Bertram, however, did. He shows us very clearly what the prevailing view was on zoning:

> One of the great principles of town-planning, of course, for convenience as well as for appearances, is that towns should be zoned for various purposes. Shops should be in one district, private houses in another, industries in a third, and so on.

Bertram opines that this is not universally a good thing, and identifies a scheme in France that might very easily be a 1990 scheme in London's Docklands. The only UK example he can point to is the inclusion of shops under flats in a Liverpool housing estate. He also explains a contemporary problem, which clearly explains the nature of housing areas that still exist today:

> Is it the duty of housing authorities to provide anything more than houses? Should they try to make communities? There is various practice in this matter. One city, for example, which builds excellent houses and grants generous sites for its schools, does not allow for churches, cinemas, shops or pubs. The result is a fringe of shoddy private enterprise around the estates.

## Post-War Development

Immediately after the Second World War the main concern was with reconstruction. However, the opportunity was taken to incorporate new developments in policy. One that was to influence the physical arrangement of development was a report by an Assistant Commissioner for Police, Alker Tripp, whose book *Town Planning and Road Traffic* (1938) recommended a hierarchy of roads, related to their function. At the same time a debate was continuing about the design and appropriate density of housing – a debate sharpened by the need to replace the houses in areas devastated by the war.

The 1944 report *The Design of Dwellings* set a range of recommended densities, from 30 persons per acre in suburban areas to a maximum of 120 for the largest cities. These higher densities almost inevitably implied the creation of flats, rather than houses. The 1946 New Towns Commission Final Act of 1946 saw the ideas of a ring of new towns around London, shown in Sharp's book, put into effect. Many adopted neighbourhood plans that followed the US model of the 1930s. Town planning was also becoming important in its own right, with the Town and Country Planning Act of 1947 requiring the creation of development plans across the whole country. For the first time all development would be controlled, and land allocation maps covered the whole local authority area, not just land for development. The Act also allowed planning authorities to grant or refuse planning permission.

It was through the control of land use that post-war cities would be given their orderly structure; major activity zones, such as residential, commercial, industrial and open space would be sharply segregated from each other (Cherry, 1988).

In fact many post-war development areas differed from these newly developing policies. In Pimlico the Churchill Gardens Estate contained 2,000 dwellings at an overall density of 200 persons per acre. The centre of Coventry was redeveloped not just with shops and offices, but with some blocks of flats over the shops and leisure uses integrated into the design. Nevertheless these are exceptions to a set of development rules which were widely if not universally adopted.

## Slum Clearance

From the 1950s into the 1970s the slum clearance, commenced in the 1930s, continued, and coupled with contemporary architecture movements saw the clearance of huge areas of Victorian housing and the creation of massive new areas of housing. As in the 1930s these often omitted other uses and were isolated from industrial areas. Increasingly they were built with system-construction techniques, with high-rise blocks as part of the development. The 1950s saw serious concern about suburban sprawl, and attempts to improve conditions and intensify development within cities. Initially the idea of massive and high-rise living, as epitomized by the inter-war designs of Le Corbusier, included services and shops within the buildings, making them self-contained and well provided with facilities. However, these were translated by construction companies into more basic structures without many (or in some case any) of the support facilities, leaving them isolated.

Town planners were concerned, in relation to land uses, with changing the residential densities, and 'cleaning up' the mixed areas to remove non-conforming industry. New towns and expanded towns were being used as a method of planned dispersion, to reduce city densities and populations. This in part was to deal with traffic congestion. The problem was that the previously close-knit communities were split up, and relied on using private transport to sustain the now looser pattern of friendships and interests, creating even greater congestion. But the response was to try to re-create the old communities in new high-rise blocks – an experiment that was eventually recognized as failing.

Some of the cleared areas were used to increase industrial development, but many of the city centre sites were developed as huge enclosed shopping malls, often with multi-storey parking. The commercial centres of cities, which were still expanding, also continued to spill into and displace surrounding residential areas. This was the era of 'comprehensive development areas' — both in the USA and in the UK. There were questions raised about the nature of these developments – particularly about their effect on vitality, safety, and traditional community networks. Planning and planners became more aware of, and concerned with, both the economic and the social impacts of their planning decisions. They attempted to try to understand the behaviour of city residents and, using the newly expanding computing power, to 'model' this activity. The community planning movement can be traced back to the hugely influential book by Jane Jacobs, *The Death and Life of Great American Cities*. Living in Greenwich Village, Jacobs opposed the prevailing view that areas such as hers should be swept away for comprehensive redevelopment. She attacked both the Garden City movement, because its 'prescription to save the city was to do the city in' (Jacobs, 1961), and the Corbusian redevelopers for the sheer brutality of their vision. As Sharp had argued in the 1930s, Jacobs thought that there was nothing inherently wrong with high urban residential densities provided this did not create overcrowding in individual buildings. Most importantly for this book, she also argued for mixed functions and land uses, both within buildings and in neighbourhoods.

The continuing growth of car ownership and use, and the increasing use of roads to carry freight, both led to larger and more intrusive road schemes. Construction of bypasses around older centres allowed the release of new areas of land for development, and this was invariably developed by specialist housebuilders for low-density or medium-density private housing areas.

## Traffic in Towns

Buchanan's report to the Government in 1963 predicted with a remarkable degree of accuracy the effect of the increased availability of the car, described as 'the impending motor age'. The Steering Group who considered the report were equally clear about the likely future. One quotation serves to illustrate the quality of the predictions in their report:

> American experience tends to contradict one of the beliefs from which people in this country are inclined to draw comfort – the reflection that traffic congestion will itself set a limit to car ownership. 'People won't go on buying cars they find they can't use them'... There is little evidence that congestion of traffic stops people from owning cars and *trying* to use them.

The solution proposed (as well as major road building) included the creation of environmental zones, which through-traffic would be kept out of. The Steering Group suggested that these 'might be predominantly residential, commercial or industrial; or they might be (and many of them should be) mixed'. The report recommended the creation of Regional Development Agencies to implement the necessary programme of work – an idea that, needless to say, was not adopted. While the main thrust of the report was about traffic arrangement and management, in analysing the problems of cities the Buchanan Report itself was ahead of its time in defining perceived benefits of a compact city:

> In a compact area, journey distances, including the all-important journeys to work and school, are kept to the minimum. The concentration of people makes it possible to provide a diversity of services, interests and contacts. There is a wider choice of housing, employment, schools, shops and recreational and cultural pursuits. It is easier in a compact society to maintain the secondary activities, such as restaurants, specialist shops and service industries which all too easily fail if there is not a large enough clientele close enough at hand.

After the Second World War, New Towns were seen as a positive contribution to the problem of the need to rebuild industry and rehouse families at lower densities. A combination of greenfield sites and expanded existing centres was followed, but in each case plans created clearly segregated areas for different uses. Other than a few local shopping centres incorporating housing, rigid zoning was applied.

But in some cities the new concerns about retaining the vitality of the city, and conserving the more important parts of the built environment, led to the development of a different approach to urban renewal. In London the Greater London Council developed Covent Garden in the 1970s with a deliberate policy (and zoning) of mixed uses – including creating housing both at fair rents and in the private sector in the heart of the West End. Community groups on London's South Bank opposed the further expansion of the City with massive office blocks lining the Thames, and put forward plans for a development of a smaller-scale scheme with a mix of uses, including a mixed use development in the Oxo Tower building.

In housing, the 1969 Housing Acts allowed a different approach to the blanket slum clearance (although this was, and still is, pursued in some places). The opportunity was created to improve the existing housing by adding facilities and repairing the fabric of the houses. Decisions to retain previously blighted housing often led to further policies to remove industry, which still existed in close proximity.

Throughout the past 50 years the property industry developed greater specialization, and the funding and property-holding institutions developed huge portfolios. Commercial buildings, industrial estates, shopping centres and housing developments were each built by companies specializing in those areas of development. The investors funded the developments with a view to either acquiring them into a portfolio of investment properties or disposing of them. This tended to rule out any development that would be difficult to dispose of because of a mixture of tenants or types of use. It also led to a preference for easily managed property; buildings had become just another commodity.

The developing economy of the past three decades has seen dramatic changes in the nature of employment. Manufacturing industry has declined in importance as other countries have developed primary resources and cheaper production plants. Service industries and commercial employment have increased steadily, and now employ significantly more people than manufacturing industry. As a result of these changes, and of the need for both industrial and office users to occupy more appropriate buildings, land uses have changed. Industry is most often now found in purpose-built plants in peripheral locations, sometimes located with warehousing, close to motorway links. Office developments have sometimes reinforced city centre locations, often through the redevelopment of earlier buildings. However, other offices have been built in campus-style 'office parks' occupying lower-density sites with a high level of landscaping. These have become more sophisticated developments associated with hotels and other business services. These too are almost always developed close to a motorway junction, and may be entirely reliant on car access, with little or no associated public transport.

## Changes in Shopping

A further effect of the continued increase in private car ownership, coupled with rising disposable incomes, was the creation of bigger shops selling a wider range of goods. Demand increased as tastes broadened through foreign travel becoming increasingly common. Town centre shops became replaced by supermarkets, then superstores, and then hypermarkets in locations that were further out of town with bigger and bigger areas of parking. The growth of home ownership led to the growth of DIY stores, then superstores, in similar edge-of-town locations, particularly as bypasses were constructed. Furniture and carpet stores joined them, then electrical goods stores, and finally almost any other high-street goods were offered for sale.

In town centres, from the 1960s developers started to imitate US experience by creating enclosed malls. Specialists like Town and City Properties acquired large areas of towns and cities, often in conjunction with the local authority, and developed (in their example) Arndale Centres with a mixture of shopping units, mostly let to nationwide chains of stores.

The logical conclusion of this development was the creation of a complete alternative high street, often linked to the other out-of-town retailing developments. These regional shopping centres sprang up (and continue to be developed) in a relatively short span of time. As retailing has continued to specialize, new angles on retailing are always being developed; the latest is discount 'factory shopping' outlets. All these developments in the past 30 years rely almost exclusively on car-borne shoppers.

## Contemporary Mixed Uses

Various policy initiatives in the 1980s and 1990s have seen the redevelopment and regeneration of former industrial areas. Through Development Corporations and similar arrangements large areas of dereliction have had new uses introduced, through the refurbishment and reuse of buildings and through new construction. Increasingly, the opportunity has been taken to introduce a wider range of land uses in cities like Birmingham, Leeds and Manchester, as is explored elsewhere in the book.

Through the 1970s and 1980s local planning policies still tended to zone sites for a specific use, and tended to group areas in the same geographical location into the same uses. However, in important central sites and city centre redevelopments there were moves to introduce a wider mix of activities: particularly leisure uses with shopping centres. The trend towards massive areas of redevelopment had lessened (except where extensive dereliction existed, as noted above), and increasingly concerns about conservation and the need for a more human scale of development came to the fore. As a Dutch publication of the 1980s noted:

> 'The intermingling of urban activities and housing types is essential for a better built environment. An intermingling of activities (with respect to their functions and locations) must always be encouraged' (Tanghe *et al*, 1984).

Only in the past few years has there been an attempt to address the concern at the way development has tended to reinforce increasing car use. Traffic congestion is also finally being seen as a problem that is not solved by the construction of further roads. Pedestrianization has been widely adopted to attempt to make town centres more attractive and civilized shopping experiences, and to try to retain activity or revitalize centres where trade has been lost – often to out-of-town locations. The environmental issues that flow from car use have led to European, government and local policy initiatives that are starting to see greater residential development in town and city centres as well as policies to require a greater mix of uses, as the rest of this book examines.

## References

Bertram, A. (1938) *Design,* Pelican, Harmondsworth.

Branson, N. and Heinemann, M. (1973) *The Thirties,* Panther, London.

Briggs, A. (1963) *Victorian Cities,* Pelican, Harmondsworth.

Buchanan *et al* (1963) *Traffic in Towns,* HMSO, London.

Carter, H. and Lewis, C. (1990) *An Urban Geography of England and Wales in the Nineteenth Century,* Edward Arnold, London.

Cherry, G. (1988) *Cities and Plans* Edward Arnold, London.

Clark, P. and Slack, P. (1972) *Crisis and Order in English Towns 1500 – 1700,* Leicester University Press, Leicester.

Clark, P. (1981) *Country Towns in Pre-Industrial England,* Leicester University Press, Leicester.

Clout, H. and Wood, P. (1986) *London: Problems of Change,* Longman, Harlow.

Dyos, H.J. (ed.) (1968) *The Study of Urban History,* Edward Arnold, London.

Dyos, H.J. and Wolff, M. (1973) *The Victorian City,* vol 1, Routledge & Kegan Paul, London.

Forshaw, A. and Bergstrom, T. (1990) *Smithfield Past and Present ,* 2nd edn, Robert Hale, London.

Greeves, I. (1980) *London Docks 1800 – 1980,* Thomas Telford Ltd, London.

Hall, P. (1988) *Cities of Tomorrow,* Blackwell, Oxford.

Howard, E. (1898) *Garden Cities of Tomorrow,* Faber, London, 1946 edn.

Jacobs, J. (1961) *The Life and Death of Great American Cities,* Penguin, Harmondsworth.

Kivell, P. (1993) *Land and The City,* Routledge, London.

Lloyd, D.W. (1984) *The Making of English Towns,* Gollancz, London.

Martin, G. (1961) *The Town,* Vista Books, London.

Miller, M. (1992) *Raymond Unwin: Garden Cities and Town Planning,* Leicester University Press, Leicester.

Montgomery, J. (1970) *The Twenties,* Allen & Unwin, London.

Mumford, L. (1938) *The Culture of Cities,* Harcourt Brace Jovanovitch, Orlando, FL, 1970 edn.

Mumford, L. (1960) *The City in History,* Penguin, Harmondsworth.

Open University (1973) *Planning and The City,* Open University Press, Milton Keynes.

Pharaoh, T. (1991) Transport: how much can London take? in *London – A New Metropolitan Geography,* (eds Hoggart, K. and Green, D.), pp. 141 – 155, Edward Arnold, London.

Pfautz, H. (1967) *Charles Booth: On the City,* University of Chicago Press, Chicago IL.

Pirenne, H. (1925) *Medieval Cities,* Princeton University Press, Princeton, NJ.

Platt, C. (1976) *The English Medieval Town,* Secker & Warburg, London.

Schofield, J. (1984) *The Building of London,* British Museum Press, London.

Sharp, T. (1940) *Town Planning,* Penguin, Harmondsworth.

Sjoberg, G. (1960) *The Preindustrial City,* Collier-Macmillan, London.

Tanghe, J., Vlaneminck, S. and Berghoef, J. (1984) *Living Cities,* Pergamon, Oxford.

Thompson, F.M.L. (1982) *The Rise of Suburbia,* Leicester University Press, Leicester.

Thorns, D. (1973) *Suburbia,* Paladin, St Albans.

Tripp, Sir H.A. (1938) *Road Traffic and Its Control,* Roadmakers Library Series.

Walvin, J. (1984) *English Urban Life 1776 – 1851,* Hutchinson, London.

Ward, S. (1994) *Planning and Urban Change,* Paul Chapman, London.

# Chapter 3

# Mixed Use Development as an Agent of Sustainability

## Helen Walker

## Introduction

The final decade of this century has seen anxiety over the deteriorating state of the global environment reach new levels. There has been both collective and individual realization of the need for urgent environmental action and the prompting of an emerging philosophy of concern for the future and for unborn generations. The problems faced by the global environment have generated a series of largely pragmatic responses at the local level, some of which are the subject of this chapter, but more particularly, the evolution and formulation of a new vocabulary to describe and analyse the condition and the possibility of its containment. Among the terms developed to articulate the problem, those of 'sustainability' and 'sustainable development' have emerged to occupy a primacy in the new language of the global community.

Chapter 1 explains that this book contains an examination of mixed use development through a range of lenses; in a text dedicated to this comprehensive approach it is axiomatic that an analysis of the relationship between mixed use development and the delivery of sustainability as an objective would be undertaken. Thus the present chapter explores the current debate over whether mixed use development should be perceived as a valid agent or tool for the attainment of sustainability, or whether this is a false hope. Following consideration of the terms 'sustainability' and 'sustainable development', the relationship between these and mixed use is traced. The links between sustainability, transport policy and travel patterns, argued by some commentators to be fundamental to the process by which sustainable development might be achieved, are explored. Finally, the land use planning system is acknowledged (by the government) as the mechanism through which any shift to mixed use development might occur; the government's use of the system to deliver this objective is briefly assessed.

### Defining sustainability

The terms 'sustainability' and 'sustainable development' derive from the World Commission on Environment and Development Report *Our Common Future* (also known as the Brundtland Report), first published in 1987:

> Sustainable development is development that meets the needs of the present without compromising the ability of future generations to meet their own needs (World Commission on Environment and Development, 1987, p.43).

While there is no single definition of the terms which has found a general level of acceptance, that of the Brundtland Report has allowed the greatest consensus. However, among the many other interpretations, it is possible to discern a duality of meaning. In the original setting above, the terms are a description of an objective, but more recently secondary definitions have developed, those of sustainable development as a principle, or code of conduct, which may guide and provide a framework for decisions.

The counter side of duality may also be ambiguity, and hence a difficulty in understanding may result from the chimeric or intangible nature of sustainable development. For some commentators the elusiveness of the term and the difficulty in reaching and agreeing clear definitions are to be regarded as an asset. Blowers for one sees this incertitude as having positive potential, noting that sustainable development is a concept, an objective or end state, whose 'strength is its vagueness' (Redclift, 1991; Blowers, 1993).

While this may be true, nevertheless it is necessary for sustainable development as a concept to develop a tangibility and currency and for sustainable development in its role as an objective to become capable of delivery. That the achievement of an objective has to be perceived as potentially viable for the concept to gain validity has necessitated further redefinition of the terms over time. Some of these definitions have greater utility than others; they range from the pedestrian (which may be seen ultimately to have devalued the term), to those of great value: for example, that produced by WWEDC, the significance of which lies in its introduction of the notion of carrying capacity, or that which the earth's ecosystems are capable of absorbing:

> Sustainable development means improving the quality of life while living within the carrying capacity of supporting ecosystems (World Conservation Union, UN Environment Programme and World Wide Fund for Nature, 1991).

With its reference to quality of life, this definition places sustainable development at the very centre of existence as an integrating concept, which brings together the two competing elements of environment and development.

In the decade following the publication of the Brundtland Report, the development of meaning and interpretation of the terms may thus be traced: sustainability has acquired an acceptance and acknowledgement as both a concept and a desirable objective. Within the plethora of definitions, it is becoming increasingly apparent that it is through what might be termed an applied understanding, or through examination and analysis of the process by which sustainability might be achieved, that a greater sense of its meaning may be derived. Thus the validity of the term will be enhanced and grow through an identification of the agents through which the concept might become a reality and/or the objective reached. In other words, what are the mechanisms through which the objective of sustainable development might be realized?

## The Earth Summit

The past decade has witnessed the emergence and growth in the significance and urgency of sustainable development as an objective. Pursuit of the concept was taken up by the world leaders attending the United Nations Conference on Environment and Development (the Earth Summit) in Rio de Janeiro in June 1992, an event intended to drive governments to confront the challenge of global environmental problems. In its title the conference marked the recognition at the highest level of the problematic relationship between the two factors, while the wording of the resulting Declaration on Environment and Development testified to the primacy at international level attained by the objective of sustainability.

A primary outcome of the Earth Summit was Agenda 21 – a programme for environmental stewardship for the twenty-first century. Among the guiding principles of Agenda 21 are subsidiarity in terms of decision making, together with intensive localized programmes of public participation. While some commentators have denigrated the outcomes of the conference – including Agenda 21 – as anodyne, nevertheless the signing of Agenda 21 provided sufficient impetus for the UK government to call for the formulation of Local Agenda 21 programmes, through the agency of local authorities, by the end of 1996.

## The European Community

At the European level, within the Community, the earliest call for environmental action was made in Article 130r of the Treaty of Rome in 1957, amended by the Single Act of 1985. This made allowance for Community action in respect of the following explicitly in urban areas:

- to preserve, protect and improve the quality of the environment;

- to contribute towards protecting human health;

- to ensure a prudent and rational utilization of resources.

The publication in 1990 by the Commission of the European Communities of the *Green Paper on the Urban Environment*, represented in its own terms 'the first manifestation of the Commission's commitment to achieve real improvements in the quality of the urban environment within the Community' (CEC, 1990). The document called for detailed consideration of the urban environment in EU policies, and broke new ground in linking environmental sustainability and the quality of urban life. Framed by the newly formed urban division, Directorate General XI, the Green Paper offered an analysis of the environmental problems facing Europe's towns and cities, discussed their origins, and proposed a number of policy directions for the future. The consultation document was intended to promote wider consideration of potential policy developments prior to further Community interventions for the improvement of the urban environment. A significant and formative discussion document, the Green Paper argued the existence of a strong policy link between urban planning and the creation of a sustainable framework for economic and social development. The Green Paper identified the 'strict zoning policies' of the planning philosophies of previous decades as the reason for the separation of land use and the subsequent development of residential suburbs: 'Mere zoning must be replaced by developing the city as a project which will assure a new quality of social and economic life' (CEC, 1990). Where a mix of development at high densities and good environmental conditions co-exist, the economic performance and vitality of the city is improved:

> The city's economic and social importance ultimately rests on the ease of communication offered by spatial density, and the sheer variety of people and institutions which can exploit this opportunity (CEC, 1990, p.21).

In addition to the radical redefinition of the urban context with its support for a mixing of different land uses, the Green Paper also contained the proposal that further urban growth should be accommodated within the boundaries of existing urban areas. These suggestions generated wide interest; while attainment and sustenance are generally accepted as desirable end states, their practicality has remained the subject of extensive continuing debate, a debate within which this chapter is located. Thus the notion of the compact city, and particularly mixed use development as a vehicle for sustainable development and as the antithesis of suburban sprawl, gained a currency over the last decade.

## Responses to the Green Paper

Support for the proposals contained in the Green Paper was given the following year in publications such as Sherlock's *Cities are Good for Us* and Friends of the Earth's *Reviving the City*. In the latter, Elkin *et al.* set out a range of policy options designed to hasten the sustainability of urban areas, principal among which is the recommendation that urban planning policy is required which would be 'based on the concepts of decentralized concentration and high-density mixed land-use' (Elkin *et al.*, 1991). The development of this emerging notion of the compact city was extended by Girardet in *The Gaia Atlas of Cities*, published in 1992. In this the author detects a changing attitude towards city form, types and density of land use. Echoing the Green Paper, he urges re-evaluation of the philosophy of zoning:

Dezoning is crucial for reducing commuting distances in cities. It means creating 'multi-nucleated' cities with districts accommodating both homes and work places ... Planners are moving toward urban layouts that provide for greater built-in proximity between homes, schools, shops and places of entertainment and leisure (Girardet, 1992, p.146).

However, while the pursuit of sustainability through modification of the urban form is seen as desirable for these commentators, the proposals contained in the Green Paper may run counter to cultural aspirations. Writing in 1992, Breheny argued that:

For the majority of people, the implication of the compact city proposal is higher-density suburban living. Given that most people have opted for low-density suburban living, it is to [be] expected that rather than welcoming the intensive urban milieu that the Commission likes so much, most urban residents would object to increased densities (Breheny, 1992, p.152).

Breheny regards the suggestion as not only undesirable but also unfeasible: 'Even if the idea were acceptable, how could it be achieved? This is an important question that the Commission ignores' (Breheny, 1992).

The report of the Town and Country Planning Association's Sustainability Study Group, *Planning for a Sustainable Environment*

*Figure 3.1*
Little Britain, London
New housing in the City of London, reflecting a new demand for convenient (and sustainable) city centre living.

published the following year (Blowers, 1993), recognized the overwhelming extent of the challenge presented by the inner city for the application of the principles of sustainable development. The sheer complexity of the inner city provides both the seed bed for the development of sustainable forms and, simultaneously, the greatest problems. Inner urban areas are close to central area employment, have high housing densities, the lowest car ownership ratios and the greatest use of public transport. However, over recent decades the inner city has proved an increasingly unpopular location either for living or working, and dispersal to the suburbs has increased. As Breheny and Rookwood noted, if the continuing trend is to be reversed, the advantages of the inner city, its compactness, higher densities and proximity to work etc. will have to be combined with other qualities. Extremely careful analysis within each individual inner urban area will be required to identify the factors that might reverse the haemorrhage of the population to the suburbs (Breheny and Rookwood, 1993).

The European Community's Fifth Environmental Action Programme, entitled *Towards Sustainability: A European Community Programme of Policy and Action in Relation to the Environment and Sustainable Development* and published in 1992, took up many of these emerging themes. The objective of the document was the transformation of 'the patterns of growth in the Community in such a way as to reach a sustainable development path' (CEC, 1992). The Programme contained the desire to break current trends – what has become known as 'trend-breach planning' – and it marks the extensive shift towards the notion of environmental capacity: targets for levels of air pollution are based on standards of environmental quality, rather than on vehicle emission standards.

In addition to the Community's Fifth Environmental Action Programme, the signing of the Maastricht Treaty, also in 1992, significantly increased the Community's commitment to environmental policy. Land use planning was adopted as an area of Community competence, and the Treaty included the 'environment first' principle, which set out the requirement that all activities undertaken by the European Community, ranging from economic development to transport, must be subject to environmental assessment. While this environmental assessment process has not yet been introduced, however, the principle has been applied to the new scheme for structural funds, transport policy, the review of the Fifth Action Programme, and the Delors White Paper on Growth, Competitiveness and Employment. The work programmes of the individual Directorates General contain the development of environmental assessment methodologies in conjunction with the newly established European Environment Agency in Copenhagen. The regional policies of the Community now include explicit reference to urban communities as part of the criteria for eligibility for Objective 2 funding.

## The Expert Group on the Urban Environment

At the end of the period of consultation following the publication of the

Green Paper, in 1991 the European Commission established the Expert Group on the Urban Environment. Two years later, in 1993, the Sustainable Cities Project was launched by the Expert Group with the aim of promoting new ideas, developing approaches to sustainability in European urban settings and fostering the exchange and dissemination of good practice on sustainability. The Sustainable Cities Project operates a network through its Charter for local government, launched at its major conference on sustainability held in Aalborg, Denmark in May 1994. Through the Expert Group the Project has produced policy reports and recommendations for Community institutions, and a report, (published in draft in two parts), entitled *European Sustainable Cities* (CEC, 1995), which is to be published in its final form at the second Sustainable Cities conference to be held in Lisbon in October 1996.

In the report the Expert Group picks up many of the proposals contained in *Reviving the City*, advocating sustainability through the Danish concept of 'decentralized concentration' whereby densities are varied with accessibility, and foci of activity are concentrated around accessible nodes. Similarly, the authors argue strongly for sustainability becoming 'a prominent goal of land use planning' (CEC, 1995). In part two of *European Sustainable Cities* they maintain that to make sustainability operational requires redefinition of the principle in order to produce a tangible set of policy options.

The Expert Group argue that, for several key reasons, a pattern of mixed use development within urban areas might present one such option. Mixed land use makes provision for local need, and may reduce the need for travel, especially short service journeys made by private car. The report maintains that residential population densities should be linked with a pattern of land use that encourages the efficient use of resources and transport infrastructure. The ageing of the population is a further sound social argument in favour of this form of development. As the ability to drive or to make use of public transport diminishes with age, short journeys on foot to locally based services become more appropriate.

While the Expert Group espoused the principle of mixed land use as a real and achievable vehicle for the attainment of sustainability, its enthusiasm for the approach was tempered by a pragmatic recognition that this form of development as a means to attaining sustainability faces three particular constraints: inertia, social and market conservatism, and ingrained sectoral thinking (CEC, 1995)

## Sustainability and Mixed Uses

The arguments advancing the societal advantages of planning for mixed use in urban areas have gained ground and have been articulated by others: for example, Friends of the Earth in *Planning for the Planet*, published in 1994:

> Mixed use of space can bring renewed life back to many parts of the
> city, and in turn enhance security in public places for disadvantaged

groups (Friends of the Earth, 1994, p.77).

In *Sustainable Cities*, Haughton and Hunter (1994) examine the argument both for and against high-density development. While acknowledging that it has been for long associated with anti-social behaviour, high crime rates and delinquency, further analysis reveals that the stress associated with living in highly dense urban cores has a greater correlation with room occupancy rates than with the number of residential units per hectare. The social components of the argument in favour of mixed use development are examined further elsewhere in this book.

In the preface to the TCPA's *Planning for a Sustainable Environment* published in 1993, Blowers argued that sustainability is an 'integrating concept' involving a set of interrelated factors. In a move towards the provision of practical measures, the book set out five 'fundamental goals', which should be applied to determine whether development is sustainable: resource conservation, built development, environmental quality, social equity and political participation. The goal of built development is concerned with the sustainable use of resources and the extent to which this may be influenced by development policy:

> Resource conservation requires patterns of development that mini-mize energy consumption, maintain the productivity of land, and encourage the re-use of buildings (Blowers, 1993, pp.6–7).

The TCPA has also refined the interpretation of sustainability as an objective, seeing it as a process requiring modification and adaptation to local circumstances:

> The size, density and location of human settlements that is most appropriate for sustainability will vary in the light of technological developments in energy, building, manufacturing and transportation (Blowers, 1993, p.7).

The issue of integration is taken up in the foreword to *Sustainable Settlements: A Guide for Planners, Designers and Developers,* which explains that the document aims to assist professionals working in the environmental field to 'convert the rhetoric of sustainable development into practical action'. Produced as part of the UK Local Agenda 21 initiative begun in 1993, the *Guide* sets out to interpret the principles of sustainability into practical policies and design solutions for factors ranging from locational choice down to the individual dwelling. Advocates of mixed use as an agent of delivery, the authors set out three 'basic principles': first, there should be a 'rough balance of homes, jobs and services'; second, commercial centres should combine 'office, retail, leisure, civic and high density residential uses in close and overlapping patterns' to increase the viability and vitality of the centre and 'facilitate multi-purpose trips'. Finally, to allow the benefits of multi-functionalism and trip sharing, the 'functional linkages between activities should be a key determinant of siting decisions' (Barton *et al.*, 1995).

## Transport and the Environment

Of the range of elements that might contribute to make mixed use development an agent in the delivery of sustainable development, it is transportation that is perhaps the most compelling for consideration. Its relationship with the delivery of sustainable development and the link with mixed use development has been the subject of extensive research over the last few years, and it is to this most fundamental factor that this chapter now turns.

It is clear that a gradual recognition of the significance of the link between land use, the environment and transport has begun to occur at all levels of policy making. Agenda 21 acknowledged the existence and importance of the relationship, while the European Commission specified land use planning as one of five key transport measures, and transport itself as a major target area in the Fifth Environment Action Programme (Royal Commission on Environmental Pollution, 1994). The Programme regards transport as fundamental to the establishment of a sustainable urban environment, and through Directorate General XI the Commission has established a research programme to explore more rational transport approaches to location decisions.

The existence of a relationship between higher-density development of the type found in the inner city core (which may or may not include mixed use) and travel behaviour has been receiving increased recognition for some while. When individuals' homes are near to their places of work, shops, schools, community and other facilities, there is the obvious potential for journeys to be multi-purpose, and for them to be undertaken on foot or by bicycle rather than by a motorized mode of travel.

## UK Government Responses

As outlined above, the European Commission's *Green Paper on the Urban Environment* identified the zoning policies of earlier periods as the reason for suburban development, which in turn stimulated commuter traffic. The Green Paper made explicit the link between high-density development (and specifically mixed use) and transport, arguing for a radical change in approach:

> We therefore need a fundamental review of the principles on which town-planning practice has been based. Strategies which emphasize mixed use and denser development are more likely to result in people living closer to work places and the services they require for everyday life. The car can then become an option rather than a necessity (CEC, 1990, p.60).

In 1990, the UK government published *This Common Inheritance: Britain's Environmental Strategy*. An extensively illustrated document of almost 300 pages, it set out 352 proposals for environmental change, and a range of targets and objectives that are subject to annual review. Described as a comprehensive strategy for the environment, the report contained the explicit acknowledgment by the government of the role of land use planning in determining travel patterns and growth. The strategy was the first in a series of White Papers that includes *Sustainable Development: The UK Strategy*, published four years later in 1994, and in which this connection is more clearly articulated. The strategy put forward a framework for a sustainable transport policy built on the following objectives:

> to strike the right balance between the ability of transport to serve economic development and the ability to protect the environment and sustain future quality of life;

> to provide for the economic and social needs for access with less need for travel (DoE, 1990 p.169).

*Sustainable Development* argues that

> the main goal for sustainable development in the transport sector must be to meet the economic and social needs for access to facilities with less need to travel... This requires... land use policies which will enable people and business to take advantage of locations which meet their needs for access with less use of transport (DoE, 1990).

As the level of empirical testimony over the relationship mounted, the Departments of the Environment and Transport jointly commissioned a study which was undertaken by ECOTEC and published in 1993. Entitled *Reducing Transport Emissions through Planning*, the Report came out in tentative support of the existence of the link:

> The limited number of studies of the impact of transport infrastructure projects on development in the UK ... warns against simple or general conclusions. (DoE, 1993).

Nevertheless, broad patterns of development indicate a permissive, if not a causal, relationship between transport systems and land use. In his book *The Gaia Atlas of Cities*, Girardet argued with conviction that the link is tangible:

> Our transport systems are unsustainable... Cities, to become sustainable, require transport policies discouraging routine use of cars. Reorganization of city layouts, with greater proximity between home, work and shops is a... priority (Girardet, 1992 p.24).

His examples include the city of Portland, Oregon, where relatively dense layout encouraged investment in public transport and resulted in 43% of the city's commuters using the bus and light rail network, a figure much higher than in any other north American city (Girardet, 1992).

In *Sustainable Development and Urban Form*, Banister examined the relationship between energy use, transport and settlement patterns, concluding that the empirical nature of the research base, together with its international nature, made comparison difficult. Like Breheny, his conclusion was that while perhaps philosophically desirable, 'notions of self-containment' of the city as advocated by Girardet and others had less validity for a post-industrialized, highly mobile, car-orientated and dependent society (Banister, 1992).

The Report of the Royal Commission on Environmental Pollution, *Transport and the Environment,* was published in 1994 following two years of preparation. The objective of the study was a comprehensive assessment of the mounting evidence that the extent of projected transport growth, particularly road transport, is unsustainable in its long-term impact. The report evaluated the conclusions of a wide range of recent research, made 110 recommendations, and proposed 17 targets. It argued the case for integration between land use and transport policy to promote a reduction in travel:

*Figure 3.2*
Devizes, Wiltshire.
Living over the shop: initiatives such as these are encouraging more residential uses of town and city centre properties.

> To ensure that an effective transport policy at all levels of government is integrated with land use policy and gives priority to minimizing the need for transport and increasing the proportions of trips made by environmentally less damaging modes (Royal Commission on Environmental Pollution, 1994).

The report acknowledged that:

> It is widely held that patterns of land use influence travel behaviour and that development density, the mixing of land uses and the location of development in relation to transport networks are related to the frequency, distance, speed and mode of travel.

The Commission also recognized that on the other hand there is an inter-relationship between the separation of activities, development densities and travel patterns. A greater segregation of land uses tends to correlate with lower development densities, which in turn generate more extensive travel patterns, or conversely: 'Higher densities permit greater choice for less travel'.

However, the Commission noted that 'the strength and significance of these interactions is a matter of some dispute...' (Royal Commission on Environmental Pollution, 1994). Since data on the effect of land use on the demand for travel derive in the main from empirically based surveys of the relationship between the two, the Commission took the view that this renders the interpretation ambiguous. Thus, as the data base is insecure and the complexity of the issue defies comparison and is anyway in part located within another set of economic and social factors, for the Commission the existence of the relationship remained unverified.

The report accepted the logic that development within urban areas tends to require a transport infrastructure less dependent on the private car than in a peripheral or rural area. The Commission acknowledged a correlation between the density of development and transport energy use, and argued that it is the planning system that should be used to break the vicious circle:

> ...the land use planning system must itself be a policy instrument in reducing the demand for travel (Royal Commission on Environmental Pollution, 1994, p.148)

In specific terms, the report recommended target cuts in the proportion of urban journeys undertaken by car, with different rates of reduction advocated for outside London and for the metropolis.

## Government Policy

In April 1995, ministerial recognition of the link between patterns of development and traffic generation was given by Steven Norris, Minister for Transport in London, quoted at the launch of a survey on air quality in the metropolis as saying that 'London authorities should introduce more mixed use areas to reduce pollution from traffic' (RTPI,

1995b). The Report, *Air Quality in London*, analysed the deterioration of the air quality in the capital between 1993 and 1994.

While the link between density, mixed use urban development and a reduction in transport is not entirely proven, nevertheless widespread acknowledgement of a considerable body of empirical evidence in support of the relationship has occurred, even at governmental level. The concluding section of this chapter traces the discernible change in governmental attitude regarding sustainable development in the aftermath of the support for the principle espoused by the Prime Minister, John Major, at the 1992 Rio Conference.

Writing in 1993, Blowers maintained that the intervention of the European Community in the environmental question marked by the publication of the Green Paper was significant in that it 're-established the old nexus between town planning and sustainable development issues'. Blowers' analysis is supported by the fact that in its publication of Planning Policy Guidance Note 12 *Development Plans and Regional Planning Guidance* in February 1992 (the same year as the Rio Conference), the UK government saw fit to recognize this connection. Using language redolent of Brundtland's founding definition, PPG12 may be held to represent the point at which formal acknowledgement is made of sustainable development as an objective of government policy and particularly of the planning system (DoE, 1992; Jacobs, 1993):

> The planning system, and the preparation of development plans in particular, can contribute to the objectives of ensuring that development and growth are sustainable. The sum total of decisions in the planning field, as elsewhere, should not deny future generations the best of today's environment (DoE, 1992).

In January 1994, the government launched *Sustainable Development: The UK Strategy*, with 'a virtually unprecedented array of Ministers' (Friends of the Earth, 1994). In the introduction to the strategy, Secretary of State John Gummer testified to the government's commitment:

> The United Kingdom is determined to make sustainable development the touchstone of its policies. We recognize that this means a change of attitudes throughout the nation... [We] shall need to revise and refine our policies so that our economy can grow in a way which does not cheat on our children (DoE, 1994a, p.5).

Despite the wide expectation that the document might have made explicit the opportunities presented by the planning system to achieve sustainability, *Sustainable Development: The UK Strategy* disappointed in this respect. While the strategy did acknowledge that 'the planning system is a key instrument in delivering land use and development compatible with the aims of sustainable development', in 267 pages the document offered little practical advice on the matter, other than listing the revisions to the Planning Policy Guidance Notes.

The Department of the Environment is revising the list of Policy Planning Guidance Notes (PPGs) in order to incorporate the increased commitment to sustainability expressed by the government. Planning policy guidance which concerns housing and retail development (PPG 3 and PPG 6) refers explicitly to sustainable development, and the latter to the vitality and viability of existing town centres. PPG 12 *Development Plans and Regional Planning Guidance* (DoE, 1992) requires plans to take account of the environment in 'all its aspects', global and local. However, it is PPG 13 (DoE, 1994c) on transport that marks the extent of the shift in the government's position. The guidance note was based on a report to the Departments of the Environment and Transport by ECOTEC entitled *Reducing Transport Emissions through Planning*. PPG 13 advises how local authorities should integrate transport and land use planning, emphasizing the need to reduce growth in the number and length of motorized journeys and to reduce reliance on the private car. However, it will require the consistent support of the Department of the Environment to uphold its aims. *PPG 13: A Guide to Better Practice* was commissioned jointly by the Departments of the Environment and Transport to disseminate examples of existing good practice. *Reducing the Need to Travel: some thoughts on PPG13* (Earp *et al.*,1995) is a commentary on the workings of the Guidance, as is Hills' paper, 'The car versus mixed use development' in which the author expressed doubt that the Guidance will be effective:

> PPG 13 cannot deliver powerful positive restraint policies against dispersed car-oriented patterns of development. Instead it must rely on essentially negative policies of development control and general exhortation. (Hills, 1994)

*Quality in Town and Country*, a discussion paper published by the Department of the Environment in 1994, is a continuation of the government's efforts to be seen aboard, if not actually driving, the sustainability bandwagon. In the preface, Secretary of State John Gummer noted that sustainable development is 'about how we develop in this generation without stealing from the next' (DoE, 1994b), thereby rendering Brundtland's classic definition into a language that presumably, were the average British citizen to see or even read the document, they might more readily be expected to understand. He continues:

> The disparate zoning of different everyday activities, working living, shopping – increases demand for travel and reduces the speed of travel... Applying the principle of sustainable development means understanding the impact of our actions upon others... It means placing civic responsibility – our duty to others, and to the future – at the centre of our lives (DoE, 1994b, pp.2–3).

At a symposium on the discussion paper, Gummer made it clear where he felt responsibility for the problem lay:

> Too much emphasis has been placed on zoning and segregation of land uses. It derives from the determined neatness of planners and has nothing to do with the proper growth of the community (RTPI, 1995a).

As in other recent government publications, the invocation of the planning system is implicit in the preface to *Quality in Town and Country*, but no more. Later in the document, however, the relationship between sustainable development and planning is articulated within the first of a number of discussion issues highlighted in the text:

> What demands does the principle of sustainable development make upon the planning of our towns and cities, and how should it influence our understanding of sustainable rural communities? (DoE, 1994b, p.5.)

What was made explicit by the document is the degradation in meaning that the term 'sustainable development' had begun to suffer at the pens of the Department of the Environment civil servants. The preface to *Quality in Town and Country* contained the 'fact' that 'quality is sustainable' together with the information that 'sustainable development means a war on waste'. Elsewhere the opportunity to express the government's firm commitment to the delivery of sustainability through the planning system falls victim to a particularly passive language:

> 'The Government is seeking to encourage sustainable urban growth both through its planning guidance to local authorities and through the spending programmes and advisory actions of its agencies and Departments of State' (DoE, 1994b).

As 1994 progressed there were intimations in the speeches of the Secretary of State John Gummer that the government, or at least the Department of the Environment, was moving towards an appreciation of the role that mixed use development might make as an agent of sustainability. By early the following year, the Department's perception that mixed land use may be one factor leading to the delivery of sustainability was receiving regular promotion. At a conference in Manchester in July 1995, the Secretary of State described the existence of an emerging consensus around the view that 'development is more sustainable if it produces a mixture of uses'. Again at pains to distance himself from the adherence to zoning practised by his predecessors, Gummer strikes a progressively more evangelical tone:

> Segregation of land uses, encouraged in the past, is not relevant now. The trend back to mixed usage brings a number of potential benefits. It ensures vitality through activity and diversity. It makes areas safer. It also reduces the need to travel, making people less reliant on cars, bringing welcome environmental benefits (DoE, 1995b).

More recently in 1996 the government has honoured the pledge contained in the *Sustainable Development Strategy* to develop and publish *Indicators of Sustainable Development for the United Kingdom*. Produced by an interdepartmental Working Group, the report presents a set of indicators on 21 topics ranging from leisure and tourism to overseas trade. In the description of indicators relating to the re-use of land the report acknowledges that commercial and residential redevelopment within existing urban areas contributes to both their vitality and viability. Support for mixed use as an agent of sustainable development is apparent, if not altogether enthusiastic:

> (Mixed redevelopment) can also improve the quality of life and also accessibility for those people without a car by increasing and widening the range of services and facilities available and thereby reducing the need for people to travel to other towns for work, shopping and leisure (DoE, 1996, p.54).

## Conclusion

This chapter has traced the evolution of sustainable development from its genesis as an objective in 1987, through perceptions of it as a process, to the formulation of policy to guide its practical application. In moving from being an iconic statement concerning the global environment to an expression combining ideal intent and pragmatic implementation, sustainable development has entered the everyday language of the nation. Within this setting a significant ideological shift within planning regarding the zoning of land use has occurred. Mixed use development has emerged both as a philosophy and as one acceptable element of the solution to the problem of delivery of sustainable development, replacing its earlier position as an inevitable consequence of *laisser-faire* development. However, as is often the case when a different perspective begins to replace the status quo, there is a danger of the new ideology becoming as rigid in its application as that which it has replaced.

While not yet universally accepted as a legitimate agent for the delivery of sustainable development, there is no doubt that mixed use development has a practical value. Its application in certain situations can provide a firm foundation for achieving the complex goals of sustainability. On the other hand, an inflexible doctrine will fail to take account of the altered expectations and aspirations of those who actually inhabit the spaces that planners seek to allocate to them. Sustainable development is a process that requires that planners are pragmatic in applying solutions, and it is within this perspective that mixed use development is emerging as an appropriate tool.

## References

Banister, D. (1992) Energy use, transport and settlement patterns. in *Sustainable Development and Urban Form,* (ed. M. Breheny), Pion, London.

Barton, H., Davis, G. and Guise R. (1995) *Sustainable Settlements,* UWE/LGMB, Bristol

Breheny, M. (ed.) (1992) *Sustainable Development and Urban Form,* Pion, London.

Breheny, M. and Rookwood, R., (1993) Planning the sustainable city region, in *Planning for a Sustainable Environment* (ed. A. Blowers), Earthscan, London.

Blowers, A. (ed.) (1993) *Planning for a Sustainable Environment,* Earthscan, London.

CEC (1990) *Green Paper on the Urban Environment,* EUR 12902, Brussels

CEC (1992) *Towards Sustainability: A European Community Programme of Policy and Action in Relation to the Environment and Sustainable Development,* COM (92) 23, Brussels

CEC (1995) Expert Group on the Urban Environment *European Sustainable Cities,* Part II. Brussels

CEC (1995) *Progress Report on Implementation of the European Community Programme of Policy and Action in Relation to the Environment and Sustainable Development* (Draft).

Department of the Environment (1990) *This Common Inheritance: Britain's Environmental Strategy,* Cmnd 1200.

Department of the Environment (1992) *Planning Policy Guidance Note 12: Development Plans and Regional Planning Guidance,* HMSO, London.

Department of the Environment (1994a) *Sustainable Development: the UK strategy,* Cmnd 2426., HMSO, London.

Department of the Environment (1994b) *Quality in Town and Country,* HMSO, London.

Department of the Environment (1994c) *PPG13: Transport,* HMSO, London.

Department of the Environment (1995a) *PPG13: A Guide to Better Practice,* HMSO, London.

Department of the Environment (1995b) Press release on Manchester symposium on quality in town and country, 24 July.

Department of the Environment (1996) *Indicators of Sustainable Development for the United Kingdom,* HMSO, London.

Department of the Environment/ECOTEC (1993) *Reducing Transport Emissions through Planning,* HMSO, London.

Earp, J.H., Headicar, P., Banister, D. and Curtis, C. (1995) *Reducing the need to travel,* Oxford Brookes University, Oxford.

Elkin, T., McLaren, D. and Hillman, M. (1991) *Reviving the City,* Friends of the Earth, London.

Friends of the Earth (1994) *Planning for the Planet,* Friends of the Earth, London.

Girardet, H. (1992) *The Gaia Atlas of Cities,* Gaia, London.

Haughton, G. and Hunter, C. (1994) *Sustainable Cities,* RSA, London.

Hills, P. J. (1994) The car versus mixed use development in *Journal of Planning and Environmental Law: Planning Icons: Myth and Practice, Occasional papers No22,* Sweet and Maxwell, London.

Jacobs, M. (1993) *Sense and Sustainability,* CPRE, London.

Redclift, M. (1991) The multiple dimensions of sustainable development. *Geography,* 76, 36–42, quoted in Blowers, A, Sustainable urban development: the political perspectives. in Breheny, M. J. (ed.) (1992) *Sustainable Development and Urban Form,* Pion, London.

Royal Commission on Environmental Pollution (1994) *Transport and the Environment,* Oxford University Press, Oxford.

Royal Town Planning Institute (1995a) *PlanningWeek,* 5 January.

Royal Town Planning Institute, (1995b) *PlanningWeek,* 27 April.

Sherlock, H. (1991) *Cities are Good for Us,* Paladin, London.

World Commission on Environment and Development (1987) *Our Common Future,* Oxford University Press, Oxford.

World Conservation Union, UN Environment Programme and World Wide Fund for Nature, (1991) *Caring for the Earth,* WCU, Gland, Switzerland.

# Case Study 3.1

# Gloucester Green, Oxford and Sandford-on-Thames

Identically worded surveys were carried out at two developments in Oxford. One is in the city centre, Gloucester Green, and the other at Sandford-on-Thames, some 2 miles beyond the city ring-road, and outside the city boundary.

Gloucester Green is a development of shops, flats and offices around a bus station and market square. Built with funding from an insurance company, GRE, the scheme has had a high profile in both the design and 'mixed use' press. The flats are located over shops and restaurants; some face onto the market square, others face the bus station.

Sandford-on-Thames was selected because the housing was of a broadly similar nature, while being located outside the city centre. The housing here is on the site of a former mill, on the riverside, and is constructed as separate units with housing over ground floor parking. The period of construction and selling prices was broadly comparable to that for Gloucester Green.

The initial hypothesis was that residents at Sandford would rely on car ownership and use, but that the city centre residents would also use their cars extensively. (Parking is available in the scheme ). We also expected that few if any families in the city centre would have children, but that there might be some at Sandford. The survey covered 24 of the 88 flats at Gloucester Green, and 12 of the 30 or so units in higher-density blocks at Sandford-on-Thames. (There are also larger family houses in the development, which were not surveyed.)

Adult occupation rates were identical in the two developments. Against our expectations, there were also three children (in two households) in the city centre, but none at Sandford. The ages and employment status of the two schemes were broadly similar; each had two households of retired people. Unexpectedly both developments appeared to be extensively let in the private sector. Only 7 of the 24 Gloucester Green flats were owner occupied, with the majority of the remainder let to students (on comparatively high rents). At Sandford-on-Thames 6 of the 12 flats were also privately let. The owners in both developments had often lived there over five years (since the schemes were completed). Not surprisingly, those who rented had stayed far less time: a year or two at most.

Neither scheme had been specifically selected by many of the occupants for any perceived qualities of the scheme itself, but rather for the convenience of the location (or in the case of Sandford, the security of the location). Obviously residents value the advantages that attach to their particular chosen location. The transport advantages of living at Gloucester Green were strongly appreciated, although several residents in Sandford also referred to the convenience (in their view) of the location – but in relation to their employment in places like Maidenhead and Didcot. Two mentioned closer employment locations (the hospital, and science park), but both used their car to travel to these.

In practice the views of Sandford residents were not expressed especially strongly either in favour or against either the location or the quality of the housing. Three respondents identified the disadvantage of having to use a car for most purposes. While some found living in a small rural community a benefit, describing it as welcoming, others in the same development (and also private renters) referred to the lack of friendliness. The one almost universal comment was in relation to the disadvantages of the lack of any village shop and the distance from the city centre.

In Gloucester Green more residents positively chose the scheme, and the benefits of the central location for its convenience for getting to work (or in many cases the university). The scheme was widely praised for its design, the 'continental' feel of the square, and the convenience of the location. Despite the fact that several respondents commented on the noise level as a disadvantage, others commented on the quiet as a positive

*Figure 3.3*
Sandford-on-Thames, Oxfordshire.
Housing created from a former riverside mill 2 miles outside the Oxford ring-road.

*Figure 3.4*
Gloucester Green, Oxford. The roadside view of the office part of the mixed use development in the city centre.

aspect of the scheme (this probably reflects different locations within the scheme). As in Sandford some occupants found living in close proximity to other occupants a problem; occupants of both schemes commented on poor acoustic separation between units. As with Sandford, contradictory views were expressed on some matters, possibly linked to direct experience. Some found the quality of construction high, and praised its solidity. Other said things 'fell apart' and were poorly built.

In relationship to the area in general, comments were far stronger than in Sandford, residents listing the convenience of different facilities (leisure, childcare and shopping amongst them). Generally, the advantages were seen as much greater than the disadvantages, although these were more comprehensively listed than at Sandford. Many of the problems were management related, and were reported as having been satisfactorily dealt with.

## Friends and Social Life

In general, residents of both schemes know only some of their neighbours, with little apparent difference between those who own or rent their home. Social patterns are, however, very different between the schemes; half the households in Gloucester Green had close friends living within a 20 minute walk (with no real difference between students and non-students), while

only one resident in Sandford had any friends in the same category.

With membership of clubs and societies and the use of facilities in the area, the differences between the two locations are even more marked. Every resident of Gloucester Green used some of the local facilities: the cinema, theatre, shops and restaurants. Half the owner occupiers, and a few of the students were also in local clubs or organizations, including a church and a local health club. At-Sandford-on Thames the only local facilities are the river walk, and a pub immediately adjacent to the housing. Two thirds of residents mentioned using the pub occasionally; one was a church member and one each in a fishing club and a rowing club.

Responses to a question on transport use for visiting friends and entertainment or sport showed a similar marked difference between the two schemes. The transport mode is discussed below, but the frequency of travel for these purposes is equally different. Two thirds of respondents in Gloucester Green were involved in sport or using entertainment facilities on a regular basis. A higher percentage visited friends or relatives, although it is significant that at least four respondents replied that friends visited them.

In comparison, a similar percentage of Sandford residents were involved in sport or entertainment (which often involved them in travelling to the city centre), but less frequently than those in Gloucester Green, and far fewer visited friends or relatives on a regular basis.

*Figure 3.5 (opposite)* Gloucester Green, Oxford. The 'continental' feel of the market place at the heart of the scheme was widely valued, despite the problems of noise that it creates for some residents.

*Figure 3.6 (below)* Gloucester Green, Oxford. Site layout.

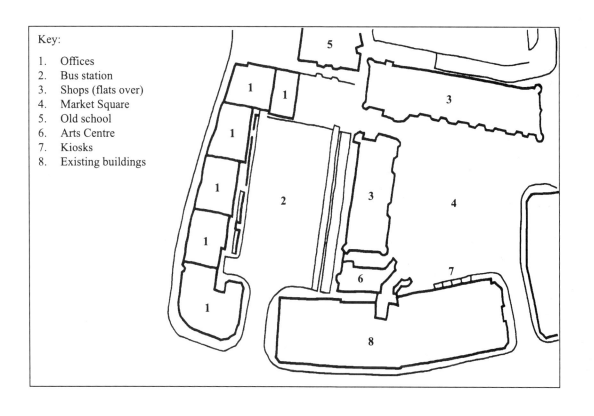

Key:

1.  Offices
2.  Bus station
3.  Shops (flats over)
4.  Market Square
5.  Old school
6.  Arts Centre
7.  Kiosks
8.  Existing buildings

## Car Ownership and Travel

One of the greatest differences is in relation to car ownership and use. At Gloucester Green there were 34 adults living in the 24 households surveyed; of these 6 households owned 7 cars and 8 bicycles. Sandford had 17 adults in 12 households; everyone had a car, and 5 households owned 6 bicycles.

Most households in Gloucester Green walk to work, to the city centre for leisure activity and to the supermarket to shop, both on a daily basis and for the weekly household shop. Just three households used a car for the main shopping; in Sandford all households used a car for all shopping trips, and for all leisure activity. One resident worked from home, one was retired, and one cycled to a station to catch a train. Otherwise all work trips are in the car. Gloucester Green residents walk to work, catch a bus, cycle or, in the case of two residents, use their car. Many residents referred to the advantage of living near the bus station for trips, particularly to travel to London (the service being seen universally as excellent).

A quarter of households in Gloucester Green used to own a car, and gave it up on moving to the scheme. The reason for doing so was either the expense involved in parking it, or the fact that it was no longer needed. One resident in Sandford who had moved from the city centre had bought a car because it was impossible to manage without one. Of the six households with a car in Gloucester Green, three appeared to use it very little, walking both to work and for shopping.

## Conclusions

There are some surprising differences between the residents of the two schemes: differences that were not expected. Clearly car use and 'sustainable' living are factors that show very significant variance between the two locations. In one way this is predictable. Living in Sandford-on-Thames offers little choice; if facilities are to be used one drives to them. But the low levels of car ownership and even lower levels of use by Gloucester Green residents were unexpected. In part this can be explained by the fact that there are more students, and the expensive parking arrangements available to residents, although there was little dissatisfaction with the arrangements. The level of travel activity of the city centre residents waws significantly greater than that of the residents of Sandford-on-Thames.

In relation questions about experiences of crime, the attitudes of the residents of the two locations showed some differences, although actual crime experienced was hardly different. It may be that people who chose to live in the city centre generally see it as safe – or at least, not unsafe – as a location, which is why they are happy or at least willing to live there. Those choosing to live outside the centre clearly feel it to be safer – to a much greater extent than actual crime would suggest is justified. Our survey group are not really representative of the population as a whole, who view the potential for crime as even greater than shown by our group. It may be that people intending to have an active social life using a range of different facilities naturally seek a location that allows them the maximum convenient access to these facilities; the city centre.

# Chapter 4

# Cities, Tourism and Mixed Uses

## Robert Maitland

## Introduction

This chapter is about the role that tourism and leisure activities can play in mixed use developments – of buildings and of whole areas of cities. It looks particularly at how tourism and 'ACE' industries – arts, culture and entertainment – can contribute to mixed use developments within a process of regeneration. It suggests that while they are no panacea, these industries can play a propulsive role in economic regeneration, add variety and vitality to areas, turn redundant buildings into assets, and play a key role in changing the image of cities.

The chapter begins by reviewing the key changes that are taking place in the economies of cities in the industrialized world, and identifying the major consequences. It looks at the rapid growth in tourism and leisure, and at the resources that cities have to attract tourists and visitors. It then looks at the contribution that tourism and ACE industries can make to mixed use development, and identifies some of the important lessons that can be learned. The argument is illustrated by a variety of examples, and by case studies of Bristol Docks and Halifax.

It is important at the outset to establish what we mean by tourism and leisure, because these terms are used by different people to mean different things. Some common definitions of tourism use overnight stay as an essential criterion. For example, the United Nations has defined a tourist as someone who stays away from home for 24 hours or more for purposes other than full-time education or semi-permanent employment (UN, 1963). This is a definition that encompasses people staying away from home for a variety of reasons. It includes leisure visitors – people taking a holiday – and also business tourists and people travelling for social reasons. Business tourists may be travelling as part of their job, for example to meet a client, or attending a conference or convention. They often use the same facilities as leisure tourists, and may be accompanied by a partner travelling purely for leisure reasons. Social tourists are people visiting friends and relations, which obviously often has a leisure element. This definition does not, however, include day visitors. Day visitors are people whose visit does not include an overnight stay – for example, spending a day in an historic city. Day visitors are an important and growing category. In many ways, they are indistinguishable from other types of tourist – they visit the same places, do similar things, and spend money in similar ways in the cities they visit (although they generally spend less than overnight visitors, because they are not paying for accommodation). This means it is more helpful to adopt a broader definition of tourism. The Tourism Society (1979) has defined tourism as:

> The temporary short-term movement of people to destinations outside the places where they normally live and work, and their activities during their stay at these destinations.

This definition includes day visitors. It embraces leisure, business and social tourism, and also other activities that may not always be seen as tourism, such as leisure shopping.

Tourism and leisure are of course closely related. Leisure tourism is one form of activity undertaken in leisure time, and tourists often use the same facilities as local residents – restaurants, theatres, parks and shops for example. Equally, business travellers and local business people will make use of some of the same services – such as conference and meeting rooms, or copy bureaux. The terms 'leisure' and 'ACE industries' are used interchangeably to include performing arts, festivals, museums and galleries, and commercial leisure such as restaurants, bars, nightclubs and cafés.

## Changing City Economies

The effects of the widespread and continuing economic restructuring of the last 25 years have been especially noticeable in cities in the UK and other industrialized countries. While cities have seen the rise of new industries and occupations, they have also been the focus of decline as previously dominant economic activities, especially manufacturing and dock industries, shrank in importance or shifted from urban areas to more rural locations or to other parts of the world. The rapidity and severity of this economic restructuring has caused strains for the populations and workforces of cities, and has required major adaptations of their physical fabric. In the UK, government strategies for cities from the late 1970s onward sought to deal with these problems through policies for urban regeneration that tackled social, physical and economic decline. The need for economic regeneration was, however, consistently seen as the key to a more general regeneration, and was the main focus of policy.

The economic changes experienced in cities and other urban areas form part of a global economic restructuring sometimes described as a shift from Fordist to post-Fordist patterns of production and consumption. The changes are poorly understood, but the main features are relatively easily summarized. They include:

- Changing industrial and employment structures, with continuing decline in manufacturing employment, and increases in service sector employment (Marshall and Wood, 1995). However, service job replacement has been insufficient to compensate for jobs lost, and new service jobs have often required new skills. The result has been persistent and high levels of unemployment, especially amongst male and unskilled workers.

- Counter-urbanization – the shift of economic activities away from cities to small towns and semi-rural locations. While the trend began with manufacturing industry (Fothergill and Gudgin, 1982; Fothergill *et al.*, 1985), subsequently some service industries, including office-based services and retailing, followed.

- The demise of the classical specialized local economy, which saw particular industries heavily concentrated in particular cities or sub-regions – for example cotton textiles in Lancashire in the UK, or in Lowell, MA. in the USA – and its replacement with a geography of corporate function. A geography of corporate function means that large corporations distribute their different functions spatially on a global basis, with, for example, routine manufacturing activities in a low-labour-cost location, headquarters in a world city such as London or Paris, and research and development in an area with a concentration of highly qualified labour and close links to leading academic research, – such as the Cambridge sub-region in the UK (Allen and Massey, 1988).

- Significant restructuring of public and private sector organizations, emphasizing the externalization of activities that used to be carried out in-house, and continuing labour force reductions ('downsizing' or 're-engineering'), and a trend towards a workforce employed on short-term contracts ('flexibility'). The effect has been to reduce the proportion of the UK workforce in full-time and secure employment, and increase the proportion in contract, casual or self-employment (Hutton, 1995). One consequence has been that traditional distinctions between industrial sectors associated with secure and well-paid jobs – for example, much manufacturing and public services – and those associated with insecure and poorly paid jobs – for example, the tourism and leisure industries – have started to break down.

These trends have resulted in fundamental changes to the character of urban areas. The extensive literature on economic restructuring in the UK has emphasized that a great variety of restructuring strategies can be adopted within these general trends, and that each locality will have a unique experience, resulting from its inherited industrial structure and the roles it plays in the new corporate geography (Massey, 1984; Allen and Massey, 1988). The experience of change is variable, with market-driven changes producing localities that gain economic activities and jobs, and those which lose them. However:

...Most of the larger cities in the industrialized world were confronted in the 1970s and early 1980s with the symptoms of what has frequently been called 'the urban crisis'. ...In the second half of the 1980s on the wave of world-wide recovery, some of the principal cities in western Europe and the United States regained something of their former leading position [but] the process of urban revival seems much more selective than that of urban decline (van den Berg *et al.*, 1994).

Policy has focused on regeneration in localities that have been losers in the process of creating 'post-industrial' cities.

Both the analysis of economic restructuring and the design of policy have generally depended – implicitly or explicitly – upon distinguishing 'basic' and 'dependent' economic activities within an economy (which may be a city, sub-region or region). Basic industries are those that earn external income by exporting goods or services to the rest of the world, while dependent industries are those that serve the local market only (Kaldor, 1966). The importance of the distinction is that basic industries are the key to growth in the economy. For any particular locality, they are the propulsive industries that generate growth, since they can expand by selling more into the external market and thus earning more external income. Non-basic industries, on the other hand, simply sell the goods or services they produce to local consumers or to other local firms. Whilst this meets market needs and demands, it does not in itself generate growth in the local economy. These industries are therefore dependent in the sense that their size and structure is ultimately determined by basic propulsive industries. It follows that the fortunes of a local economy are determined by basic industries. A decline in basic industries – through closure of mines or manufacturing plants, or out-movement of mobile firms – will result in direct job losses and also consequential job losses in dependent industries as income earned from the rest of the world falls. Equally, growing basic industries will propel the whole economy, creating jobs themselves and also further employment in dependent industries. As a result, the analysis of economic change and the focus of economic policy has been on those industries identified as basic, with dependent industries seen as relatively unimportant.

For many years, this translated into a preoccupation with manufacturing industry as the key to local regeneration. In principle, basic industries can be part of the extractive, manufacturing or service sectors, but manufacturing has conventionally been seen as much the most important. Fothergill and Gudgin (1982) estimated that most manufacturing industry was basic, but most services were dependent. This meant that despite the continuing growth in service industries and jobs (Marshall and Wood, 1995), most service industries were seen as, at best, unimportant in economic regeneration and, at worst, parasitic activities, which did not provide 'real jobs' (Williams, 1994). Those service industries that clearly were basic – like many of the financial services in the City of London – tended to be regarded as exceptions. As Urry (1990a) argues: 'Implicit in the restructuring ... literature is a presumed hierarchy of industrial sectors, with extractive-manufacturing seen as basic ... and service industry as relatively unimportant'.

Williams (1994) points out that, over the last decade, this view of services has begun to break down. First, a wider view is now taken of what constitutes basic services. Producer services, frequently closely associated with manufacturing, are now widely acknowledged as trading inter-regionally (and internationally), and thus as income-earning basic industries: business and financial services are examples. In addition, some consumer services have been recognized as basic, because they attract consumers into the locality where they spend money, earning external income for the locality. Tourism is the most widely recognized 'basic consumer service' industry, but some leisure and retailing – part of our wide definition of tourism – fall within the same category. Tourism is capable of generating income from across regional and national boundaries, and is thus an export industry in the fullest sense. Second, services are propulsive and contribute to economic growth if they prevent the leakage of income outside the locality. They can do that by providing consumer services that otherwise could only be purchased elsewhere. Thus a city's shopping and leisure facilities are basic to the extent that they result in residents spending money in the city that they would otherwise have spent elsewhere.

The presumed hierarchy of industrial sectors is thus based on inaccurate assumptions. Services are of increasing significance in regeneration, and consumer services as well as producer services can have an important propulsive role. What are the changes in city economies that mean that regeneration is required?

## Consequences of Economic Change

Radical and rapid change in city economies from the 1970s onwards meant that there was an increasing concern to generate new investment and to attract mobile economic activity. That in itself was not new. National and local government, and local business interests, have traditionally been concerned to attract new investment to areas where industries are in decline. The novelty arose from the fact that economic change was sufficiently rapid, widespread and severe to prompt innovative responses from policymakers. There were three main factors involved in the UK.

First, there was an increasing awareness that total manufacturing employment would continue to decline while competition between cities to attract mobile investment would intensify both nationally and internationally. As a result, individual cities could not expect that job losses in traditional manufacturing (and associated extractive and distribution industries) could be made good by new manufacturing investment. Conventional policy responses based on luring in new manufacturing firms through subsidy and the provision of premises were thus at best a partial solution. This forced policymakers in the late 1970s and early 1980s to look creatively at other sources of potential employment and regeneration, and this focused attention on activities lower down the conventional hierarchy of industrial sectors – consumer service industries such as tourism and leisure. In 1980, the English Tourist Board was able to review a series of examples of tourism-based regeneration initiatives, and argue that whilst tourism was not a panacea for inner city problems, it could play an important role in creating employment and income and in revitalizing an area (ETB, 1980). In many cases, however, tourism and ACE industries were promoted with reluctance and for the want of alternatives. There was a view that service jobs, and leisure jobs in particular, were 'candyfloss', not real jobs. This perspective was partly based on a culture of manufacturing and heavy industry that defined 'proper' jobs, and partly on the reality that many leisure and tourism jobs have been of low quality – in terms of pay, security or working conditions. In the mid-1980s, the Civic Trust's initial programme for regeneration in Halifax was modified to exclude an initial emphasis on the promotion of tourism because public consultation showed there was a feeling that 'job creation in tourism and retailing was a poor substitute for the employment in manufacturing that had been lost' (Lockwood, 1993). These ideas have persisted, and even in 1994 Williams was calling for an end to 'erroneous prejudices' against service jobs in local economic development, and arguing that 'the service sector must be reconceptualized as a vibrant dynamic sector which can strengthen the health of a local economy'.

Second, the intense competition for inward investment led to a concern with city marketing and promoting a positive image of a locality. Promoting the (alleged) advantages of locating in a particular town or city was not new. The 1950s and 1960s had seen local authorities advertising the availability of new industrial units and serviced sites, and in the 1960s and 1970s most places found some means to claim that they were located at the heart of Britain's motorway network. The novelty of city marketing was that it sought to promote a place to investors not through specific industrial or 'business' attributes like sites and roads but with overall image, and the general virtues of the place as somewhere to live or to visit. 'Place marketing [came to be] recognized as a key component of the post-industrial city' (Smales, 1994). This concern naturally meant an increasing interest in those aspects of places that were attractive to visitors or potential investors, which created positive images, or which could be used effectively in marketing.

Third, the loss of traditional industries left a legacy of vacant buildings and sites: empty warehouses, mills, market buildings, railway stations, and factories. These vacant buildings and derelict sites were very visible signs of economic decline, and an obviously wasted resource, leading to pressure to create new and productive uses. In many cases, buildings and sites were ramshackle and polluted, attractive only to the most dedicated industrial archaeologist, so solutions required clearance and redevelopment. However, there were also many instances of buildings with clear potential. Frequently they were of historic interest (whether or not they were statutorily listed); well known locally and symbolically important; structurally sound and adaptable; clustered in recognizable districts; within or close to city centres; and cheap (Beioley *et al*, 1990; Urry, 1990b). In such cases, the need for economic regeneration was not translated into proposals for comprehensive redevelopment, as would have been the case in the 1960s. Attitudes to the built heritage had changed, public money was scarce, and such proposals were mostly far too risky for the private sector to undertake without public guarantee or subsidy. Instead, the requirement was to find new activities and uses that could capitalize on the potential of the inherited stock of buildings. Ideas of 'adaptive re-use' of buildings (Cantacuzino, 1975) became widespread, often drawn from early US initiatives such as Baltimore's Harbour area or Boston's Quincy Market (Urbed, 1994; Colquhon, 1995).

The stock of redundant buildings is continually replenished as

*Figure 4.1*
The Corn Exchange, Leeds. An imaginative conversion of a historic but redundant city centre building for retailing and restaurants by Speciality Shops plc with the support of Leeds City Council.

economic change continues, and the process is not confined to industrial buildings. The most significant recent changes in city economies have affected service activities, including office-based services. Reductions in employment, the shift of 'back-office' functions to new locations, and the existence of large amounts of unlet new office floorspace constructed during the boom of the 1980s have meant that many older office blocks have become vacant. In many ways, this stock of redundant buildings represents more of a challenge than did the older industrial buildings, because the structures are usually less adaptable, less attractive and much less liked. As Chris Marsh points out in Chapter 5, these buildings do have the potential to be re-used, but the market has so far made little progress in achieving change.

The combination of these factors led to attempts to identify types of

*Figure 4.2*
Pearl Assurance, Holborn, London. Redundant offices (following relocation of the company to Peterborough) awaiting re-use, possibly as a hotel.

economic activity that could use the built heritage of past industry and so turn it into an asset and a new source of competitive advantage, which contributed to a positive image for the city. Above all, there was a concern to create new jobs, and an interest in industrial sectors that were growing rapidly in post-industrial circumstances. This inevitably led to an interest in tourism and ACE industries, which are large and rapidly growing, both in the UK and on a world scale. The growth and requirements of the tourism and leisure industries are discussed in the next section.

## Growth of Tourism and Leisure

Tourism and leisure industries have grown strongly, and that growth looks set to continue. Worldwide, over 500 million international tourists were recorded in 1993 – 20 times the volume in 1950. These tourists spent US$324 billion in the countries they visited, and according to the World Travel and Tourism Council (1993), tourism now accounts for 10% of global GNP and employs 204 million people, making it the world's largest employer and accounting for 1 job in 10. World employment in tourism is estimated to grow to 348 million by 2005.

In the UK, employment in tourism-related industries in 1993 was around 2.5 million (Department of Employment, 1994). This exaggerates the importance of tourism, because many tourism-related industries cater for their host population too – transport, pubs and restaurants are obvious examples. A more realistic estimate of employment attributable to tourism would be around 1.5 million jobs (Morrell, 1985). Total leisure spending in the UK is around £60 billion a year (Mills, 1989), and the arts are estimated to employ some 500 000 people and contribute £4 billion to overseas earnings (Myerscough, 1988).

This rapid growth meant that tourism was seen as a means of replacing jobs lost in other declining industries. Almost 20 years ago, the GLC's study of London's tourism industry argued that although in many parts of the industry pay was low and working hours inconvenient:

> ...the industry is giving employment and hence higher incomes to London's poorer families and to workers whose employment prospects have suffered so much in London's population decline (Lipscomb and Weatheritt, 1977, p.17).

During the 1980s, as Hart and Shaw (1992) point out, the UK government took up with enthusiasm the idea that tourism and leisure were a source of employment growth. The White Paper *Employment for the 1990s* (1988) pointed out that increases in real incomes led to increased demand in the leisure and recreation industries, which had seen a growth in employment of 28% in the previous 10 years.

These are impressive figures – which is why there is a strong interest in tourism and ACE industries as sources of economic activity and regeneration – but they should be treated with some caution. Optimistic projections of continuing growth in tourism and leisure, often derived from industry sources, together with the genuine difficulty in defining the industries and their impacts (Goodall, 1987), naturally lead sceptics to argue that their significance may be overestimated. Even from a sceptical point of view, however, it is clear that tourism and ACE industries are already a substantial part of the UK economy, have grown rapidly, and seem likely to be a comparatively rapid growth sector in the future. They potentially constitute a basic consumer services sector which can propel the growth of city economies. A city will enjoy this effect, however, only if it is able to attract visitors from elsewhere, and to retain the leisure spending of its own population. What are the attractions that are required to achieve this?

It is conventional to break down the elements that contribute to the 'total tourism product' (Middleton, 1988) that attracts visitors. One way of doing this is to separate the resources, or primary product – which constitutes the initial attraction – from the services, or complementary product – which makes a visit possible (van den Berg *et al.*, 1994; Davidson and Maitland, 1996). In the case of a traditional resort destination this distinction is fairly clear cut. Resources include natural characteristics like sun, sand and sea, together with facilities provided specifically and mainly for visitors, such as casinos, theme parks and entertainment districts. Services include the transportation required to get to the destination – such as charter flights – and the hotels and other elements of the hospitality industry needed to make a stay possible.

In the case of cities, separating resources from services, and defining resources provided for or attracting mainly tourists and leisure visitors, is much more difficult. The range of destination resources is extensive. It can include:

- **Physical characteristics and setting** — coastal or river locations, or proximity to attractive countryside have particular potential.

- **Built environment and the urban fabric**. Architectural heritage has long been important in historic towns and cities like Chester, Norwich or York (EHTF, 1995), but a growing public interest in Victorian heritage has meant that the nineteenth-century industrial architecture of cities such as Bradford, Glasgow, Halifax and Manchester has become an attraction for visitors. Industrial engineering and artefacts can also be turned into tourism attractions: for example, the Transporter Bridge in Middlesbrough (English, 1995).

- **History, archaeology, and literary associations**. Attractions may be of varying degrees of authenticity. They can be based on 'real' historic buildings and sites – castles, cathedrals, ruins or interpretations based on real sites and artefacts – such as the Jorvik Viking Centre in York, or museums and interpretation centres. However, they may be themed entertainments based on elements of a past – such as the London Dungeon, a 'truly horrible experience' housed not in a dungeon but in railway arches under London Bridge station – or a mix of historical and literary inspiration, like the Canterbury Tales Experience, loosely based on Chaucer and the idea of pilgrimage.

- **Shops**. There has been a continuing growth in shopping generally, and in 'leisure shopping' in particular (Cairns, 1995). Leisure shopping is undertaken not just to purchase goods, but because the experience is enjoyable in itself. It thus excludes routine food, grocery and convenience goods shopping. For most holiday makers, shopping is rarely the prime purpose of travel, but it 'tends to be a predominant time-use for many tourists, irrespective of their primary travel motive' (Jansen-Verbeke, 1994). Leisure shopping is generally a more important element in the motivations of day visitors, and in the case of some cities, it can be the main motivation for the visit — whether a day visit or overnight stay — or at least a secondary attraction (EHTF, 1995).

  Some of the growth of leisure shopping has been accounted for by new monocultural retail developments. Many out-of-town shopping malls, or the growing factory outlet developments, have no significant mix of uses, and are often closed entirely outside shopping hours. However, for many people, leisure shopping requires a mix of shops with some unique qualities (real or illusory), a positive image, supporting amenities – like pubs and restaurants – nearby, pedestrian areas and 'multi-functionality of the environment which guarantees the place feels alive' (Jansen-Verbeke, 1994).

- **Cultural, entertainment and sporting facilities**, which can include museums, cinemas and theatres, arts centres, sports stadia, concert halls and night clubs. A number of these elements may be combined in leisure complexes including, for example, cinemas, bowling, nightclubs, bars and restaurants; and new types of entertainment centre are being developed, such as Segaworld at London's Trocadero. Attractions may be created by packaging or marketing elements of a place's social characteristics to form a leisure experience: for example, Bradford's Flavours of Asia, which includes introduction and guides to the city's Asian shops and restaurants, and a 'Curry Tour' (Smales, 1992; Smith and Maitland, 1996)

- **Characters and events**, whether real or literary. Middlesbrough has used its association with Captain Cook (who was born there) in marketing and as the basis of several visitor initiatives, while also promoting its association with fiction through the 'Catherine Cookson Country' (English, 1995). Authors, works and characters as diverse as the Brontes, Emmerdale, and Sherlock Holmes have been used to help create images of places. In some instances, the 'place' to which tourists are attracted may be an artefact – such as Granada's *Coronation Street* studio set.

  Regular events such as festivals can be a major and long-lasting attraction, as the Edinburgh Festival illustrates. There has, however, been a growth of interest in high profile single events, which generate visitation, spending and a high profile, and which contribute to changes in image. Garden Festivals, Glasgow's year as European City of Culture (1990), Manchester's bids for the Olympic Games (and securing of the Commonwealth Games) and Greenwich and Birmingham's rival bids for a Millennium Festival are examples.

- **Facilities for business tourism and conferences** such as hotels, conference and exhibition centres, and support services. Business and conference tourism has grown rapidly over the last decades, and is particularly important to cities. Business tourists generally spend more per day than leisure travellers, and are sought after. While the supply of business and conference facilities is the most important attraction, an attractive physical environment, a range of other attractions, good evening facilities and a good image are also important (Law, 1993).

The tourism and leisure resources of cities, then, are complex and interlinked. The attraction for visitors frequently arises from the combination of several or all these elements in the right place at the right times. Visitors are attracted to a well-defined area (or areas) offering a range of activities, for much of the day and evening. There are several implications.

First, it is difficult to separate elements of the 'total tourism product'. What appear to be services or complementary elements – such as shopping – may in fact constitute a major part of the attraction of visiting the city or remaining there for leisure activities. It may be most sensible in cities to see primary and complementary elements together forming total 'urban leisure supply' (Margot Jokovi, 1992). Second, it is difficult to separate clearly those elements that cater for overnight visitors, day visitors and others, and many facilities will be used by all of them.

Many of the aspects of the city that are attractive to visitors are also valued by others – whether residents or potential investors. Third, tourism and leisure resources are also potentially flexible and changeable,

*Figure 4.3*
City centre, Oslo, Norway, September 1995.
Sitting outside is becoming a universal experience for tourists and business people, seemingly irrespective of latitude.

because they derive from users' perceptions. The marketing of industrial cities, for example, has involved changing negative images to positive ones – in the case of Bradford, from one of derelict mills set in a decaying industrial wasteland to one of interesting Victorian heritage surrounded by magnificent open countryside with strong literary associations. Both images include a mix of reality and interpretation.

Finally, there is a clear and strong association between tourism and leisure uses and mixed development. Because the attraction of the city for visitors, and for residents seeking entertainment, depends strongly on a combination of attractions that can be found in an area that is convenient and coherent from a user's point of view, mixed use areas have obvious potential advantages.

## Tourism, Leisure and Mixed Use Development

Tourism and leisure uses can play a crucial role in creating a mix of uses – both within buildings and within areas. Re-use of buildings and regeneration of areas are of course interlinked; it is easier to achieve the development of a particular building if is located within an area generally perceived as attractive for investment, and conversely, a major flagship building may affect the fortunes of a whole area. Nevertheless, it is convenient to examine buildings and areas separately.

Because changes in city economies have created a large stock of vacant buildings, many with historic, heritage or architectural value, finding suitable new uses has been a continuing challenge. Tourism and leisure uses have often been seen as important parts of the answer. There are a number of reasons for this. First, and most obviously, as growing economic activities, they require space. Any growth industry interests those seeking new uses for vacant floorspace, and tourism and leisure uses have often been the outcome of attempts to find some viable function for an historic building that has been 'saved' (Beioley, *et al.*, 1990).

Second, they may capitalize directly on the building's history, its form or status as part of the city's history and heritage. There has been a very rapid growth in the number of museums, heritage and interpretation centres. Urry (1990b) points out that a 1987 survey found 1 750 museums in Britain, of which half had been started since 1971. The building itself may be an integral part of the museum or interpretation – as when a textile museum is housed within a former textile mill, and attempts to re-create industrial processes using authentic or original plant and equipment (Lowell in the USA, Styall in Cheshire and New Lanark all offer examples). Equally, it may be less directly associated with exhibits, but be appropriate in a more general way. Manchester's Science and Industry Museum, for example, is housed partly in a railway station and railway warehouses, but also in a former wholesale market – not directly related to science or industry, but part of the city's industrial past. Glasgow Development Agency's planned conversion of the George Square post office is a mixed use scheme involving not only a philatelic museum but also a gallery of Scottish art and design, as well as offices. Finally, many leisure uses gain interest and potential selling points from being housed in older or historic buildings. Hotels, bars, restaurants and shops can all gain from such locations and associations, although these advantages may be offset by high costs of conversion and operation compared with purpose-built premises. Some showpiece developments, such as Terence Conran's conversion of the former Michelin building in London to a shop, restaurant and offices, illustrate the potential.

Third, some leisure uses may attract public or non-commercial funding, especially those involved in arts and entertainment. The National Lottery is now an appealing source of cash for projects that would not meet commercial funding criteria – for example, the Tate Gallery's proposed conversion of the former Bankside power station. Public funding may be for setting up or operating the activities – some museums or galleries, for example – or to assist in the costs of conversion of historic buildings. In either case, this may permit the conversion of a building that would not be viable on purely commercial criteria: the publicly funded use can act as an anchor tenant, or capital costs of conversion can be reduced or developer confidence may be increased. The tourism elements of Liverpool's Albert Dock development – which included offices, shops, a studio, maritime museum and art gallery – can be seen in this light. (Beioley *et al.*, 1990).

Fourth, many tourism and leisure uses are good neighbours, especially for office, retailing and professional service activities. The need to attract visitors means they pay particular attention to their physical environment, and often place a premium on good design. Some uses,

*Figure 4.4 and 4.5*
Butlers Wharf, London (left) and Brindleyplace, Birmingham (right). Examples of increasingly imaginative use of waterside sites (the River Thames and the canal respectively) to offer more interesting places to locate restaurants in a mix of other uses.

such as museums and galleries, may add to their neighbours' status, and visitor facilities including cafés and restaurants may be used by people living and working in the area. High volumes of visitors, on foot or coach-borne, can cause difficulties in heritage cities, but rarely seem to be a problem in industrial cities.

Finally, tourism and leisure uses often attract local support. By re-using and revitalizing buildings associated with industries that have declined or vanished, they offer a positive response to de-industrialization, which can be an antidote to feelings of social and cultural loss (Urry, 1990c). Bringing such buildings back into use for tourism also fosters the view that the city has something to be proud of, and which is attractive to the outside world. When residents of Manchester and Liverpool were asked about the redevelopment of former industrial areas for tourism, over 80% said that the developments were something to be proud of. (Beioley *et al.*, 1990).

But tourism and leisure uses represent more in the changing economy of cities than just a growth industry that can help bring vacant buildings back into use. As we argued earlier, consumer service industries should be seen as basic industries, capable of earning external income and thus of driving growth in the local economy. With the decline of traditional industries, tourism and leisure will become an increasingly important part of the economic base of cities. As this happens, they become more important not just in their own right but because of the effect they have on other economic activities:

> ...such developments are increasingly important in determining the character of individual places. Tourism, including arts and leisure, has become central in forming people's experience of place, of the natural and built environment, the range of services available locally, the transportation infrastructure, the degree of congestion and the attractiveness that such a place has for inward manufacturing investment (Urry, 1990c, p.279).

This widening importance, and the significance of the character of a place for investment, points to the link between mixed use areas and tourism and leisure.

Tourism and leisure uses both require and make possible areas of mixed use. They require them because, as suggested above, visitors and people at leisure revel in a variety of activities in city centres. They want to be able to shop as well as visit museums, to eat and drink and just sit around as well as going to a gallery, and they want to go to a club or theatre or both in the evening. In other words, some types of tourism and leisure experience require the presence of other people – visitors and locals alike – to be enjoyable. Urry (1990c) distinguishes between 'romantic' and 'collective' conceptions of tourism. In the romantic case, the value of the tourist experience derives from unspoilt beauty, solitude, and an authentic experience away from other people – being able to wander lonely as a cloud. Growing numbers of visitors threaten to destroy such experiences – you cannot wander lonely in a crowd. Collective tourism experiences, on the other hand, incorporate other people as part of the enjoyment; it is hard to imagine that a day as the sole visitor to Blackpool Pleasure Beach would be much fun. Equally, the attractiveness and glamour of cities derives partly from the large numbers of other people, including other tourists, and the exciting and cosmopolitan atmosphere that this can create.

Critics argue that, far from promoting a lively mix of uses, – multifunctionality which makes the area feel alive – tourism leads to its own form of sterile mono-culture:

> Walk around Windsor on a summer weekend, and you find yourself in a world which exists solely to cater for people who never spend more than a few days in the place (Sudjic, 1996).

This can be a real danger in small areas subject to intense tourist pressures, and the problem is discussed below. However, Sudjic goes on to argue that larger cities like York are also damaged, and that catering for tourism means their centres are dead at night after visitors have gone. This seems much less convincing, and misunderstands the processes taking place. Tourism means that during the day – the peak period for visitors – cities like York support a much more intense level of activity than they otherwise would, given their resident population. As visitors leave, activity reverts to closer to the norm for the population size. Tourism is increasing daytime activity, not reducing night-time activity. The challenge for a livelier night economy is to encourage visitors to stay longer.

Looking at tourism as a collective experience means that there is a real synergy from a mix of uses – the whole that is created is greater than the sum of the individual parts. This has long been recognized, if not always put into practice. The GLC's regeneration of Covent Garden in the 1970s, for example, was centred on using the former wholesale market buildings for retail and leisure uses. Although the development was intended to produce a commercial return, differential rents were used to ensure that a mix of different types of shops, stalls, eating places, cafés and so on was achieved in the Market, rather than simply accepting those that could pay the highest rents. This helped to promote a vibrant and mixed centre, which encouraged the regeneration of the rest of the area.

Tourism and leisure can make possible areas of mixed use in a variety of ways. First, because visitors themselves provide a market for a range of services – cafés and restaurants, bars, shops, nightclubs and so on – it seems reasonable to suppose that a range of uses will be promoted in the vicinity of major attractions (Jansen-Verbeke, 1994). While this seems to be borne out anecdotally – for example, the concentration of family restaurants near Madame Tussaud's in London – no research evidence seems to be available.

Second, tourism and leisure promote areas with an attractive physical environment, the re-use of historic buildings and the conservation of heritage, as these are key assets for the industry. More cities are seeking to do what many historic cities have always done:

What the major UK tourist cities have in common, notably cities such as York, Bath and Edinburgh, is an ability to make the past an integral part of the present and a major contributor to the local economy (Smales, 1994, p.37).

Such areas can prove attractive to many non-leisure users. The regeneration of the Castlefield area of Manchester, for example, was based on tourism development and rehabilitation of historic buildings. In the process the area became more attractive for other activities – for example, professional services like architects and designers – who began to move into the area, thus promoting a variety of uses (Beioley *et al.*, 1990). The whole process is facilitated by a third impact of tourism and ACE industries – image changing. Tourism and leisure uses are frequently high profile and well publicized, so they not only help change an area, they also increase awareness of that change. This can affect potential investors and decision-makers, who may visit a city as a business or leisure tourist and have their view of it altered as a result. This in turn may mean that inward investment in non-tourism uses is encouraged. The case studies of Halifax and Bristol illustrate these points.

Tourism and leisure clearly have the potential to promote lively areas with a mix of uses as they play an increasingly important role in city economies. What are their drawbacks? Commercialization and inauthenticity are potentially problems, and relate to a wider debate about

*Figure 4.6*
Riverside, Leeds.
Converted industrial buildings and warehouses have been successfully converted to flats, offices and (on the right of this picture) a hotel and restaurant. Nearby are new tourist facilities, including Tetley's Brewery Wharf and the Royal Armouries Museum.

the extent of and requirement for authenticity, especially in a post-modern environment (Urry, 1990b; Hewison, 1987). Law (1992) summarizes the issue:

> The sanitized environment that tourists want may completely change the character of a place ...Roy Worskitt [points out] 'Once you take the Disneyland approach to towns you kill off the idea of a town as a place which changes and you devalue the historic buildings'

While it is not clear that tourists necessarily want a 'sanitized environment', the general problem can be a real one, especially in smaller towns and villages. While it is unlikely that the whole of a city centre would succumb to these pressures, particular areas might, and an interesting mixed use area could degenerate into a tourist trap. It might be argued that, as a result of changing policies, this process is now well under way in Covent Garden, for example. Such changes are associated with another potential problem – the displacement of uses that cater mainly for local needs and markets and which may be driven out by leisure and tourism activities able to pay higher rents. The loss of butchers and bakers and the growth in souvenir shops is a frequently quoted example. How far such potential effects are a real problem is hard to say, because clear evidence is hard to acquire. On the issue of displacement, for example, it is clear that butchers, bakers and other local shops have disappeared in large numbers everywhere in the UK; the alternative to souvenir shops may be vacant premises.

Although tourism may lead a process of regeneration that ultimately leads towards sanitization, other activities exert similar pressures. Changing image and increased footfall can make an area attractive to image-aware office users such as advertising agencies and design studios, and to major or chain retailers. They may then drive out marginal office users and independent specialist shops, which gave the area some of its original character. This again can be observed in Covent Garden, and raises the interesting issue of how prospering mixed use areas can be managed so that they do not become victims of their own success.

On a similar theme, very large visitor flows (and the associated coaches or cars), or a dominance by particular kinds of visitor, can be disruptive: foreign schoolchildren have a particularly bad reputation in a number of historic cities, for example (Davidson and Maitland, 1996). A lively and cosmopolitan atmosphere can too easily become one that is noisy and trashy. All these potential problems raise issues of management and planning, which are discussed in the following section, and in Chapter 9.

Finally, there is a danger that tourism and leisure may themselves become the victims of their own success. Cities desperate to find ways of regenerating their economies may develop exaggerated expectations of the role that tourism and leisure can play, and underestimate the public resources and time required for significant effects to be achieved (Law, 1992). An allied danger is 'me-tooism'. Ideas that seem to have worked well in other cities – in Britain or elsewhere – may be imported without clear consideration of whether they are really appropriate. As Smales

(1994) says, this can too easily result in the creation of 'urban environments that are little more than a kit of badly assembled, dangerously fragile parts'. In either case, attempts to use tourism and leisure to lead broader mixed use regeneration are likely to be unsuccessful.

## Tourism in the Mixed Use Development Process

The growth of interest in tourism and leisure as a means of regenerating the economies of cities since the late 1970s has been one that had its origins in strategic opportunism rather than plan-led development. At central government level, there was generalized support for the growth of tourism, and enthusiasm for its job-creating potential, but there was

*Figure 4.7*
Gloucester Green, Oxford. Managed to encourage a range of smaller specialist shops and restaurants in a highly aclaimed mixed use scheme with flats, offices and the market.

no overall strategy (Goodall, 1987). There was some support for tourism and leisure projects through the inner city programme, but projects were usually initiated by local authorities, often with the support of tourist boards (Maitland, 1991).

At the local level, too, an interest in tourism and leisure derived not from a strategic appraisal of opportunities but from a combination of responses to specific problems – what to do with vacant buildings of historic interest, how to capitalize on areas of economic growth, how cities' images could be changed – and a willingness to experiment in the absence of alternatives. Some tourism developments and initiatives in the early 1980s arose from innovators devising solutions to particular problems, and finding the means to carry them through – whether in terms of physical developments or marketing campaigns. (At the start of the 1980s the idea of Bradford seeking to attract tourists under the slogan 'Bradford – a Surprising Place' was itself pretty surprising.) Some form of strategy often followed later, and helped keep the process going (Beioley et al., 1990). Since these pioneering initiatives, an increasing recognition of the role of service industries, including consumer services, in the city economy has meant that tourism and leisure initiatives have joined the mainstream of economic development.

There was a parallel growth of interest in the whole idea of city image as an important element in economic decision making. While 'selling' places to inward investors is not a new idea – Ward (1990) shows that local authorities have been doing it at least since the inter-war period – it became more pervasive and sophisticated in the 1980s. The idea of attracting investment to towns and cities by promoting them as good places to live, first used by new town corporations such as Milton Keynes, Peterborough and Telford, was adopted by local councils in established cities. Promotion was often linked to specific events, such as garden festivals, city of culture designations, or attempts to secure major sporting events.

The combination of an opportunistic approach to regeneration strategy, making the most of potential assets and a concern with improved image led to a focus on tourism and leisure, and on mixed use development – even if these were not explicit goals, as the Halifax case study illustrates. The success of some of these initiatives and a developing reappraisal of the most important industries in city economies encouraged a more deliberate focus on the role of tourism and leisure.

Developing experience of the role that tourism and leisure can play in changing city economies suggests that there can be a mutually supportive relationship with mixed use development. A number of elements seem to be important in gaining the maximum benefits.

First, tourism and leisure uses need to be strongly linked to other local firms and to other initiatives to generate the maximum benefits. In this they are like any other propulsive industries: the stronger the links to local as opposed to outside industry, the greater the multiplier effects on the local economy. More broadly, tourism attractions can bring in visitors who like to use other facilities and services, which can then become attractions in themselves.

Bradford's National Museum of Photography, Film and Television is a major draw in its own right, with 850 000 visitors a year. Visitors are encouraged to explore nearby Asian restaurants, and thus help promote the city's Asian cuisine as an attraction in its own right. Policies to promote such cooperation and reinforcement are necessary to realize maximum benefit, and may be achieved through partnerships of various forms (Bailey, 1995).

Tourism and leisure projects can form an important element in such partnerships, especially when mixed use development and regeneration are sought. They are potentially highly visible, are directly related to an area's image, and can add excitement and zest to proposals, and so generate commitment to change. This can be especially important when public authorities are attempting to secure beneficial change with very limited resources. In South London, for example, the Greenwich Waterfront Development Partnership has had to adopt an essentially promotional strategy aimed at attracting private sector and central government funds to aid the area's regeneration for the benefit of local people. The high profile that tourism gives the area, the potential to attract Millennium events because Greenwich is the home of the zero meridian and Greenwich Mean Time, and the possibilities of leisure and tourism uses as anchors in development schemes, have been used to attract outside interest and attention and to raise confidence in the area

*Figure 4.8*
Pelikan-Viertel, Hanover, Germany.
The conversion of a historic industrial complex into a mix of uses incorporates new restaurants in the former boiler house. See case study in Chapter 10.

(Greenwich Waterfront Development Partnership, 1995).

Second, the role of public agencies is fundamental. When the aim is to use tourism and leisure as part of a process of regeneration, public investment, grant-aid and infrastructure improvement are usually necessary to induce investment by the private sector. Private sector entrepreneurs who are prepared to take the risk of initiating a process of mixed use development are rare. There are few parallels with Jonathan Silver and Salt's Mill (Chapter 9). Public investment is common to a wide variety of regeneration strategies. A particular advantage of some arts, culture and leisure initiatives is their ability to access funds outside the regeneration budgets. For example, the Royal Armoury museum (below) benefited from a £20 million grant from the Department of National Heritage, while refurbishment of buildings for leisure uses in Greenwich town centre benefited from £1 million from English Heritage. A clear programme to guide and coordinate public and private investment and initiatives, with responsibility for delivering it, is also a key element for success.

Third, competition for key tourism and leisure activities has increased as their importance has become more widely recognized. New or footloose arts or tourism attractions are now courted as enthusiastically and competitively as new car plants or micro-electronics facilities, and the same techniques of lobbying and financial incentives are employed internationally (for example, the competition for Disney Europe) and nationally. For example, Leeds made considerable efforts to secure the Royal Armouries museum, a major visitor attraction originally considering locating in Sheffield. The campaign, which included lobbying and the provision of a financial package of £25 million from the City Council, the Development Corporation and private sources, was successful, and the museum is to be used as a focus for regeneration on one edge of the city centre (Smales, 1994).

Finally, effective initiatives need to be realistic. The real potential of tourism and leisure means that there is the risk of its being oversold as the key to unlocking difficult problems, or the guarantee of lively and enjoyable developments. It is neither, and 'me-too' policies that are inappropriate for local circumstances are likely to fail.

# References

Allen, J. and Massey, D. (1988) *The Economy in Question,* Sage, London.

Bailey, N. (1995) *Partnerships Agencies in Urban Policy,* UCL Press, London.

Beioley, S.J., Maitland, R.A., and Vaughan, R. (1990) *Tourism and the Inner City: An Evaluation of the Impact of Grant Assisted Tourism Projects,* HMSO, London.

Cairns, S. (1995) Travel for food shopping – the fourth solution. *Traffic Engineering and Control,* **36** (7/8), 411–418.

Cantacuzino, S. (1975) *New Uses for Old Buildings,* Architectural Press, London.

Colquhon, I. (1995) *Urban Regeneration,* Batsford, London.

Davidson, R. and Maitland, R. A. (forthcoming) *Planning and Managing Tourism Destinations,* Hodder, London .

Department of Employment (1988) *Employment in the 1990s,* Cmnd 540, HMSO, London.

Department of Employment (1994) *Employment Gazette.*

EHTF (1995) *Historic Towns – Mixed Uses and Vitality and Viability,* English Historic Towns Forum, Bath.

English, R. (1995) Tourism for economic regeneration: the Middlesbrough experience, in *RTPI Summer School Proceedings,* 36–41.

English Tourist Board (1980) *Tourism and the Inner City,* ETB, London.

Fothergill, S. and Gudgin, G. (1982) *Unequal Growth: Urban and Regional Employment Change in the UK,* Heinemann, London .

Fothergill, S., Kitson, M. and Monk, S. (1985) *Urban Industrial Change: the causes of the urban rural contrast in manufacturing employment trends,* HMSO London.

Goodall, B. (1987) Tourism policy and jobs in the United Kingdom. *Built Environment,* **13** (2), 109–123.

GWDP (1995) *Greenwich 2000 Tourism Development,* Greenwich Waterfront Development Partnership, London.

Hart, T. and Shaw, T. (1992) An overview, in *The Role of Tourism in the Urban and Regional Economy,* 1–4, Regional Studies Association, London.

Hewison, R. (1987) *The Heritage Industry,* Methuen, London.

Hutton, W. (1995) *The State We're In,* Jonathan Cape, London.

Jansen-Verbeke, M. (1994) The synergy between shopping and tourism: the Japanese experience, in *Global Tourism – The Next Decade,* (ed. W.F. Theobold), Butterworth-Heinemann, Oxford.

Kaldor, N. (1966) *Causes of the slow rate of growth in the United Kingdom,* Cambridge University Press, Cambridge.

Law, C.M. (1992) Tourism as a focus for urban regeneration, in *The Role of Tourism in the Urban and Regional Economy,* 11–18, Regional Studies Association, London.

Law, C.M. (1993) *Urban Tourism,* Mansell, London.

Lipscomb, D. and Weatheritt, L. (1977) Some economic aspects of tourism in London. *Greater London Intelligence Journal,* **42**, 15–17.

Lockwood, J. (1993) Holistic regeneration: the experience of Calderdale, United Kingdom, in *Urban Regeneration, Property Investment and Development,* (eds J.Berry, S. McGreal and B. Deddis) E. & F.N. Spon, London.

Maitland, R. (1991) *Tourism and urban regeneration: the contribution of tourism to economic development in inner city areas in the UK,* paper to Planning Transatlantic Conference, July, Oxford.

Margot Jokovi, E. (1992) The production of leisure and economic developments in cities. *Built Environment,* **18** (2), 138–144.

Marshall, N. and Wood, P. (1995) *Services and Space,* Longman, London.

Massey, D.B. (1984) *Spatial Divisions of Labour: Social Structures and the Geography of Production,* Macmillan, London.

Middleton, V. (1988) *Marketing in Travel and Tourism,* Heinemann, Oxford.

Mills, S. (1989) Tourism and leisure – setting the scene. *Tourism Today,* **6**, 18–21, quoted in Urry (1991a).

Morrell, J. (1985) *Employment in Tourism,* British Tourist Authority, London.

Myerscough, J. (1988) *The Economic Importance of the Arts in Britain,* Policy Studies Institute, London.

Smales, L. (1994) Desperate pragmatism or shrewd optimism? The image and selling of West Yorkshire, in *Reinventing a Region: Restructuring in West Yorkshire,* (eds G. Haughton and D. Whitney), Avebury Press, Aldershot.

Sudjic, D. (1996) Can we fix this hole in the heart of our cities? *The Guardian,* 13 January.

Tourism Society (1975) *Handbook and Members List,* London.

UN (1963) *UN Conference on International Travel and Tourism,* Rome.

Urbed (1994) *Re-using Derelict Urban Buildings,* Department of the Environment, London.

Urry, J (1990a) Work, production and social relations. *Work, Employment and Society,* **4** (2), 271–280.

Urry, J. (1990b) *The Tourist Gaze,* Sage, London.

Urry, J. (1990c) The consumption of tourism. *Sociology,* **24** (1), 23–35.

van den Berg, L., van der Borg, J. and van der Meer, J. (1994) *Urban Tourism,* Erasmus University, Rotterdam.

Ward, S.V. (1990) Local industrial promotion and development policies 1940-1988. *Local Economy,* **5** (2), 100–118.

Williams, C.C. (1994) Rethinking the role of the service sector in local economic revitalisation. *Local Economy,* **5** (1), 73–82.

World Travel and Tourism Council (1993) *Travel and Tourism Report,* WTTC, Brussels.

# Case Study 4.1

# The Piece Hall, Halifax

This development illustrates how historically and architecturally important buildings can find a new lease of life in a different use. The Piece Hall in Halifax dates back to 1779, when local hand-loom weavers traded 'pieces' of cloth in the two- and three-storey stone-built colonnaded building. The trade was very valuable, the cloth highly regarded, and the building suitably impressive. However, the weaving trade declined, and the building came into use as a fruit and vegetable market. By the mid 1960s this use had also ceased, and along with the adjacent Square Chapel the Hall was considered for demolition, to make way for a town centre car park.

Calderdale Council voted (by a margin of one) to keep the buildings and find alternative uses. The central courtyard, once used to graze sheep, is now a thriving market. The various small dealing rooms have been combined to create retail units, all taken by individual traders selling a wide variety of crafts and gifts as well as books and antiques. One side of the building is linked to an adjacent former mill building, and the whole complex now forms an Industrial Museum featuring the trades and industries of the locality. An art gallery and a restaurant complete the uses in what has become a successful and popular development, which has retained the character of the building without superfluous or inappropriate additions.

A variety of events are held in the courtyard, including classical, rock and folk music. The adjacent Square Chapel is an Arts Centre, which is still seeking funds for a complete refurbishment but which still offers a wide variety of dance, music and cultural performances. Building on the successful transformation of what was a very run-down and unattractive location, the adjacent railway station now hosts the 'Eureka!' project, a experiential science museum which attracted over a million visitors in 1994. As Comedia in the report *The Art of Regeneration* (1996) comment:

> The Council's recognition of the potential for the architectural gem in their midst was hard won, at a time when other towns were demolishing historic buildings which are much regretted. ... The buildings provided a physical and symbolic focus for an important part of the town, and have helped underline richness of the cultural experience which Halifax can offer resident and visitor.

*Figure 4.9 (opposite)*
The Piece Hall, Halifax.
Specialist shopping, a market,
art gallery and industrial
museum in a converted
historic building.

The Piece Hall is one positive example of a local authority transforming unwanted buildings. Elsewhere in Halifax, Dean Clough Mills shows a private entrepreneur taking a huge former textile factory and re-using that too. Here Ernest Hall (with Jonathan Silver for a period) has created employment, a home for various arts companies, rehearsal space and other facilities including a restaurant. Halifax is, perhaps surprisingly, one of the best examples of successful urban regeneration.

# Case Study 4.2

# Bristol Docks

There have been a number of regeneration projects associated with the Floating Harbour that runs through the centre of Bristol. One of the earlier schemes shows both the public/private partnership approach and a successful mix of uses. The Arnolfini Gallery is a converted nineteenth century tea warehouse on a quayside about 400 m from the city centre. The gallery, used for performances as well as exhibitions, occupies the bottom two floors and includes a bookshop and bar/restaurant. The top four floors of the building are known as Bush House, and are commercial offices serviced by an entirely separate entrance.

*Figure 4.10*
Bush House, Bristol.
Home of the Arnolfini Gallery
as well as commercial offices.

The scheme was started in 1974, with the gallery funding their part of the work on the building in partnership with local developer JT Group, who carried out the work and retained the commercial space. The costs (at 1975 prices) were £1.1 million, with the Gallery funding £372 000 with a combination of donations and grants. In its 21 years on the site the Arnolfini has established itself as an important part of Bristol's cultural life.

The Harbourside project is the latest scheme which Bristol City Council hope will strengthen that cultural activity. Based on the largest area of the Floating Harbour that remains undeveloped, Harbourside is made up of a variety of commercial and cultural elements. These include an 'electronic zoo' christened 'Wildscreen World', a science centre (building on the city's existing 'Exploratory', a similar project to 'Eureka' in Halifax) and a Centre for the Performing Arts. Again a public/private initiative, Harbourside is much bigger, involving landowners (including British Gas, Lloyds Bank – who have their new headquarters on the site – and the JT Group) with Bristol City Council. An accord between the interested parties was signed in 1994, designed to build on the development framework agreed in the same year. The £300 million scheme has already received Millennium Commission support for some elements of the project. To fund the necessary infrastructure the City Council is supporting the provision of

*Figure 4.11*
Harbourside, Bristol.
A plan of the possible layout for the Harbourside project, with: a mix of uses across the site, but few mixed use elements overall.

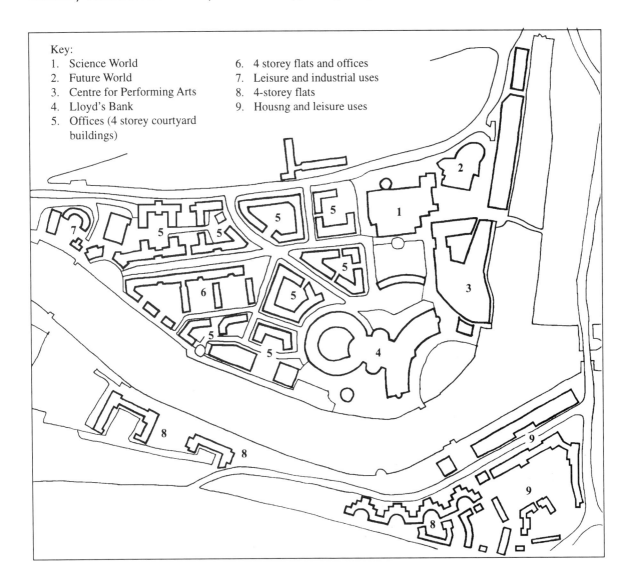

Key:
1. Science World
2. Future World
3. Centre for Performing Arts
4. Lloyd's Bank
5. Offices (4 storey courtyard buildings)
6. 4 storey flats and offices
7. Leisure and industrial uses
8. 4-storey flats
9. Housng and leisure uses

There are two groups of interrelated explanations to address:

- the criteria traditionally used to evaluate investment and thus development opportunities; and

- the characteristics and especially the limitations of property appraisal and valuation methods.

Unlike the approach adopted in some countries where private investors are significant, the property investment market in the UK has long been dominated by institutional investors.

The investing institutions include pension funds and life insurance companies whose objective is to invest their contributors' premiums in safe, reliable investments, which yield solid returns over an extended period. Property companies, banks and other investment vehicles are also important investors in property. Indeed,

> ..the increased exposure by banks to the commercial property market has been central to banking difficulties in many countries (Lewis, 1994).

However, pension funds and insurance companies are crucial in two respects:

- their ownership of commercial property – that is, offices, shops and a variety of business spaces – is very extensive and thus a fundamental market characteristic; and

- their perception of the prospects for property tends to determine the level and type of activity in the property market, not least by their willingness to forward fund or more commonly acquire completed developments. Consequently, their attitudes are major determinants of property value.

Therefore in considering the outlook for mixed use development, a useful starting point is to identify the factors that are most likely to influence investors in selecting particular investments. We can then examine mixed use schemes in the light of changing market circumstances and determine the extent to which those developments may meet investors' requirements in the foreseeable future.

There are a number of ways in which potential investors may view investment criteria. Predictably, these are complex and constantly evolving, but they can be summarized in a number of ways.

## Current Portfolio Composition

Inevitably, investors' decision-making regarding property will be influenced by past performance when compared with other investment options such as gilts, bonds and equities, together with current levels of exposure. Generally, property investment has performed well in comparative terms [1]. Over the last 25 years, property has enjoyed real returns of around 4% per annum, and recent research confirms that:

...property can significantly improve diversification [within a portfolio] if included as an asset to balance equities (IDP/Fuller Peiser, 1995).

But average returns are bound to mask wide variations in the performance of particular funds. Indeed,

...in the early 1990s, the international property market finds itself in the throes of the worst crisis this century. Prices of all types of property have collapsed across the major capitalist economies, resulting in negative equity for many homeowners and in widespread losses in commercial real estate (Coakley, 1994).

The unfortunate fund manager who acquired an office block at the height of the market may now be seeking to disinvest from the sector and minimize losses. The cash-rich counterpart, however, may perceive the same building as relatively cheap today and likely to achieve good returns in the future (though not necessarily without refurbishment or change of use). In other words, different investors will assess individual properties differently depending on their circumstances.

|  | December 1980 | September 1995 |
| --- | --- | --- |
| UK equities | 45 | 54.9 |
| Overseas equities | 9 | 22.6 |
| UK bonds | 21 | 5.9 |
| Overseas bonds | 0 | 3.9 |
| UK index linked | 0 | 3.0 |
| Cash/other | 5 | 4.6 |
| **Total excluding property** | **80** | **94.9** |
| UK property | 20 | 4.9 |
| Overseas property | 0 | 0.2 |
| **Total assets** | **100** | **100** |

*Table 5.1*
Pension fund weightings (%)
source:
WM All Funds Universe

Overall, however, institutional investors have been steadily reducing their exposure to property (as demonstrated in Table 5.1), mainly on the grounds of better performance from bonds and equities and their comparative liquidity.

While some commentators believe that pension funds (unlike life funds) will eventually abandon property entirely, others maintain that the shift away from property has gone far enough,[2] on the grounds that equities may be due for a pricing correction, bond yields are expected to fall, property's expected returns of 10% for the next three years are attractive, and its comparatively low volatility is useful in diversifying a portfolio.

Nevertheless, the immediate effect on property, especially after the recession, has been that funds have become much more discriminating in identifying appropriate investments but, as will become clear, this strategy not only generates greater competition for the best properties but also opportunities for property companies and other investment vehicles to fill the void. This prospect is important in advancing the cause of mixed development.

*Figure 5.1*
Dorrington House, Leather Lane, London.
Offices over shops, previously owned by an institutional owner in the Midtown area. Bought by property developer Sapcote for around £1 million in early 1996 for residential conversion.

## Comparative Investment Opportunities

While investors are influenced by long-term trends, short- to medium-term prospects will prompt constant monitoring and review of the investment portfolio. In 1995, UK pension funds recovered strongly after a poor showing in 1994, achieving average returns of 19%. This reflected particular advances in bonds and equities: UK equities, for example, provided a return of 24%. Only equities in the USA exceeded this figure, while the average return from Japanese equities was under 2%, highlighting market turmoil in that country. Over the last five years, however, UK equities with an average return of 16% have been beaten by every leading overseas equity region with the exception of Japan. Most notably, the Pacific rim countries averaged a remarkable 27% return, and not surprisingly remain the focus of many investors' attention.

Property, having been successful in 1994, recorded a disappointing return of 5% in 1995 and although pundits are more optimistic about property prospects in 1996 and beyond, property's comparative position in the global market is clearly central to investment decision-making.

## Prime and Secondary Property

Property of course is not a single investment entity capable of comparison as a whole with other forms of investment. Some properties will be more attractive than others. Particular properties can be categorized in terms of their attractiveness to investors, principally by distinguishing 'prime' from 'secondary' investments. Prime property, while not subject to an absolute definition, can be considered as the best and therefore the most highly valued property from an investor's viewpoint. As such, prime property has specific characteristics, which can be identified as follows:

- they are located in the best possible position to meet their function. For example, prime retail property in Oxford Street, London, will be located close to Bond Street and Oxford Circus underground stations, where pedestrian flow is most concentrated.

- the structure of the building and the facilities provided in and around the building will best meet occupiers' requirements.

On the assumption that the physical criteria are met, the building to be considered a prime investment must then attract:

- a high calibre, financially well-founded tenant (that is, a good 'covenant'), prepared to enter into an institutional lease (that is, a long lease with regular upward-only rent reviews).

Obviously such properties are rare, and come to the market infrequently. The vast majority of properties are thus secondary: that is, they lack one or all of the characteristics listed to some degree. This does not imply that secondary properties are of no interest to investors, but it does suggest that greater risk is associated with them and, as a result, their value is adversely affected. The notion of prime property is complicated by the following;

- No two properties are alike in investment terms. Adjacent shops in Oxford Street will vary slightly in location, structure or covenant, any or all of which will affect their prospects and value.

- Prime locations are not necessarily fixed. The building of a new supermarket at one end of the high street may well change consumers' shopping habits and shift the location of prime property.

- Unlike other forms of investment, while locations are fixed, buildings can be refurbished or ultimately redeveloped and thus may have the potential to reinstate investment prospects.

## Property Sectors

Just as property investments can be classified as prime and secondary, the market must also be assessed in terms of use. The office, retail, industrial and business space markets are not necessarily coordinated. Some sectors (or elements within them) will be more attractive than others at any point in time. Indeed, each sector may be situated at different points in the investment cycle. In the early 1990s, for example, during the depths of recession when the office market in particular was collapsing dramatically, the warehouse sector remained strong as corporate demand for logistical efficiency in distribution networks generated new property requirements.[3] For the fund manager, therefore, identifying likely areas of future growth and committing resources accordingly in anticipation of increases in value is a crucial contributor to overall performance.

## Capital and Rental Growth Potential

While rental income provides a basic return on capital invested in property, it is growth potential over and above inflation that attracts the investor. This will be reflected in increases in a property's capital value and/or its rental value. There are a number of factors that may generate growth, but the most obvious is scarcity. When particular types of property are scarce or likely to be scarce in the future, and demand for that property type is strong, then risk from the investor's stance is reduced and values are likely to increase.

Various events may prompt this situation. For example, in the aftermath of the property recession of the early 1990s, very little new office development has taken place in London, and while vacancy levels remain high, much of that stock is poor-quality secondary property. In 1995/6, demand for good-quality new space has started to re-emerge. The result is a shortage of prime office accommodation and some rental growth, despite the continued glut of secondary space. Consequent competition between investors for prime buildings is then reflected in capital values.

Government can affect growth potential. For example, revisions to Planning Policy Guidance Note 6 issued by the Department of the Environment in 1995 seek to revitalize town centres, especially the retail element, in part by adopting a more restrictive position on new out-of-town shopping developments. Car-borne consumers' preference for such schemes has not diminished however, and therefore, from an investor's viewpoint, restricting supply in the face of strong demand equals growth. Competition between retailers for available space in new and existing schemes has intensified, rents have improved and capital values benefited.

Traditionally, growth in property investments has also been underpinned by the institutional lease with its pattern of five-yearly upward only rent reviews. While growth in earnings is collected only every five years, two advantages accrue to the investor:

- In a balanced portfolio, rent reviews for different properties will be spread over time, and therefore, overall, rental income is likely to rise, even when market rents are temporarily static.

- The tendency for the institutional lease to lock in the tenant for an extended term provides the investor with a hedge against the effects of occasional market slumps. The significant falls in rents from property in the early 1990s did not benefit tenants committed to long leases. The effect is that many tenants occupy buildings that are now over-rented. The owners of such buildings are hardly likely to complain as long as the occupier remains in business.

Nevertheless, the growth prospects of property investment are not assured. An extended period of low inflation in the national economy, for example, might well affect property returns. Similarly, the effects of the property recession on the institutional lease – for example the acceptance of shorter lease terms and break clauses by landlords – may prove a permanent feature of the market and thus make property less attractive comparatively to investors.

## Portfolio Management Questions

It has already been made clear that managing an investment portfolio requires constant evaluation and adjustment. However, different types of investment require different types of management.

The equities and bond markets are characterized by high levels of liquidity and comprehensive market information. Investors, especially institutional investors, rarely become actively involved in, say, the companies in which they invest. In contrast, investors in property cannot be passive. Apart from strategic decisions common to all investments – buy, hold or sell – day-to-day property management is unavoidable.

From the investor's viewpoint, the ideal position would be to let a whole building to a single tenant with good covenant and transfer all the responsibilities for its maintenance and associated outgoings to that tenant the 'full repairing and insuring lease' (FRIL). The investor's responsibilities are minimized. The investment is especially attractive.

Where the building cannot be let to a single tenant, not only is the net lettable area (and thus rental income) of the building reduced by the need for common areas to service separate tenants, but the landlord has to become more actively involved in managing the building, maintaining and cleaning the structure and providing security. Service charges will offset these costs but organization and administration is implicit. The greater the number of subdivisions in the building necessary to attract tenants, the higher the costs, while more tenants occupying small spaces increases the risk of vacancy and therefore lost income. The lesson for most investors is clear. The more management an investment requires, the less attractive it becomes.

This picture, however, ignores one important scenario, namely the role of 'active management'. Active management is a loose term, which can be applied to those investors who view property investments not in terms of current income and growth prospects but in terms of potential income and returns, following some degree of upgrading. Improvements will range from the modest to the substantial, but in all cases the objective will be to improve facilities and the image of the development in order to make it more attractive to occupiers and users. At one extreme, this may involve painting the foyer of the office block, placing planting in the shopping centre or changing the industrial estate's name to 'Greenfield Business Park'. At the other extreme, substantial refurbishment or renovation may involve considerable expenditure on the building's structure and surroundings, possibly including changing use wholly or in part. Such actions involve sensitive calculations comparing current returns with potential returns following specified outlay. Not surprisingly, the risks associated with these projects will be high and only of interest to specialist investors. Nevertheless, they have become increasingly common. Indeed, ultimately, such calculations are inevitable. While the land on which a building is located may increase in value (assuming locational preferences have not changed), the structure itself will gradually incur functional and/or physical obsolescence. In those circumstances, every owner/investor will eventually be presented with a range of refurbishment/redevelopment options and a difficult decision.

## Investment Criteria and Mixed Use Development

How then has mixed use development matched up to investors' traditional expectations to date? The obvious answer is that it has generally failed. Certainly those estates dominated by older buildings in central areas such as the Grosvenor, Portman, Portland and Howard de Walden estates in London have a legacy of mixed uses where they have sought to manage such buildings positively, but their experience is unusual. The vast majority of investors have conscientiously avoided mixed use schemes, and the explanations are not hard to find.

While there is a wide range of investors interested in property, from the institutional funds and property companies to local estate holders and individuals, all are conservative in assessing risk (albeit to varying degrees). The role of the developer in identifying market opportunities, initiating the project, completing the building, letting the space and achieving good returns before selling on a proven investment is one obvious way of minimizing risk to the investor. The developer will therefore normally be required to 'pioneer' new forms of development, arrange appropriate short term funding and carry all the risk. Once the scheme becomes established and is seen to be successfully performing, then the investor will step in.

On the face of it, this process of generating investment credibility in new property types would appear protracted at best and impossible at worst, but this is not necessarily the case. For example, up to the mid 1980s, investors, especially at the institutional end of the spectrum, largely ignored warehouses. In less than ten years, however, attitudes have totally changed in response to corporate concentration on increased efficiency in distributing goods; a rapid rationalization of outlets by many firms, and a concentration on a small number of very large distribution centres; their changing property requirements and the successful initiatives of specialist developers such as Gazeley Properties. Suddenly, investors are competing fiercely for such schemes and forward funding projects when opportunities arise.

In contrast, while examples are beginning to appear more frequently, mixed use developments are still going through adolescence in market terms and have yet to achieve a recognized track record of investment performance. This is hardly surprising. For many investors, mixed use schemes reflect an obvious failure to attract a single use or user. They are therefore by definition secondary, and more likely to be found in non-prime, fringe locations. On both counts, they are obviously less favoured, and so, in the interim, risk in pursuing such schemes must be largely internalized by the owner and/or developer. As the example of warehouses demonstrates, however, circumstances can generate changes quickly, and this possibility will be explored later in this chapter.

Unfortunately, in the case of mixed use developments, overcoming habitual antipathy is complicated by the particular characteristics of such schemes, which continue to be dissuasive factors. Many may be regarded as petty management issues but their effect on value and thus their effect on investor perception remains considerable.

For many occupiers, differing neighbouring users within the same building will be viewed as intrusive and potentially problematic. The much reiterated property agent's tale of the overflowing bath in upper-floor housing damaging computer hardware in lower-floor offices is symptomatic of attitudes in general but nevertheless based on not unreasonable concerns. Different tenants have different needs and expectations, especially in common areas, which are often manifest in disagreements about service charges, all of which increases management responsibilities and thus costs. Separating services and insulating users from each other (literally) are invariably necessary but often difficult to achieve, especially in older buildings. Even new multi-use buildings have to be very carefully designed in order to minimize conflicts. Physically, this almost always involves providing separate accesses to, for example, ground floor offices and upper floor residential, and that can constrain internal layouts, complicate statutory requirements such as fire escapes, reduce otherwise rentable floorspace, and increase construction costs.

Even where uses are complementary, different lease terms may reflect different legal frameworks, most obviously in landlord and tenant law.

The outcome is predictable, and reflected in both market characteristics and valuation practice. For most occupiers (and therefore landlords), mixed use buildings have been avoided wherever possible. Where unavoidable, rents are traditionally discounted because the market believes that mixed use occupiers have tended to be poorer covenants, less inclined to enter institutional leases, and more likely to move on or simply fail. Vacancy rates therefore tend to be higher, and difficulty in finding replacement tenants means longer voids and lost rent. Not surprisingly, all these factors adversely affect yield (i.e. the multiplier used to calculate the capital value of a building). A valuation of a mixed use building or an appraisal of a mixed use proposal will mirror these considerations. Lower rents and higher yields (i.e. riskier investments) mean lower capital or development value. Higher costs and profit to offset greater risk will reduce residual land value. Therefore, even if developers did favour mixed use schemes, they might be unable to compete in land value terms with a single use project, not least because funding mixed use projects would certainly be more difficult and more expensive. Investor preferences in such circumstances have been understandable, so how can a brighter future for mixed use developments be justified?

On the face of it, the evidence against mixed use developments is irrefutable. Schemes characterized by a combination of poor returns and higher costs have inevitably failed to compete with better, simpler and more acceptable property investment and development options elsewhere. Is this pattern set to continue, or will a combination of structural changes in the nature and outlook of property investors, the effects of the worst property market recession since the mid 1970s, and the efforts of a small but intrepid band of mixed use development pioneers change investors', developers' and occupiers' perceptions of mixed use schemes?

## Changing Property Market Prospects

An improving property investment and development market in general is an important prerequisite to any change in attitude towards mixed use schemes. However, having anticipated rental growth in commercial property and a housing market recovery numerous times since 1989, the market has continued to be disappointed. While values in all the main sectors stopped falling overall in late 1995 (subject to local variations), only exceptional buildings in particular locations have exhibited growth. In comparison with property performance in the late 1980s, results appear very poor but this is somewhat deceptive.

> With inflation running at an average of over 8% over the last 30 years, high nominal growth was required just to maintain real values. In the lower-inflationary environment of today, 4 or 5% rental value growth is actually very attractive (Patterson, 1995).

The consumer, however, has not been reassured, at least not so far. The so-called 'feel-good' factor remains latent, which continues to restrain the housing market. It is perhaps therefore surprising that not only have banks returned to lending money for commercial property but on terms almost as favourable as at the height of the property boom in the late 1980s. On the face of it, this is encouraging for mixed use schemes, not least in financing projects during the transitional period to more general investor acceptability. However, in 1996, there are important differences in lending characteristics that need to be noted:

- Most bank lending is set against revenue-producing properties, not developments, and although by early 1996 lending criteria were slightly more relaxed, financing speculative development remains very difficult.

- Lending against a property sector with very much lower value levels is clearly less risky. Put simply, there is less to lose and less likelihood of losses occurring when values are deflated.

- Borrowers can no longer expect to raise funds against anticipated increases in property value. Income from the building must cover loan interest, and the lender may also require additional insurance to cover other possible rising costs such as higher interest rates.

- Most important of all, a potential lender's view of a property will be heavily influenced by the strength of covenant. Indeed, with so many household as well as little-known company names disappearing from the property map since 1989, some analysts now argue that lending is so linked to covenant that the property itself is of minor importance.

While these characteristics tend to suggest a much more discriminating stance on the part of the banks, which would not appear to help the cause of mixed use schemes, the overall level of lending has in fact increased noticeably.

The Bank of England figures (Table 5.2) show the largest increase in lending by UK banks since 1990 and a major change in attitude by some banks. There is also considerable competition between banks for the right property, and this has reduced borrowing rates. While this may not directly influence attitudes to mixed use schemes, it does represent an important more general re-entry into the property market by lenders, which is essential[4] prior to institutional involvement.[5]

Nevertheless, for banks who saw the value of, say, City of London offices fall by over 50% during the recession of the 1990s, and who are now faced with shorter lease terms, break clauses, overrented properties and uncertainty about future yields, lending decisions can still be fraught with difficulties. Predictably, in these circumstances lenders seek additional loan protection.

One slightly more encouraging sign for mixed use schemes, however, concerns covenants from the lender's viewpoint:

The property owner's ideal of letting a building to a single tenant still holds good if the covenant is absolute top quality. Properties of this kind can be financed without a problem. It is a different matter when the single tenant is of lower standing. A portfolio of mixed covenants, in which some are less reliable than others, will be easier to finance than a single-tenanted property with only a moderate covenant. Income risks have to be spread unless the risk is extremely low in the first place (Brett, 1995).

Although this approach clearly applies to a mixed portfolio rather than a single mixed use property, it does suggest that a good covenant in part of a building could still be attractive.

While mixed use schemes are likely to remain less attractive to institutional investors until proven, UK banks and bank loans are not the only source of finance. Overseas lenders, while by no means predominant, are nevertheless influential. In particular, many such interests not only come from an investment culture less myopic regarding mixed use schemes but have also avoided the worst excesses of the UK property recession. Addressing today's market conditions without being influenced by a portfolio of non-performing loans from the recent past, may well generate a more enthusiastic view of mixed use properties.

Overall, it would obviously be foolhardy to suggest that the property climate has so changed in the post-recessionary property market that mixed use schemes are now easy to finance. Clearly, that is not the case. However, the right mixed use scheme in the right place with a solid covenant base may well find support from lenders, and certainly there is actual evidence to call upon.

There is also a general consensus amongst property analysts that the direct property market will begin to recover in 1996. Thus, for example:

> ...rental growth will be stronger in 1996 than in 1995 (based on a benign mixture of economic growth and the declining availability of desirable space). This, together with a small improvement in yields, would be sufficient to give a total return of 13.5% and make property the best performing UK asset class of 1996 (SBC Warburg, 1996).

|  | September 1995 | Annual change | Market share (%) |
|---|---|---|---|
| UK banks | 20.22 | 3.86 | 62.74 |
| US banks | 0.92 | 5 | 2.87 |
| Japanese banks | 3.06 | -9.79 | 9.49 |
| Other banks | 8.03 | -2.94 | 24.9 |
| **Total** | **32.23** | **-0.69** | **100** |

*Table 5.2*
Bank Lending to Property Companies, £bn.
source: Bank of England

## Property Market Circumstances

Although the general attitude of lenders towards mixed use properties may still be at an early stage of recognition, particular market circumstances suggest increasing opportunities for the sector. Clearly, if a choice exists, investors, especially institutional investors as well as property companies, will always opt for prime properties if possible.

For example, competition for absolutely prime property was perhaps best epitomized by the efforts (eventually successful) of John Ritblat's British Land to secure the acquisition of the Broadgate development, London EC3, following the collapse of Stanhope and Rosehaugh. Such schemes are exceptional.

In contrast, Chesterton reported in their third quarter survey (1995) of Central London office space, that take-up had fallen for the third successive quarter and was down 22% on the equivalent quarter of 1994. Chesterton claimed that:

> the lack of choice for major occupiers seeking new, high specification office space in Central London [was] now critical and [was] acting to depress overall take-up levels (Chesterton, 1995).

Occupiers seeking space in excess of 9 300 m$^2$ (100 000 ft$^2$) had very limited choice while vacancy rates had fallen from 12% to 9.8% year on year (albeit with sharp local variations). Demand, it was stated, had remained relatively stable at about 743 500 m$^2$ (8 million ft$^2$) with almost three-quarters targeted at new or refurbished second-hand space. At the same time, Chesterton reported that office space in the pipeline had increased to 4.8 million m$^2$ (52 million ft$^2$) following the grant of planning consents totalling 334 570 m$^2$ (3.6 million ft$^2$) in the third quarter.[6]

The lessons from such analysis are clear. Prime markets will continue to be active, with some large space needs being frustrated in the short run, making development of the latter phases of projects like Broadgate, or new schemes like Spitalfields viable. These will generate shortages in some sectors, creating some improvements in values: a fact reflected in forecasts (see Table 5.3). More generally, however, the excessive level of space in the pipeline will halt overall growth. While modest growth is essential to maintain activity, pre-let or pre-sold developments will still be required before development will be attempted in all but the best locations:

> The last thing we want now is unwarranted and irresponsible speculative development (Slade, 1996).

The obvious conclusion from this situation should be that the prospects for secondary property must improve. Indeed, many owners of such properties continue to hold on to this hope (and thus defer any more radical strategy, including an acceptance of mixed use within their buildings). If demand and take-up is strong but net availability is about the same, then increasingly the space on offer is secondary or worse. Research covering 19 centres outside London in 1995 suggested that

250 000 m². (2.69 million ft²) of new office space and 1.2 million m² (12.9 million ft²) of secondhand space was available.

While these statistics may provide some hope for building owners, other research is less optimistic.[7] For example, a report commissioned by the London Planning Advisory Committee[8] warned that London is facing a serious threat of over-supply of land with planning permission for office developments, suggesting that there are more than 400 office permissions and applications that are unlikely ever to be built.

London really does need to look at the implications of downsizing and delayering in many of the office sectors and consider the future in terms of the core office areas. We may be seeing some contraction in land use terms. The question is how that provides other mixed use opportunities, like turning offices into hotels (Simmons, 1996)[9].

*Table 5.3*
Property Value Forecast
Changes (%) 1995/96
source: Atkins and Jones,
1996, p.16

| | Rental values | | Investment yields | | Capital values | |
|---|---|---|---|---|---|---|
| **Offices** | 1995 | 1996 | 1995 | 1996 | 1995 | 1996 |
| All | 0 | 3 | 8.2 | 8.2 | -2 | 2 |
| London | 2 | 3 | 7.6 | 7.8 | 1 | 1 |
| South East | -3 | 2 | 9 | 8.9 | -5 | 2 |
| Rest of UK | -1 | 2 | 9 | 9 | -5 | 2 |
| **Retail** | | | | | | |
| All | 1 | 3 | 7.2 | 7.1 | -4 | 5 |
| Shops/centres | 0 | 2 | 7 | 6.8 | -5 | 5 |
| Retail warehouses | 3 | 4 | 8.1 | 8 | -1 | 6 |
| **Industrial** | | | | | | |
| All | -2 | 1 | 10 | 9.9 | -6 | 1 |
| London | -3 | 0 | 9.6 | 9.6 | -5 | 0 |
| South East | -3 | 0 | 10.3 | 10.2 | -6 | 2 |
| Rest of UK | 1 | 2 | 9.9 | 9.9 | -5 | 1 |
| **All property** | **0** | **2** | **8** | **8** | **-3** | **3** |

| | Nov 1994 | May 1995 | Nov 1995 | Annual % |
|---|---|---|---|---|
| Shops | 252 | 251 | 251 | -0.5 |
| Offices | 204 | 204 | 204 | 0 |
| Industrial | 198 | 199 | 202 | 2.2 |
| **All property** | 222 | 221 | 222 | 0.1 |

*Table 5.4*
Secondary property rent index
(Base: May 1994 = 100)
source: Hillier Parker

| | Nov 1994 | May 1995 | Nov 1995 | Annual movement |
|---|---|---|---|---|
| Shops | 8.4 | 9 | 9.3 | 0.9 |
| Offices | 9.5 | 9.5 | 9.6 | 0.1 |
| Industrial | 10.5 | 10.5 | 10.6 | 0.1 |
| **All property** | 9.8 | 10.1 | 10.3 | 0.5 |

*Table 5.5*
Secondary property yield movements.
source: Hillier Parker

Certainly, market value evidence to date has not been reassuring. While secondary property rents have been stable overall, yields have weakened (Tables 5.4 and 5.5)

Clearly, the prospects for the best secondary property may be better but more generally, the distinction between prime and the vast majority of secondary locations and building stock may well increase, not least as the pace of corporate relocations releasing more secondary space increases in 1996.[10] This will place further pressure on the owners of secondary buildings to explore alternative futures. In many of these situations, rents and capital values will be too low to warrant redevelopment now or in the foreseeable future. A refurbishment/change of use option is likely to be the only feasible strategy: a view confirmed by a recent report of the Government Office for London,[11] which advocates the conversion of redundant offices to alternative uses on the basis that much accommodation is unsuitable for modern business needs. (Pointedly, the report recommends the encouragement of mixed use developments near transport nodes which could lead to opportunities for regeneration.) This process has already started. Thus, for example, converting secondary offices into residential blocks and former industrial

*Figure 5.2*
Teziac House, a 1960s office
block in the City of London,
now known as Cathedral
Lodge, developed as
apartments by Barratt in
1995.

premises into live-work units is increasingly common.

In February 1996, the first residents moved into Cathedral Lodge, London EC1, where Barratt's converted 53 000 ft² at Teziak House, former offices into 50 flats ,which sold quickly. For the former owner of the unlettable office block, the sale provided an exit strategy and prevented further losses. For Barratt, the acquisition at a modest price and the subsequent conversion provided an immediate return, and by setting up a tenants' management company, the developer could on completion pass over all future responsibility for the property. This approach to development is underpinned by demographic changes and has a bright future.

Specifically, the forecast of a serious housing shortage over the next ten years is also an important factor in determining the future of mixed use, especially in London. The Department of the Environment's latest household projections for England for the period up to 2016 were published in March 1995 and prompted concern. They showed a sharp increase in forecast households over the 1989-based projections – 737 000 more than the 1989 figures. The predicted growth by 2016 now totals 4.4 million households, and presents difficult questions about how to accommodate this anticipated growth. A Government Discussion Paper on available options is expected in 1996[12]. Nevertheless, one major research project[13] has already suggested that this revised forecast, together with restrictive planning policies could result in a shortage of between 80 000 and 100 000 units in central and inner London alone by the year 2005. Demand for smaller non-family units is already strengthening, and that, together with the possibility of further reductions in Housing Association Grant and thus activity, suggests rising prices and rents. For first time occupiers, the outlook is difficult. For developers and investors constrained by land availability especially in inner areas, opportunities beckon in expanding conversions of existing properties.

*Figure 5.3*
Warner Lofts, Clerkenwell, London.
The conversion of a 1930s industrial building, Warner House, into residential 'lofts'.

This view was confirmed by a recent survey,[14] which suggested that on 1st January 1996, only 2000 private homes were available in central London. By the end of the century, 11 400 should be added to this total, with supply peaking in 1997. While 70% of all units with planning permission are in Docklands, where demand is possibly lower, the report concludes that most new homes in central London will come from commercial and industrial conversions.

Clearly, the prospect of the population of central and inner areas rising is to be welcomed. Not only would it counter long-standing outmigration and contribute to the achievement of sustainability objectives, but it would facilitate the (re)introduction of a wider range of facilities and services into areas that were previously dominated by single uses. Furthermore, it would provide genuine and much-needed development and refurbishment options to investors currently locked into depreciating assets with poor or nil income flow.

However, wherever possible, conversions of this type retain one overriding characteristic, namely that the objective for most (though not all) investors and/or developers is to sell on the completed scheme. As noted earlier, this is clearly facilitated if the building in question is converted to a single use (as in the example of Teziak House above). Indeed, in the short to medium term, a converted and occupied mixed use building may be no more disposable than in its previous life. Here, the building's owner will probably have to accept the rental income flow (and the management responsibilities and costs involved) for the time being, at least until mixed use properties' investment 'credibility gap' is bridged.

Overall therefore, in particular locations, the property market is accepting the notion of mixed uses (albeit perhaps somewhat grudgingly), but single use buildings will still be preferred whenever possible.

## Planning and Legal Considerations

The property market's perception of mixed use schemes has also been influenced by central government's stance on planning and development issues, changes to the law of property (in particular the provisions of the Housing Act 1988) and, occasionally, the availability of grant aid to make viable otherwise marginal or loss-making schemes.

While planning policy regarding mixed use is considered elsewhere in this book, it is worth noting at this point the property market's reaction to recent planning initiatives, in particular since 1991.

The influence of property-based organizations and the property professions on central government was considerable during the Thatcher years and found a sympathetic ear. The planning system was presented as an obstacle to development and thus economic growth,[15] and this prompted the government to relax the process in various ways in order to facilitate development. By 1991, however, the planning regime was being presented in a more positive light by the Major administration, in part in response to increasing concern about environmental and infrastructure considerations, but also, ironically, in order to provide greater certainty to the property development industry – then in the grip of the worst recession since 1973. The product, however, went well beyond the expectations of the property world. The introduction of mandatory nationwide coverage of local plans in 1991 (for the first time in the history of town planning in the United Kingdom), the emphasis placed on the status of up-to-date plans by the revised section 54A of the Town and Country Planning Act, 1990, the expansion and strengthening of national policies through Planning Policy Guidance Notes and ministerial statements supporting greater control of development (occasionally implemented through the planning appeal process) predictably prompted trepidation in the property industry. While the actual effects of these changes have not been as dramatic as the market feared – a stronger planning system cannot in itself generate demand – in areas where there are development pressures and adopted policies promoting mixed use, there is a greater likelihood of such policies being implemented.

Ironically, the interaction between the planning and development processes can actively work against mixed use even where local policies encourage it. Planning gain is now a widely accepted part of the planning process, with increasingly clear government policy[16] and developing consistency in legal application[17] and, according to the Royal Town Planning Institute,

> ...cannot be abandoned without reconsidering the whole system of planning (RTPI, 1982).

This process, operating within a planning system characterized by administrative discretion, inevitably involves negotiation between developers and planning authorities, and in this respect the provision of planning gains off-site is often presented as controversial. Off-site gains in the form of, say, road infrastructure requirements will obviously be consequential on the development proposal in question. However, where there is a sound planning framework to support mixed use development, it has often been in the developer's interest to seek to provide the 'secondary' use off-site too. Not only will it be financially advantageous to intensify the principal commercial element of the scheme but, as noted earlier, 100% commercial schemes have consistently been preferred by investors, and this favouritism has been reflected in higher values.

Market perceptions of mixed use developments have also been influenced by changes to the law of property, which address traditional developer and investor reluctance to include residential elements in commercial schemes. Not only was residential development an area of activity in which most commercial development companies and surveyors had little or no experience, but residential inclusions were invariably considered to be fraught with legal complications, as was noted in a recent editorial: 'Investors and their professional advisors rarely cross the divide between commercial and residential property' (*Property Week*, 20.1.96, p.52).

In particular, the effect of rent control legislation on most residential lettings entered into prior to the Housing Act 1988 was a major disin- centive to investors. The effect of artificially controlled rents producing passing rents which would eventually amount to a fraction of actual open market value clearly badly affected valuing such an investment on the basis of income stream. This, combined with the tenants' security of tenure by virtue of the Rent Act 1977 , effectively '... limited the possibility of increasing the income stream and made the reversionary interest a very distant and sometimes unobtainable prize'. [18]

Many developers and their advisors also remember residential rent freezes in the early 1970s, and have since considered residential tenancy as an area subject to undue political intervention (and thus investor uncertainty) and not worthy of serious consideration. This attitude has now been partially alleviated following the introduction of the Housing Act 1988. Since 15th January 1989, landlords have been able to adopt new tenancy vehicles such as the 'Assured Shorthold Tenancy', with which it is possible to let residential property at open market rents and on terms that would not grant security of tenure to the tenant. In these circumstances, it is reasonably certain that vacant possession would be easily gained at the end of the term within a relatively short period, whatever the actions or intentions of the tenant. While this change certainly hasn't revolutionized the residential rented market, it does

*Figure 5.4*
Inveresk House, The Strand, London.
One of a number of empty office buildings in the West End being considered for conversion to a hotel.

provide the possibility of removing a further hurdle to mixed use schemes.

Ultimately, however, the success of the government in promoting mixed use developments can be measured only in terms of direct funding of appropriate projects; here the record is variable. Reductions in, for example, grant support to housing associations are a constraint on mixed use schemes (housing associations have been partners in some mixed use schemes and have been actively involved in developing and managing mixed schemes themselves). However, grants made available through various funding programmes, especially those aimed at inner city areas, have enabled some mixed use developments to go ahead.

## Mixed Use and the Market – Future Prospects

It is hopefully clear from the discussion above that the property investment and development market in the UK has long-established attitudes and practices that are difficult to change, even in the face of market slumps. However, in the light of the steady reduction in institutional investors' exposure to property over the last 20 years, it is possible to envisage market perceptions being slightly less conservative in the future, especially as property becomes increasingly international and thus subject to foreign investor interest, perhaps less constrained by our traditional favouritism for single use buildings. The emergence of a new breed of property company and, in particular, indirect property investment vehicles should also contribute to a slightly more relaxed and perhaps more opportunist view of property. Certainly, a recovery in property market fortunes is an essential prerequisite to any change in market attitudes, and there are, after innumerable false dawns in the early 1990s, reasonably good prospects for prime property. The right building in the right location with the right tenant in occupation will continue to yield good returns and attract investor interest.

The prospects for secondary property, however, (including buildings and locations previously regarded as prime but no longer so classified), are far less secure, and it is here that opportunities for mixed use developments to become established as an acceptable sector for investors are most obvious. All sectors of the property market are characterized by an increasing gulf between prime and secondary property, perhaps most obviously demonstrated in the central business district office market. Here, not only did the boom of the late 1980s seriously over-supply many towns and cities with potential space, but much of the glut of secondary space has become unmarketable in any condition. Despite 'downsizing' and 'delayering', (the latest property jargon), interest is likely to be maintained in the concentrated central business districts of cities. This is despite continuing corporate relocations to more environmentally attractive locations with better infrastructure. The high expectations of property owners and speculators in City fringe locations, at the height of the market, have proven for the most part to be unrealistic. It is here that alternative development scenarios are most likely to emerge at least in the short to medium term. Owners of secondary space plagued by high vacancy rates and high costs are increasingly looking towards change of use/refurbishment options as a means of securing returns, and here market circumstances are conspiring to be helpful. In particular, rising demand for housing developments, especially from small households content to be located in city fringe areas, which conveniently parallels broader sustainable planning objectives, is presenting owners of secondary property with serious investment possibilities. If property yields remain relatively high and interest rates relatively low, then significant change-of-use refurbishments may well be self-financing. This does not of course imply that all vacant or part vacant buildings suddenly have a secure future; far from it. Poor locational characteristics, structural limitations of the building and difficulties in securing planning and building regulation consents as well as funding problems will always limit the number of buildings with alternative futures; but, for some, the outlook is more cheerful.

Does the potential in refurbishing secondary property or for that matter redeveloping sites in secondary locations equate with a better future for mixed use developments? The answer is yes, in some cases! But the fact remains that if a single use development is viable and fundable, then it will continue to be the preferred option for most investors. It does, however, appear likely that single use schemes, especially in inner and city fringe areas, (although rarely in central business districts), will be less feasible in the future, and mixed use buildings will begin to prove more acceptable in some circumstances.

## Conclusions

As a whole, the property investment and development market is conservative. Its traditional practices and attitudes are difficult to change, and thus any comments on the prospects for mixed use schemes from the market's standpoint must reflect some caution. Having said that, there is certainly no shortage of examples of such schemes, as the case studies demonstrate. The issue therefore from the property market's position centres on whether we are witnessing a short-term development fashion or the beginnings of a more substantive, longer-term change in market perception of mixed use developments.

Certainly, the 'short-term fad' school of thought does reflect the views of many property professionals, and is perhaps easier to justify. It is argued that traditional preferences for prime property remain, and shortages of such property will generate rental growth in the short term. That in turn will prompt redevelopment and/or refurbishment of poorer buildings and provide the owner/investor of existing secondary stock with a possible means of realizing otherwise depreciating and unsaleable property assets. This scenario, however, rests on spiralling demand for commercial use and a certain bravura on the part of the property development and investment community. Pundits suggest otherwise.

Perhaps unfortunately, there remains a danger that investment institutions and property companies will ignore opportunities, for example, to convert empty offices into housing developments.

Fear outweighs greed; mainstream developers are missing out on a mini-boom in housing demand because they don't understand the market (Marsh, 1996).

While Marsh's criticism reflects traditional preferences and the professional demarcation that tends to separate commercial from residential activity, the implication of his comment suggests alternative viewpoints. Certainly, there is evidence of some successful conversions, but most are to a single use. The contention therefore is that completed mixed use developments will remain a rarity, and where they do occur, particular local market considerations will be the catalyst.

Supporters of the longer-term, substantive change school of thought regarding market perceptions of mixed use development are in the minority, at least for the moment. Nevertheless, the evidence is mounting, with increasing numbers of mixed use schemes being implemented in many towns and cities. Although in some cases the underlying motive is disposal, the case studies do suggest that, founded on a slightly less conservative funding climate, there is a broader recognition beginning to emerge of the benefits of mixed use. While the driving force for many investors and developers may be a gradual acceptance that the large-scale commercial office market will not provide endless opportunities in the future, the more positive aspects of mixed use schemes are starting to be recognized too, not least (somewhat ironically) in the bastion of the office market, the City of London.

Providing retail on the ground floor is one way of making a scheme stand out from the competition. [For example] Marks and Spencer's unit on the corner of Gracechurch Street and Leadenhall Street did not deter Sun Alliance from taking the offices above at a record rent of £70.00/ft². Nor did it halt the sale of the combined investment to Legal and General for £120 million at a net yield of 5% (Hargreaves and Morgan, 1995).

This view is particularly important in that it clearly presents a mixed use development not as a fall-back or exit strategy, but as providing a positive competitive edge in a market where occupiers have considerable choice. Clearly, in this example, both the occupier and the institutional investor agreed. This certainly lends credibility to the notion of structural change in the property market in favour of mixed use developments.

To date, mixed use buildings have only very occasionally achieved the elevated status of 'prime property'. The prime property characteristics of location, building quality and covenant will be especially important in mixed use schemes if they are to secure long-term success. Design considerations will be critical, and it is likely to remain rare to find a mixed use building in isolation. Mixed use areas may well prove to be an essential prerequisite to individual mixed use developments.

Overall, despite these reservations, it is not unreasonable to suggest that the outlook for mixed use development is improving, and that such schemes could well be a prominent feature in the next investment and development cycle. However, to secure an extended life for mixed use buildings will require a further radical change – user flexibility – designed into the development at the outset. The ability to accept different users into buildings without major expenditure in response to market developments in the future can certainly be facilitated if prioritized in the initial design. The benefits for investors are obvious, and should ensure that mixed use does not prove to be a mixed blessing.

## References

Atkins, J. and Jones, R. (1996) in *Property Week,* 4 January, 17.

Bennett, M. (1978) Mixed use development in the inner city. *Estates Gazette,* 18 March, 920–923.

Brett, M. (1995) Once bitten, twice shy? *Estates Gazette,* 19 August, 34–35.

Chesterton (1995) *Central London Office Survey*, Chesterton, London.

Coakley, J. (1994) The integration of property and financial markets. *Environment and Planning,* **26**.

Hargreaves, C. and Morgan, T. (1995) Mixed blessings. *Estates Times Office Review,* 17 November, 45–46.

IDP/Fuller Peiser (1995) *Risk and Return*, Fuller Peiser, London.

Lewis, M.K. (1994) *Banking on Real Estate*, Discussion Papers in Economics No 9416, University of Nottingham.

LRS (1996) *London Residential Development,* London Research Services, London.

Patterson, A. (1995) Converging forces raise prospects for expansion. *Property Week,* 12 October.

RTPI (1982) *Planning Gain*, Royal Town Planning Institute, London.

SBC Warburg (1996) *Property; Review of 1995 and Prospects for 1996*, SBC Warburg, London.

Simmons, M. (1996) London land use policy is failing to fuel regeneration. *PlanningWeek,* 8 February, 6.

Slade, M. (1996) Four telling the future. *Property,* 4 January, 17.

## Further Reading

Baum, A. and Crosby, N. (1995) *Property Investment Appraisal,* 2nd edn., Routledge, London.

Cadman, D. and Topping, R. (1995) *Property Development,* 4th edn., E. & F.N. Spon, London.

Scarrett, D. (1995) *Property Asset Management,* 2nd edn.,E. & F.N.Spon, London.

## Notes

1   See for example the regular research reports that monitor property market perform-ance, published by leading surveying practices such as Jones Lang Wootton, Healey and Baker and Hillier Parker amongst many.

2   See for example Baring Houston and Saunders UK Property Report 138, November 1995.

3   For a fuller explanation of property cycles and their significance, see Barras, R. (1994) Property and the Economic Cycle: Building Cycles Revisited., *Journal of Property Research,* **11** (3), 183-197.

4   For a more detailed analysis of property sector borrowing, see DTZ Debenham Thorpe's *Money into Property* surveys.

5   For details of the property investment market's expectations of property market per-formance, see the Investment Property Forum's annual review. For a commentary, see French, N. (1995) Property – love it or leave it? *Estates Gazette,* 7 October, p.126.

6   See also Jones Lang Wootton (1995) *Central London Offices Quartely Review, Fourth Quarter 1995,* JLW.

7   For example, Healey and Baker's *Quarterly Market Report* (4th Qtr,1995) suggests that while prime rents will grow by 6–8% in 1996 compared with 3.25% in 1995, secondary property will have another slow year.

8   LPR (1996) *London Office Policy Review.*London Property Research.

9   See also Joanna Wood (1995) *Office Politics,* Licensed and Leisure Property Supplement, Winter 1995.

10  See for example Jones Lang Wootton (November 1995) *Decentralization of Offices from Central London,* which suggests that following a low level of relocations in 1995, 267 000 m$^2$ is due to be released in 1996, thus contributing to the 'overhang of available secondary space'.

11  DoE (1996) *London in the UK Economy: A Planning Perspective.* Department of the Envionment.

12  For a further discussion of the issues involved, see Gordon, M. (1996), Problems arising from the projections. *Planning Week,* 16 February.

13  See LRR (1995) *Residential Development in Central and Inner London,* London Residential Research.

14  See Savill's *Survey of Major Central London Developments* (January 1996).

15  Note for example the title and content of the Government's White Paper, *Lifting the Burden* 1985.

16  See the Draft Revision to DoE Circular 16/91 published in December 1995 and the Scottish Office's Draft Circular on Section 50 Agreements published in November 1995.

17  The planning gain policies contained in government circulars were found to be legal by the House of Lords in *Tesco Stores Limited v Secretary of State for the Environ-ment and others* (1995) 1W.L.R.759; (1995) All ER 636.

18  Reference to interview with Andrew Youens ARICS, principal of Andrew Youens and Company, specialist surveyors in this area.

## Case Study 5.1

## The Howard deWalden Estate

The deWalden estate is one of the historic London estates established in the eighteenth and nineteenth centuries, which are responsible for the style of much of London's West End. The estate is still owned by the deWalden family, and run as a commercial operation with a staff of surveyors and managers. The estate covers an area between Marylebone Road to the north, Baker Street to the west and southwards nearly to Oxford Street. The unique character of the deWalden estate is due to the significant medical element, with much of Harley Street and the surrounding streets forming part of the estate. Approximately half the estate is residential in use, with commercial uses forming the next largest use (almost all relatively small office buildings or suites), and medical and retailing forming the smallest percentages. There are one or two other uses, including two hotels.

Almost all the estate is in a conservation area, and many of the buildings are also individually listed, leading to significant complications in managing and modernizing the buildings. Altogether there are about

*Figure 5.5*
Welbeck Street and Queen Anne Street, Marylebone, London.
A typical block in the Howard deWalden Estate.

1200 contiguous properties. Very little opportunity exists for comprehensive redevelopment, but the estate is in a permanent state of flux, with refurbishment or limited redevelopment constantly being initiated in most months. Individual buildings may include a mix of uses, and this aspect of the estate is one that is actively being managed for change.

The problems of having a mix of different uses in the same building can be significant. Security can be a problem, particularly if the different uses share the same entrance. As the buildings cannot easily be altered (or sometimes, where listed, at all), it may not be possible to have separate entrances. If this is so, internal access doors must be made secure, which can also be a problem if the doors themselves form part of the listed fabric. Much of the commercial space in the estate is let to professionals. Both medical and legal practices are reluctant to have tenants able to gain access to the building. There is an additional problem if the building has a lift that exits directly into the office floors as well as the residential elements above.

The estate also faces difficult (and sometimes expensive) decisions where there are mixed uses. Common areas – particularly hallways and entrances – would normally be maintained to different levels of service, and decorated differently. Legislation applies differently too; the Landlord and Tenant Act imposes requirements on the number of quotes for maintenance work that differ according to the use. A further management problem arises where plant or equipment is shared; hot water systems or lifts can cause particular problems. There can also be related difficulties with service charges; occupiers of lower-floor offices are very unwilling to pay towards the lift that serves upper floors. There can also be particular problems with day-to-day management issues such as noise; where the building has an Adam ceiling and the floorboards are listed it is hard to introduce noise reduction measures (other than requiring

*Figure 5.6*
Wimpole Street and New Cavendish Street, Marylebone, London. A corner block in the Howard de Walden Estate where different uses (offices and flats) have separate entrances on different streets.

thick carpeting!)

Wherever possible, therefore, the estate is attempting to regionalize uses. This does not mean losing the mix of uses in the estate as a whole, or in any one street; rather it involves attempting to get individual buildings into different, discrete uses, or, where possible, to provide separate entrances for those uses. The estate sees distinct advantages in retaining the mix of uses; the area sees continuous use and activity with a degree of (at least perceived) security. There are also distinct financial benefits; the estate takes a long-term view of the valuation, which has fluctuated quite dramatically between different uses over relatively short periods. Currently residential property lets at a higher rate per square foot than offices, although historically this is not the case. Lettings in 1989 raised as much as £55/ft$^2$, while current lettings are closer to £20/ft$^2$. As a result of having a mix of both uses, severe fluctuations in rent stream can be avoided.

Indeed, the estate is keen to see the mix strengthened and are currently involved in negotiating to acquire a derelict site behind shops in Marylebone Lane. This would be developed as a supermarket (currently lacking in the area), with other shops, and possibly housing above. A further development will see the Conran Shop opening their first London outlet other than the Fulham Road flagship, accompanied by a Conran restaurant.

The ideal refurbishment takes place with corner blocks. These are illustrated here; the Wimpole Street entrance serves one use, and that on New Cavendish Street the other. Similarly, at 49/51 Queen Anne Street the ground floor and upper parts form one building, while the two basements were combined with a separate access from Welbeck Way. There is no stairway between the two uses.

Particular management problems can arise with restaurant uses; the planners impose opening restrictions in what is a strongly residential neighbourhood, and the estate also have a similar provision in the lease. Ducting and air conditioning can also be difficult to install; the Conran example is in fact completely new built behind a retained facade.

# Case Study 5.2

## Tesco, Brook Green

This development represents a new style of mixed use development that has not been seen before, and which may well be replicated in future in a similar form (see case study 6.1). The development of a former industrial site, the Osram factory, at Brook Green in Hammersmith, sees an unusual combination of new-build housing association property provided on the roof of a supermarket for Tesco. This is not a token couple of flats, but 96 units of between three and five storeys, mixing houses and flats.

The site was originally the light-bulb factory for Osram, who operated the site from the 1890s (from the 1940s for the manufacture of cathode ray tubes), and was closed down in 1988. After a number of changes of ownership an application was approved for B1 (business) use totalling 37 000 m² (400 000 ft²) in 1990. By 1993 it was apparent that office use was unlikely to proceed; two other major commercial projects on the nearby Hammersmith roundabout had been built, but not let.

The architects for the scheme, Corstorphine and Wright, had been offered the design work in 1991, if they could find a use for the site. The owner at that time was a trader, who acquired sites with development opportunity, found a viable use, and then sold on to another developer. In the architect's view retail use was the only financially viable alternative

*Figure 5.7*
Tesco, Brook Green, London.
The architect's artist
impression of the scheme.
*(Corstorphine and Wright).*

to offices, but this was not initially acceptable to the planners, who were unwilling to lose potential employment-generating uses to a supermarket.

The architects realized that to make the scheme possible they would need to find a way of making the project more acceptable to the planners. By adding a significant element of affordable housing they hoped to gain consent, which was indeed forthcoming in 1993. They put together the two elements of the scheme, contacting both Tesco (who had been looking for a site in the area) and the Peabody Housing Trust.

The scheme was slow to develop, in part because the relationship between the two different clients had to be developed, and because, in design terms, each had quite different (and in some cases opposing)

*Figure 5.8*
Tesco, Brook Green, London. The completed housing over a Tesco supermarket, with the original factory tower incorporated on the left of the building.

requirements. Additional complexities arose because Peabody were funding their part of the project through two Business Expansion Scheme (BES) companies (a financial vehicle which is no longer in operation), which in turn would be then bought with Council funding by Peabody. This meant that the Council were also involved in the detailed design prior to the planning approval stage. Eventually Higgs and Hill became the developer for the scheme, initially building the store for Tesco (who retain ownership), and then the podium and housing, which become a 'flying freehold' over the store. The only retained element of the former industrial building was the corner stair tower, which now serves as a pedestrian access to the housing.

The design required fairly strict segregation between the uses; both horizontally within the building and in relation to entrances and access points. To ensure absolute segregation horizontally a void has been constructed above the supermarket, the roof of which forms the base of the podium level on which the housing was then constructed. This void, which is 1.5 m. deep, takes all the services for the housing and provides an additional waterproof barrier. With hindsight the architect's consider that void may be more than is needed; in any future project they think Tesco might well accept some services passing through their structure in dedicated ducts. The scale of the structure was vast, and consequently quite expensive. One beam spans 26 m., is solid reinforced concrete and is 2 m. thick. As a result the store has just four columns on the sales floor.

Services are located in the basement, utilizing the existing factory basement, also used for car parking. The store totals 4 152 m² (44 675 ft²) with a sales floor of 2 480 m² (25 685 ft²). There are 111 car spaces under the building, another 156 outside, and the housing has 37 car spaces on the podium, with 8 integral garages and 22 further ground floor spaces accessed from a different street from that for the shoppers car parking.

While there were a number of local objections to the scheme, mostly in relation to the generation of traffic, these did not prevent it going ahead. It was argued that the store would only capture trade that otherwise might go elsewhere – probably involving driving further. The roads are already effectively at full capacity; few further problems can therefore be created, and the previous approved office use had more parking anyway.

There were no obvious problems with the scheme regarding building regulations, although the requirements mean that there are no staircases common to the two uses.

# Chapter 6

# Mixed Uses and Urban Design

## Marion Roberts and Tony Lloyd-Jones

## Introduction

Urban designers have long supported mixed use as a necessary ingredient of successful urban design. From Jane Jacobs onwards, key urban design texts have expounded the importance of mixed uses in providing the foundations for a lively, safe and interesting neighbourhood.

While Jacobs' ideas are now being given more currency than hitherto through policy guidance, ideas about mixed development require further elaboration in design terms. The concept of mixed uses has been promoted in a British context by certain key figures, of which the writing and work of the late Francis Tibbalds (1992) and that of Richard MacCormac (1987) forms a landmark. Nevertheless, as a recent report on *London's Urban Environment* (DoE, 1996) acknowledges, the idea of mixed uses has been ill defined, most notably in current unitary development plans.

Bentley *et al.* (1985) sought to expound Jacobs' ideas on mixed uses in their design primer *Responsive Environments*. This book was written from the context of the medium-sized British town and is addressed primarily at the problems raised by that milieu. In a North American context, Murrain (1993), working with Duany & Plater-Zyberk, has extended his work in the *Responsive Environments* team to the design of new settlements. Meanwhile Calthorpe (1993), also working in the USA, has elaborated his ideas for mixed use sustainable settlement form with his concept for transit-oriented development. More recently Barton and Guise (1995) have developed guidelines for sustainable settlements based on British policy and practice.

It is within this arena of detailed consideration and refinement of the spatial concept of mixed use development in a range of urban contexts that this chapter lies. The argument is that simple formulations of mixed use development are insufficient in terms of design guidance. Elaboration must be offered taking into consideration notions of scale, grain, intensity of use, pedestrian experience, the disposition and nature of uses, definitions of public and private, conflict and security.

Clearly, it is also the case that mixed uses are not just a question of design, and many practical problems in implementation have to be faced. These include conflicts between uses and requirements for health and safety including fire separation, means of escape and sound insulation. These last building requirements can provide obstacles to the conversion and re-use of existing buildings and, in some instances, to the design of new mixed use buildings. In the main, our investigation has indicated that these impediments can be overcome in practical terms, but may create financial problems for the creation of a viable project.

As well as these more practical problems, broader factors work against the production of the type of fine-grained, mixed use environment which was typical of pre-modern urban development. The trend of contemporary city development for large-scale, simply managed projects may provide a stumbling block to the design characteristics of successful mixed use.

The aim of this chapter will be to set out the urban design rationale for mixed use development, stressing the logic that should inform the design approach rather than providing detailed design criteria. The intention is to concentrate on the reasoning rather than to set out a prescriptive set of 'rules', which may not be applicable to more than one context. The chapter argues that current British practice in design control lacks sufficient refinement to be able to prescribe the key components of a successful mixed use area. It is written from an experiential point of view, because a thorough review of British design control has been carried out by others (Punter *et al*, 1994a; Punter *et al.*, 1994b; Carmona, 1996). Rather it makes suggestions, from direct observation and drawing on the work of established urban design theorists, as to the issues and concepts that should inform a re-drafting of design guidance with regard to mixed use development.

Such reasoning cannot be offered, though, without at least a preliminary consideration of the benefits of mixed use development. The arguments in favour of promoting mixed use development in urban design are various but the most important are connected with safety, environmental quality and environmental sustainability. The issues of quality and safety are interrelated. They are both, in a large part, aspects of the notion of vitality: that is, the intensity and diversity of pedestrian-based activity in the public realm and the pattern of such activity over time. The issue of sustainability, although more topical, is also more contentious, and this will be considered first.

## Sustainability, Mixed Uses and Urban Design

As seen in Chapter 3, Planning concerns have increasingly focused on the issue of environmental sustainability, and it is within this context that much of the more recent debate about mixed-use development has taken place. The central proposition is that mixed use developments combining residential and employment functions will allow people to live close to their workplaces and so reduce the amount of travel in cities. This idea has gained wide acceptance, and underpins the thinking behind the European Union's promotion of the 'compact city', urban villages (Aldous, 1992), and the government's Planning Policy Guidance Note 13 on accessibility (DoE, 1994).

In design terms, the urban village concept stresses the planning of new settlements and a network of urban quarters that would allow people to walk to work, to local services and to public transport systems, and therefore also emphasizes the importance of the pedestrian environment. While it seems obvious that a reduction in movement should result from this type of mixed use spatial planning, there are many problems with the idea.

These have been dealt with elsewhere in this book. They might be summarized as the contrast between a pre-industrial culture where home and work was of necessity in close proximity and a post-industrial society where economies of scale and the comparative advantage of different locations pull apart home, work and leisure. While many of the (often idealized) features of an early industrial culture are attractive, it is not clear that it is feasible to return to them in the context of contemporary economic and social conditions. Current debate within the urban design profession would tend to support this view (Lloyd-Jones, 1996).

Faced with this argument against returning to a pre-industrial townscape, proponents of the living/working proximity in mixed use stress the growing importance of homeworking and telecommuting. Working from a terminal at home clearly has little to do with urban design to accommodate a mix of uses. It has more to do with the colonization of domestic space by workspace, with perhaps as many potential disadvantages as advantages for the household concerned. While there will be long-term implications for the form of cities should widespread home-based teleworking begin to occur, the immediate implications for design are limited to domestic space planning.

There is another argument, however, if a more subtle one, that favours mixed used development over large-scale zoning in cities in terms of resource efficiency. This suggests that with the more even and fine-grained distribution of uses across the urban landscape, traffic movements will be correspondingly more evenly distributed. With the migration of many traditional central city functions to the suburbs and the growth of inter-suburban commuting, this trend is already established. Some reduction in the tidal flow of commuters from suburbs to central locations means that transport systems could be designed to accommodate smaller peak flows and be subsequently less under-used during the off-peak periods (Roberts *et al.,* 1995).

The authors of this chapter remain sceptical about many of the conventional arguments for increasing the sustainability of cities to a significant degree through the effect of mixed use development on commuting patterns. It certainly seems unlikely that large numbers of households will choose to live in high-density urban villages – if such developments could be created in sufficient numbers to meet housing demands. As a consequence, the design criteria that are given importance in this chapter are those that relate more directly to the issues of vitality and urban quality, and to the enhancement of the pedestrian experience.

It should be added that increasing the pleasure of walking may in itself encourage greater use of this means of movement, thereby reducing pollution and energy consumption.

## Vitality in the Public Realm

The key characteristics of a successful mixed use environment were set out by Jane Jacobs (1961) in the first two sections of her book. These findings may be confirmed by observation in the traditional quarters of almost any Western European city. They might be summarized by the concepts of 'fine grain' and intensity of use.

The main thrust of Jacobs' argument in favour of the traditional, mixed use urban street form over the mono-functional forms that resulted from modernist town planning ideas was that mixed uses promoted vitality. In particular, it was her argument that the traditional street provided security through its high degree of natural, collective supervision that has received most recent attention (Trench *et al.*, 1992). In Jacobs' view, a balanced mix of working, service and living activities provides a lively, stimulating and secure public realm, and by this means also promotes a sense of community within a neighbourhood.

Although this idea provides the core for many current initiatives on

*Figure 6.1*
Richard McCormac's designs
for redeveloping Spitalfields.
*Richard McCormac
Partnership*

safety and security (Trench *et al.*, 1992; URBED, 1994), its efficacy in terms of lowering crime rates has not been proved in the context of town centres (Shaftoe, 1997). Indeed, evidence gathered for this book (Chapter 7) casts doubt on the inevitability of a connection between surveillance and a reduction in crime. It would seem, again, that the reasoning for promoting mixed use development is more safely grounded in issues of environmental quality and vitality than in possibly ungrounded assertions about safety.

Arguments for mixed use often focus attention on the composition of uses within and across development sites. The argument about vitality in the public realm, however, is concerned with an appropriate mix of uses in relation to activity in the street or other public spaces and not necessarily within the city block. For a neighbourhood to support an intensity of pedestrian use and to have an essential vitality, it requires a multiplicity of uses, attractions and routes. Attractions may comprise shops, small commercial outlets, bars, restaurants, clubs, hotels: in short, uses that offer opportunities for the public to enter and leave both the street and buildings on the street, and to interact.

The principle of providing a fine grain may be observed in the design of contemporary shopping malls. While shopping malls are highly specialized spaces, and a mixed use area would be, by definition, more generalist, it is interesting that the concept of forming a number of relatively small-sized retail spaces is still used. The designers of shopping malls have perfected the art of arranging small commercial and retail outlets with larger 'magnet' department stores to extract the maximum in sales from shoppers (Crawford, 1992). In such carefully crafted spaces it is not uncommon to find the same retail chain siting two or more boutiques at different ends of the mall, the first to tempt the shopper and the second to clinch the purchase. Such a phenomenon may also be observed in London's West End; Oxford Street provides more than one example of such practice.

In their planning of 'magnet' stores, shopping mall planners make some use of the 'multiplier' effect that Jacobs set out in her chapter on 'The need for mixed primary uses'. By primary uses, Jacobs means residential and major employment or service functions: that is, any land use that generates a large number of people moving through an area. Primary uses produce the demand for secondary uses – shops, restaurants, bars and other small-scale local facilities – which serve the primary users.

Such movement will occur at different times, forming 'tidal' ebbs and flows. The consideration of the activity schedules of people engaging in different activities is fundamental to Jacobs' argument, and should inform any urban design approach to mixed use development. If a public space is surrounded by one type of land use it will be used only at certain periods during the day. Combining the primary activities of living and working implies a better distribution of demand over the day, and will support a greater variety of secondary facilities, all of which add to local diversity and an even spread of activity in the public realm throughout the day and evening (Jacobs, 1961).

While Jacobs provides us with one set of tools for a more refined consideration of uses, invoking the categories of primary and secondary, the concepts of local and global, well known to social geographers (Harvey, 1993; Massey, 1994), are also relevant. Richard MacCormac (1987), has provided an elaboration of these concepts in terms of urban design .

## Local and Global Transactions

Large office development has proved one of the worst offenders of any building type in terms of producing dull, mono-functional areas. The sheer bulk, size and anonymity of many office areas led to a popular revulsion against such developments in the 1960s and 1970s (Booker, 1973; Anson, 1981). The problem of accommodating such uses in a lively, mixed use district does not only relate to the issue of scale, as Richard MacCormac (1987) points out. The problems are also related to the activities specific to large institutions themselves. Such activities he classifies as local and global transactions.

Through the use of these concepts, MacCormac offers another, more spatial, perspective on the relationship of primary and secondary uses. From this he has developed his own methodological approach to urban design, which aims to produce vitality in the public realm and accommodate the needs of a local resident community.

MacCormac makes the point that transactions are the essential glue that holds urban life together. By transactions he does not mean only the exchange of commodities, which is sometimes portrayed as if it is the only viable public activity. He also includes other types of human exchange, such as conversations in cafés and restaurants and in the street, and cultural and religious activities. Civilized behaviour depends upon these activities and our participation in them.

The problem with the big commercial organizations which require large offices is that their transactions tend to be regional, national or transnational, and have little relation to the local area in which their office is based. While it might be true that the 'movers' and 'shakers' within these organizations require face-to-face contact with others nearby in order to make the key decisions, many of the transactions taken by, say, the financial services sector rely on national and global connections.

These organizations exist in contrast to smaller and medium-sized enterprises, which often may have more local connections. Thus a small printing company may rely on local suppliers and distributors and have local as well as regional trade as customers. The accessibility of such enterprises to a local population has, as MacCormac points out, an immediate effect on the street. Even in specialized districts of London such as Hatton Garden or Temple Fortune, which are both connected with the jewellery trade, or the clothing workshops of Brick Lane and Savile Row, there is an interchange between the business and the street that gives vitality to an area.

Of course, large offices support a number of smaller businesses simply by virtue of the requirements of their workers for sustenance. The City of London, for example, has a number of sandwich shops, pubs and restaurants. These are used only at certain limited periods during the day, and because land values in the City are so high, it is not possible to have the café society that exists in parts of Westminster (where there is also a residential population to support these services), let alone other public activities such as art galleries and cinemas.

The notion of global and local transactions gives some useful clues as to how a specification for a mix of uses that would guarantee vitality might be drawn up. To reinforce the theme of this chapter, 'use' is too crude a category to be insightful in terms of design; other categories need to be added to refine the description. Thus far, a notion of the scale of activities, primary and secondary uses and of local and global transactions has been introduced. The relationship of this to public and private space and the issues of spatial diffusion and linkages will be considered next.

## Public and Private in Mixed Use Urban Design

In terms of vitality, the basic design objective should be to match the flow of pedestrian activity to the capacity of the public realm to achieve the required intensity of activity levels. A corollary is that the intrusion of the motor vehicle in the street should be controlled to allow ease of pedestrian movement and ease of pedestrian interaction (Whyte, 1988). This might involve considerations of the dynamic management of public space as well as its design. For example, streets could be closed to vehicular traffic during the periods when they are subject to particularly heavy pedestrian use.

More detailed design criteria might include consideration of directions of pedestrian flows at different times, and whether interactions between

*Figure 6.2*
Street cafe, Oslo, Norway. The public realm extended into the street through removing traffic, creating vitality.

different activity groups are desirable or undesirable. In general, urban designers tend to regard social interaction in the public realm as beneficial *per se,* but clearly there are situations where controls may need to be exercised, as, say, in the location of football stadiums.

In the past, the distinction between the private and the usually municipally managed public realms was apparently straightforward and determined by the traditional pattern of public streets and private city blocks. In the European cultural tradition, all private buildings had their public face clearly defined and marked with entrances fronting on to streets, which formed a focus of social life. This structure of clearly defined fronts and backs and public and private realms led to a rich tradition of public street architecture through the effective means of private buildings 'addressing' the street (Rowe and Koetter, 1984). The vitality of the traditional street was composed of the combination of this architectural expression with the movement of people and social interaction derived from a concentration of building entrances along the edges of streets.

From the point of view of mixed use design, it is the manner in which private spaces link to the public realm that is critical in helping to influence the vitality of the latter (Hillier and Hanson, 1984). This is not just a question of design, of a straightforward consideration of the position of entrances; it also involves larger issues of who owns the public realm. Arguments for a lively public realm with high levels of pedestrian density assume that such a realm exists. Contemporary arguments about the public realm have shifted from criticisms of the undifferentiated semi-public wastelands that surround many housing estates (Jacobs, 1961; Newman, 1973; Coleman, 1986) to the privatization of the public realm (Punter, 1990; Davis, 1992; Tibbalds, 1992). Here the concern is over the degree of control that owners of semi-public spaces such as shopping malls, airports and transport interchanges and office and hotel atria exercise in excluding 'undesirable' members of the public from their hallowed establishments.

Certainly mixed use development at a large scale does not preclude the design and construction of such newly privatized zones. Indeed, Chapter 10 explains how mixed use mega-developments set up precisely these type of 'tame zones'. In the context of the fine-grained mix of uses that this chapter advocates, it is more difficult to see how such zones could be owned, developed and managed, apart from by either a very large public–private consortium or a public authority. It is also difficult to imagine how patterns of appropriate policing, other than those usually provided for, could be supported. Where a large number of property owners are involved, and the intention is to create a democratically accountable public realm, then the logic of a democratically controlled police force becomes inescapable.

Even with an active pedestrian-oriented police force, it would be impossible to provide 24 hour control of all public places. In such situations, physical pointers and symbols that help to promote civilized conduct acquire greater importance. The arguments of theorists such as Rowe and Koetter and Newman become pertinent in their suggestion that pedestrians be given a series of psychological cues to guide their movement and behaviour. In this way the management and security of an area can be lent a greater degree of informal control. The psychological cues need not necessarily be the post-modernists' incantation of streets and squares (Krier, 1984), but could incorporate new concepts of urban space, as in MacCormac's proposed arcades for Spitalfields (see below) or the parks in Barcelona. The Moll de la Fusta in the harbour area of Barcelona, for example, provides a fine marine walk with palm trees and cafés and skilfully constructed bridges over four lanes of fast motorway traffic. The use of cobbles and tarmac, vegetation and pedestrian bridges provides clear guidance about vehicular and pedestrian movements without the excessive use of signs and notices.

Other crucial psychological cues are the definitions of fronts and backs of buildings and the screening or setting apart of the private dwelling, either by a basement or a small garden or patio, or by a different sequence of reminders to indicate where space moves from public to semi-public to private. Newman suggests that gateposts, small courtyards and decorative bollards, to name a small number of devices, can all help to provide an appropriate set of clues as to ownership and control. In this way potential conflicts over the use and management of public space within a mixed development scheme can be ameliorated.

## Permeability

In her discussion of the necessity for small blocks Jacobs (1961) makes the point that for a neighbourhood to support a number of small commercial outlets there is a need for a multiplicity of routes, permitting pedestrians choice and variation in their journeys. Bentley et al. (1985) pursued this idea and refined it in their concept of permeability – the notion that good urban development allows a 'democracy' of choice in pedestrian movements through it.

The idea of maximizing pedestrian choice through increasing permeability may not necessarily be congruent with increasing vitality in the public realm, as Jacobs appears to assume. At a certain point, a multiplicity of routes is likely to dilute pedestrian activity and to reduce the concentration of demand for secondary, derivative services in critical locations below a sustainable level.

The issue of permeability, in relation to intensity of pedestrian activity in streets and demand for local services, is a relative one, which involves a considered design approach to the layout of streets in cities. This implies examining not only the potential numbers of pedestrians and the distances they are likely to travel, but also the number of junctions and changes in visual axis that they are likely to face on their chosen routes. According to the space syntax theory of Hillier and Hanson (1984), which uses the number of shifts in the visual axis along a route as a measure of spatial integration, this last factor can be more significant than distance in determining pedestrian activity, and is critical in shaping the allocation of uses across the city grid.

*Figure 6.3*
Tower Bridge Plaza, London.
Another new public space,
but of limited success because
of poor permeability; the
route out of the square is
under the buildings through a
narrow and obscure alleyway.

## Scale and Grain

In relation to mixed uses, permeability is bound up with the notions of urban scale and urban grain. The British development plan system has tended to consider scale in terms of crude measures such as plot ratio and housing density. The problem with limiting discussion to these measures is that they are insufficient parameters of urban quality. The over-simple system of use class orders compounds this problem. In traditional urban centres, attractive environments may be achieved with buildings of six or more storeys and high densities. Conversely dense, high mono-functional development may be monotonous and dreary. A more precise measure of scale and size is required that can permit a multiplicity of uses.

The Building Code employed by the City of Paris since the late eighteenth century provided densely populated but attractive thoroughfares by controlling the relationship of the street width to the building height. Successive regulations throughout the nineteenth century permitted greater storey heights and hence higher densities, but used architectonic measures such as hiding the extra height in an attic storey and retaining a common cornice line to achieve a pleasant ratio of street width to height of building (Loyer, 1987). More recently, the 1977 regulations even lowered the maximum permitted height in the historic centre, the precise measure varying according to neighbourhood (Loew, 1994).

A further measure might be that of urban grain, which considers the size of the urban block and the subdivision of the block. A useful technique for exposing urban grain lies in the 'figure-ground' diagram. This is a diagram in which all the major constructed elements are coloured in black, thereby exposing areas of public, semi-public and private space. The figure ground plan makes possible a study of the urban 'tissue' or 'fabric': that is, the size of the average block or unit of development. It expresses the physical grain of an area within which the potentially finer grain of land use may be constrained.

Within given height limitations, the scale of any development is determined by the size of the site or plot. Taking into account the type of consolidation of plots through purchase that has occurred in the commercial centres of cities in the past, the scale of future developments may ultimately be constrained by the grid of public streets. In many comprehensive city centre redevelopments, and in most urban renewal schemes involving large-scale public housing schemes in the recent past, the existing street pattern was ignored. In this situation, the scale of development was constrained only by the level of investment available. A strong argument in favour of making city blocks small, and enforcing the grid of public streets thereby created, is that it limits the potential size of single developments. This increases the potential variety of urban forms and the likelihood of a diverse use pattern in any area – although it clearly works against the institutional investor's preference for ever larger parcels of development.

Opinion about the size of the ideal urban block varies. Jacobs advocated small blocks, but did not specify a size. It is worth noting here that Jacobs generalized from a particular urban morphology: that of the Manhattan block which is some 400 m long by 50 m wide. This inflexible form produces a particularly monotonous distribution of uses, with all the residential activities concentrated on the long, secondary cross streets and all of the commercial activities housed in the unsuitable short ends of the blocks over great distances along the main longitudinal streets. The notion of breaking up the blocks with new streets clearly made sense in terms of giving local residents a greater choice of routes. This would allow a better distribution of retail and commercial facilities, making use of the new corner site opportunities that would be thus created.

The growth in absolute size of urban enterprises, as experienced from the 1920s to the 1980s, from department stores to corporate headquarters, and the desire for efficiency in management and control, have meant that it is more difficult to return to the fine grain of mixed uses that characterized many early twentieth century neighbourhoods. This problem is being felt acutely in Berlin, for example, where areas of the city centre are being rebuilt after unification. The Director of Housing and Building Construction has proposed that these be 'critically reconstructed', with requirements to follow nineteenth-century building lines, eaves heights and block dimensions, as well as a requirement for a mixture of uses (Stimmann, 1995). He ruefully comments, though, that critical reconstruction is easier to require than to implement. To reinforce a point, one of the critical problems that he identifies is that of scale, where the individual developers of blocks or a number of blocks are unwilling to permit subdivision in ownership or management terms, and architects are forced to use more visual, cosmetic devices to ensure visual variety.

Jane Jacobs argues for an urban fabric consisting of various types and ages. This results in a range of rentals with cheaper, lower-grade buildings able to accommodate uses and users who would otherwise be driven out of an area by high rents. Building booms, driven by what Jacobs calls 'cataclysmic money', often sweep through an area with comprehensive renewal and standardization of its building forms and uses when demand for a particular, usually commercial, use is high. Worse still, the boom can peter out having destroyed the existing diversity of uses before replacing them with new, more uniform development. A contemporary example of this process occurred in the old entertainment centre of New York's Times Square, which was destroyed by the 1980s boom. Once-popular old cinemas stood empty while the new office blocks failed to materialize (Zukin, 1995).

A fine-grained urban structure does not preclude the effects of such development pressures. Nevertheless, it probably does constrain such change by making such 'clean sweep' planning (Ravetz, 1980) more difficult. The medieval pattern of streets and blocks in the City of London, for example, probably had some effect in reducing the impact of the massive commercial renewal of the late 1980s. Similarly, conservation legislation can limit the effects of such damaging development.

As an aside, it might be noted that the UK suffers from having legislation that preserves buildings rather than uses. Legislation in France, for example, permits the fixing of rents so that small shops may still survive in central locations.

It is not only the size and scale of the block that are important. The extent to which it can be subdivided vertically for different uses is also significant. Large blocks may provide an acceptable urban environment if they can accommodate a series of smaller-scale retail and commercial uses at ground level. Conversely, mono-functional buildings or blocks may still provide an acceptable, lively environment provided that they are small enough to offer a variety of attractions through their collective diversity. In traditional urban development, fine-grained development was made possible by the potential of the urban block for subdivision. In medieval development this took the form of the narrow-fronted, terraced shop-dwelling. In later development the vertical divisions, instead of running continuously through the block, could be changed from ground to upper levels. Current cultural preconceptions on the part of owners and tenants make this form of urban development harder to manage and let.

## Density

Mixed uses and issues of scale and grain cannot be divorced from the questions of density. The intensity of activity in streets is clearly dependent on the numbers of users as well as the mix of uses. Jacobs, (1961), who stresses the importance of density in her chapter on 'The need for concentration' (pp. 213–234) suggests that medium to high residential densities of between 100–200 dwelling units to the net acre are necessary to maintain vitality in cities. In Jacobs' view, greater densities still are possible but only with multi-storey buildings requiring monotonous, standardized forms of construction. Much lower densities are acceptable in suburbs, where conditions are very different, but where such low-density residential areas are engulfed by the city, they lack the necessary vitality and diversity, and are destined to become 'grey areas'.

Opinion about urban densities is conditioned by cultural circumstances. Traditionally, UK planning practice has favoured a suburban density and spacing of housing where possible. There has also been an in-built bias towards single-family housing throughout the first six decades of this century (Roberts, 1991). This can be challenged both by reference to changing demography, such as the growth of one- and two-person households, and by good design practice aimed at accommodating families at high densities, which is certainly more common in cultures that have a tradition of metropolitan living. Even current proposals made by organizations such as Friends of the Earth (1994) for higher densities in urban centres favour no more than three to four storey heights.

*Figure 6.4*
Redcliff Wharf, Bristol. The presence of water can allow high-density development to succeed. Here buildings are used for offices, housing and ground floor retailing.

There is obviously room for argument on this matter, but the important point, as before, is to consider the logic of an approach towards height, scale and intensity of activity rather than to dogmatically assert specific standards. Within Jacobs' urban districts in New York and Boston, high densities were achieved without resorting to standardized forms of housing, and the urban form consisted of diverse city blocks with a high degree of ground coverage and fairly small areas of courtyard. Jacobs contrasts these with modern, standardized housing estates where the ground coverage is as little as 25%, resulting in the familiar large, dead areas of unmaintained open space.

Urban density is not just a question of planning and design but obviously also interacts with economic factors. Land values tend to spiral upwards in the centre of cities and other particularly accessibly locations. The more certain types of use congregate in one place, the more likely they are to create a critical mass of demand, which increases development pressures raising land values still further. Thus city centres invariably attract those commercial uses that give the highest value-added to a parcel of land and exclude those that do not. Apart from destroying the diversity of uses in such areas, such development pressures create a need for substantial areas of floorspace for a project to provide a financial return. Problems of high density and over-development may be perceived as a particular problem with central area mixed developments that incorporate an element of cross subsidy: that is, where higher-than-average commercial floor areas are needed to 'compensate' for the inclusion of low-return uses. (See case study 6.1.)

## Mixed Use within City Blocks.

In this section we deal in more detail than hitherto with the design issues relating to the mix of retail, small office and residential uses in the city block. Given the current concern with the decline of town centres and high streets, it is important that architects, planners and developers alike give thought to the design factors that may be holding back mixed use development in our declining commercial centres. A starting point in considering the design of mixed uses in city blocks is offered in the role of retail services. Retail uses, in certain cases, bring the highest rental returns, and it is normal that the most intensively used street frontages will be occupied by shops and showrooms. In many cities, traditional high street shops have suffered from competition by car-accessed, stand-alone supermarkets, superstores and retail warehouses. Nevertheless, in other locations, the traditional high street remains remarkably robust, even where occupied by lower-grade, short-lived retail and local service activities in some low-income areas or, conversely, by highly specialist 'up-market' facilities in more central areas.

The development of the small pedestrian-accessed city supermarket by major retailers, such as Tesco's Metro stores, may help to revive the fortune of the urban shopping street. This type of store requires only a limited area of street frontage for the entrance in relation to its floor area, unlike the smaller shop, which requires a maximum of street front display area in relation to its floor area. This new category of supermarket may not therefore contribute to 'active' street frontages in the same manner as traditional shops, because many of its transactions are hidden from the street.

The model of the medium-rise (four to ten storey) perimeter block typical of the nineteenth-century development of cities in continental Europe and parts of North America supports fairly continuous retail and service use along the more prominent streets. Variations of this form were also built in many of the larger UK cities, and it is a particularly common building type in Scotland, where walk-up tenement buildings are a more typical form of residential development.

The scale and nature of the local retail developments that can be supported depend on both the size and the income levels of the local community. With a given density of development, retail facilities will naturally be sparser in lower-income areas, as well as being of poorer quality. In such areas, street frontages may be characterized by low rental activities such as workshops, garages and other low grade non-retail services, interspersed with cafés, bars and occasional local shops. This is a mix more typically found in the side streets of higher-income areas.

Most retail activity is confined to the ground floor. Only high-value shops can support the staff costs and provide the enticements in terms of

*Figure 6.5*
Quayside, Cambridge.
A riverside development:
originally intended to include
housing, it now consists of
offices over retailing and
restaurants. The design
suggests separate buildings
built over many years, but the
whole scheme was built in the
1980s.

goods and displays to lure customers up or down levels. Department stores and specialist goods stores are rather special cases but even a shop such as Marks & Spencer is usually confined to two levels and exceptionally, in the UK, reaches three. Mixed use in the city block fronting a busy street derives from the logic of this situation. To realize the maximum value of the site, the building should be multi-storey, with uses other than retail on the upper floors.

This gives rise to the typical high street block, with offices and flats above shops. The design problem here is that of providing access to upper levels from the main street, which reduces valuable retail front-age, or from the rear access, which is often blighted by goods access to shops. Spacing of vertical access to upper floors will depend on use and ownership. In Victorian terraces, each vertical unit within the terrace typically was under a separate leasehold, and each plot incorporated its own separate staircase.

Where a strip of units forms part of a single development, then various forms of shared access are possible, with less frequent vertical access points linking up to corridors or access balconies. In this case the size and layout of units as well as means of escape requirements become critical. With upper-floor offices, current demand is likely to determine the size of units required in a new development and thus the spacing of vertical access points. While some flexibility may be designed into the layout, this is limited where a subsequent change of use is involved. It would be difficult to convert larger office units above shops into residential units at a later date, for example, without having to construct new vertical circulation routes .

In terms of structural design, the grid of residential development tends to determine the spacing of retail units. With small retail units the spatial requirements of the different types of use can be easily coordinated with a frame or cross wall grid of between 5 m and 7 m. Modern supermarket retailers, however, have a strong preference for large, open floor areas free of structural obstructions. This can lead to the need to incorporate heavy, widespan bridge structures into the building fabric, as in the Gillingham Street development, together with the additional design requirements of accommodating large areas of customer car parking.

The development logic behind the vertical mix of uses in the traditional city block is the same spatial logic that encourages the development of the site to its maximum extent horizontally as well as vertically. Shops are built to the back of the pavement line, whereas the demands of privacy require that the ground floor of residential buildings needs to be set back. Typically, shop units are deeper in plan form than residential units, with servicing and storage areas to the rear of the customer area. Thus a common building profile in a Victorian high street terrace is an upper block of two to four storeys and 10 m or so deep above a ground floor storey fronting onto the pavement, with a single-storey extension accommodating the back section of retail units at ground floor level.

Sometimes the development is reversed, with the shop extending forwards in front of the main residential frontage above. This can be the result of the later conversion of ground floor residential to retail, and is commonly found on broad arterial routes such as Kingsland Road in East London. This configuration gives some advantage in partly cutting off the residential frontage from the noise and pollution of the street. With the sheer-fronted perimeter block, environmental pollution of upper-floor residential units and, to a lesser extent, office units can clearly be a problem, although the advantages of a fashionable and accessible location seem to overcome these drawbacks in the case of continental cities like Paris or in parts of central London.

Where mixed use city blocks incorporate residential uses, these tend to be critical in terms of determining the minimum width of the block.

*Figure 6.6*
Stephen Bull Bistro, Clerkenwell, London. An unusual solution to the problem of providing access to the upper floors, the upper-floor offices have a central door between the shopfronts of the restaurant.

Minimum overlooking distances between habitable rooms, laid down in planning standards, determine the position of residential blocks. The more stringent spatial and environmental requirements for residential developments may be a further reason for investor resistance to mixed use development in high-value areas. The requirements of existing buildings in terms of overlooking or rights to light can also have a major influence on the form of new mixed use development, whatever uses they incorporate.

In many older mixed use city blocks, both in the UK and in mainland Europe, dwellings are characterized by a lack of outdoor private space, overlooking, poor light and ventilation conditions, often with windows opening out onto tiny courtyards and light wells. These problems are increased as the height of the blocks increases in relation to the width of light wells and courtyards. As with dwellings overlooking busy streets in central locations, poor environmental conditions are frequently coupled with high property and rental values as the desirability of a location is traded off against its drawbacks.

As a further relaxation of planning constraints may prove necessary if mixed developments are to be encouraged in city centres, the inclusion of dwellings in central area developments is critical in providing a full range of daily activities, demand for local services and an essential vitality.

## Other Mixed Use Configurations

Thus far the focus in the discussion of mixed use city blocks has been on a mixture of residential, retail and primarily small offices. Each of these uses can normally be reconciled with the other in terms of unit size and circulation requirements. Other combinations of uses are of course possible, and indeed common. Along with retail services, which are mainly confined to daytime use, local residential populations will generate a demand for evening social and leisure facilities, including pubs, clubs and restaurants. In terms of the spatial morphology of an area, such uses are unlikely to have a major impact, although they obviously have an effect on and contribute to the general character. They may, however, be a source of potential nuisance to the immediate residential neighbourhood, and thus have particular environmental design implications. In tourist areas, such facilities become a primary use, being a major source of income and employment. Where there is an established residential population, conflicts of use may become critical, whether these are environmental in character or questions of access.

Light industrial and workshop uses are often located on separate sites because of environmental conflicts with other uses in terms of noise and pollution. They are commonly found on industrial estates and low-grade urban land, that is not suitable for other uses, such as railway land and in railway arches. While such uses may be sometimes viewed as dirty and undesirable, they nevertheless contribute to diversity in a neighbourhood, and many of the environmental problems can be dealt by careful urban design.

Some types of workshop and studio use are not environmentally intrusive, and can be mixed in with residential and retail uses to provide a diversity of functions and employment opportunities. The creation of the B1 use class was, in a sense, a recognition of an established urban building type, the flexible small workshop unit that can be adapted to a variety of uses – office, storage, light industrial or studio – depending on current demand and environmental requirements. With the increasingly common conversion of defunct office, warehouse and workspace use to residential 'loft' space, and the increasing popularity of living–work spaces, some architects and developers are now arguing for a merging of the B1 and residential use classes.

Typically, in long-established city blocks, back yard areas gradually came to be filled up with these types of workshop and multi-purpose 'sheds'. An interesting morphological variation particular to eighteenth- and nineteenth-century urban development in Britain is the mews. The mews originally provided the stabling space for the middle and upper class households in adjacent terraced town houses. As the motor car took over as the prime means of private transport, mews were increasingly given over to garages and car-servicing facilities. Subsequently, as land values have increased, the number of garages has diminished and focused on an ever more select market of luxury car owners, while an increasing number of units have been converted to residential and office use. In the most expensive areas, mews have long since been transformed into desirable residential locations.

*Figure 6.7*
Baker Street, London. This 1920s block, despite its bulk and location on a heavily trafficked main road, has a mix of luxury flats, offices, shops and an Underground station.

Many other uses tend to be accommodated in large volumes, which occupy a city block or part of a city block as a separate single use building. As has been noted, such large buildings can have a deadening effect on the surrounding area. Where a large building occupies part of a block with other smaller-scale uses, this raises site planning issues such as questions of security, rear access, parking requirements and the over-looking of adjacent residential development.

The urban solution to the problem of large offices and indeed other uses that require a large land-take, such as supermarkets and other types of business, does not necessarily reside in expelling them to the peripheries of our built-up areas. Large offices can be 'civilized' by the inclusion of other uses at their own periphery, thereby employing an approach to form that emphasizes the public realm rather than sheer height or bulk. Ancillary uses can be integrated into the urban fabric through the skilful use of architectonic urban elements, such as atria, arcades, colonnades and courtyards.

MacCormac Jamieson Prichard and Wright demonstrated the feasibility of this approach with their proposed masterplan for the Spitalfields Market redevelopment. This scheme represented two and a half years' work and the coordination of the ideas of a number of contributors, combined with negotiation with elected representatives, local groups and the Royal Fine Arts Commission. Their proposals for development on the site of the former Spitalfields vegetable market also had to respond to a land valuation based on the provision of a high proportion of office accommodation. The former Spitalfields vegetable market occupies a key site of transition in London's urban hierarchy, as it is situated between the affluent development of Broadgate at the edge of the City and the deprived zones of Brick Lane and Commercial Road. It is surrounded by some fine examples of eighteenth-century housing, and Hawksmoor's Christ Church is adjacent.

Rather than proposing a single, bulky landmark building or a simple over-sized perimeter block, they elevated the offices above the site, only allowing them to come down to the ground as foyers. Courtyards and a central galleria enabled the offices to face inwards. To the north an arcade development of small business and flats faces a small perimeter block of new housing, which integrates the development into an existing eighteenth-century conservation area. A crèche and other community facilities provide services to the local population. To the east, a public square, museum and food court provide another magnet to draw people through the site. The offices have a galleria as their centrepiece. The ground floor of the galleria is occupied by retail space, providing shops for the thousands of City workers in the area. A theatre acts as a hinge between the public square in the east and the galleria, which leads off Bishopsgate. A further square accommodates a Sunday street market, and a jazz club is also proposed adjacent to the food court. Housing is provided at upper levels at the perimeter of the office development, tactfully disposed in gatehouses to the office courts so that the unity of the corporate façade is not threatened.

In this way the commercial uses act as a presence both day and night, a presence that would be positive and act as a catalyst for a new urban milieu. A variety of leisure facilities are provided for all sections of the population, with a similar potential for the retail facilities, ranging from specialist boutiques for City managers to a Sunday market for those on low incomes. The masterplan succeeds in reaching the objectives of its authors, which were

> ...to reconcile commercial needs with the re-creation of a lively and inviting public environment, attractive to the working population, the local population and to the wider catchment of London as a whole, with scale and character sensitive to the locality (McCormac, Jamieson, Prichard and Wright, 1989 p. 2).

Regrettably the masterplan has not been adopted by the owners of the site. As a document it remains as one of the most ambitious attempts to plan a mixed use scheme for a site at the heart of a world city, and rests as evidence that such a feat lies well within the bounds of contemporary capability. Indeed, its production suggests that Rowley's conclusion (1996) that new mixed-use development may be difficult if not impossible to achieve may be overly gloomy, for with a buoyant property market the Spitalfields masterplan might well have become a reality.

## Aesthetics

Jacobs limits her comments about visual order largely to a discussion of the structure of the gridiron street system and stressing that 'the city cannot be a work of art' (p. 386). It is the case that certain building types can accommodate a variety of functions, and aesthetic arguments tend to be highly subjective, with one person's complexity representing another's chaos. This chapter's comments have therefore focused on quality in terms of vitality, pedestrian use and enjoyment and viability.

It could be that a well-designed mixed use area may not in fact, be beautiful. A number of examples spring to mind, mainly conversions or infill schemes, which although skilfully executed, take a robust rather than elegant setting as their starting point. Farrell's Comyn Ching triangle in Covent Garden provides a case in point. In these authors' view, whatever the demerits of any successful mixed use scheme or area in formal terms, it is likely that it will become loved, merely through the intensity of use and a richness of association. Evidence for this point of view has already been given in the type of local resistance that was offered to some of the comprehensive development area schemes that were proposed in the 1960s and 1970s. Again, Covent Garden provides a good example of the height of esteem with which people regarded such areas.

## Concluding Comments

This chapter has attempted to provide an overview of an urban design rationale for mixed use development, focusing in particular on the relationship of such development to the public realm. It has been argued that sustainability may not prove to be an adequate justification for the advocacy of policies towards mixed use development, but that arguments that relate more directly to improving the vitality of cities and the quality of the pedestrian environment are sufficient in themselves.

Rather than setting out a series of guidelines for successful mixed use development in urban design terms, the chapter has sought to elaborate the rationale behind such prescriptions. Detailed attention has been given to the issues of pedestrian intensity, the classification of use,

*Figure 6.8*
Ching Court, Comyn Ching, Covent Garden, London. The interior courtyard of Terry Farrell's refurbishment with new additions of a triangular city block (see also Chapter 9).

permeability, density, scale and grain. Consideration has been given to the urban forms that most commonly accommodate high-density mixed use development.

Reference has been made to the problems of providing new mixed use developments in terms of conflicting uses and design requirements. It has been suggested that many of these problems may be overcome, and that the principal objections to mixed use development lie in the preferences of investors for large-scale development and simplified management combined with a cultural aversion to living at high densities.

The planning policy implications in terms of codes and standards have been touched upon, and some remarks may be made as to future development. Jane Jacobs criticized all aspects of the town planning ideas of her time, implicating both zoning and the neighbourhood unit idea. She described the city as a structure of organized complexity, a view shared by Christopher Alexander (1965) in his influential paper, 'A city is not a tree'. Alexander described how the natural pattern of cities, as opposed to the artificial cities created by planners, consisted of a complicated network of overlapping catchment areas for different activities and functions. Attempts to control this activity by confining it to single use zones or in strictly delineated, multi-use neighbourhood units would destroy the natural vitality of the city. While Jacobs favoured the natural city over the planned one, she also recognized the tendencies of the market to eliminate diversity, and was therefore in favour of some planning interventions to counter such trends.

While the system of land use classes in use in British planning practice is not as prescriptive as the zoning schemes of the past, it is still largely based on the idea of defining particular uses for particular sites. Extreme proponents of the deregulative approach to planning suggest that there should be only one land use order – 'space' – with any potential conflicts between neighbouring uses being dealt with by environmental health regulations (Wang, 1995). This may raise uncertainties for land owners and purchasers regarding the future effects of neighbouring developments, and would undermine property values.

A more flexible approach, adopted in some American cities, is to list a series of acceptable uses for particular sites. A new approach adopted in some Australian cities is based on defining broad performance requirements for development sites. This seems to lie somewhere between an environmental health and a multi-use zoning approach. Clearly there is room for a variety of ways of dealing with development control, having recognised the failures of past and present practice. In line with the approach taken in this chapter, it would seem that urban design controls or guidelines might have a wider application to the primary elements of a city's public realm, with more flexible, performance-based guidelines being set out for the less significant areas. This would contrast with the current approach of restrictive design rules for 'heritage' areas and the rather clumsy standards that apply to non-conservation areas.

It has been suggested that current mechanisms for assessing urban quality such as crude measures of density are not sufficiently sensitive to provide for lively mixed use areas. Rather it is hoped that urban design guidelines could more specifically control measures that directly affect urban quality. These might be directed towards such matters as relationship to the building line, height, ground floor uses, the distribution and nature of 'primary' uses and the grain of development in terms of the layout of streets and permeability throughout the city. By contrast other controls, as has been suggested above, could be given greater flexibility.

In conclusion we would assert that the British planning system has a long way to go in terms of incorporating urban design considerations (Carmona, 1996; Punter, 1996). A detailed consideration of the design implications of mixed use development schemes might provide a fertile starting point for the evolution of such measures.

# References

Aldous, T. (1992) *Urban Villages*, Urban Villages Group, London.

Alexander, C. (1965) A city is not a tree, in *The City Reader,* (1996) eds. R. LeGates and F. Stout, 118–131, Routledge, London.

Anson, B. (1981) *I'll Fight You For It!: Behind the Struggle for Covent Garden,* Cape, London.

Barton, H. and Guise, R. (1995) *Sustainable Settlements: A Guide for Planners, Designers and Developers,* The University of the West of England and The Local Government Management Board, Bristol.

Bentley, I., Alcock, A., Murrain, P.,McGlynn, S. and Smith, G.P. (1985) *Responsive Environments: A Manual for Designers,* Butterworth Architecture, London.

Booker, C. (1973) *Goodbye London: An Illustrated Guide to Threatened Buildings,* Fontana, London.

Calthorpe, P. (1993) *The Next American Metropolis,* Princeton Architectural Press, New York.

Carmona, M. (1996) Controlling urban design – Part I: A possible renaissance, *Journal of Urban Design,* **1** (1), 47–74.

Coleman, A. (1986) *Utopia on Trial,* Hilary Shipman, London.

Crawford, M. (1992) The world in a shopping mall, in *Variations on a Theme Park: The New American City and the End of Public Space,* (ed. M. Sorkin), 3–30, Hill and Wang, New York.

Davis, M. (1992) Fortress Los Angeles: The militarization of private space, *ibid.* 155–182.

Department of the Environment (1993) *Planning Policy Guidance Note 6: Town Centres and Retail Developments,* HMSO, London.

Department of the Environment (1994) *Planning Policy Guidance Note 13: Transport,* HMSO, London.

Department of the Environment (1996) *London's Urban Environment: Planning for Quality,* (Building Design Partnership) HMSO, London.

Friends of the Earth (1994) *Planning for the Planet: Sustainable Development Policies for Local and Strategic Plans,* Friends of the Earth, London.

Harvey, D. (1993) From space to place and back again: Reflections on the condition of postmodernity, in *Mapping the Futures: Local Cultures, Global Change,* (eds J. Bird, B. Curtis, T. Putnam, G. Robertson and L. Tickner.), Routledge, London.

Hillier, B. and Hanson, J. (1984) *The Social Logic of Space,* Cambridge University Press, Cambridge.

Jacobs, J. (1961) *The Death and Life of Great American Cities,* Penguin, Harmondsworth (page refs. from 1984 edition).

Krier, R. (1984) *Urban Space,* Academy Editions, London.

Lloyd-Jones, T. (1996) Report of Urban Design Group Panel. *Urban Design,* **58**, 7–8, April.

Loew, S. (1994) Design control in France *Built Environment,* **20** (2), 88–103.

Loyer, F. (1987) *Paris XIX^e L'Immeuble et La Rue,* Hazan, Paris.

MacCormac, R. (1987) Fitting in offices. *Architectural Review,* **181** (9), 50–51.

MacCormac Jamieson Prichard and Wright (1989) *Masterplan: Spitalfields Market Redevelopment,* for the Spitalfields Development Group, January.

Massey, D. (1994) A global sense of place, in *Space, Place and Gender,* (ed. D. Massey) 146–156, Polity Press, Cambridge.

Murrain, P. (1993) Urban expansion: look back and learn, in *Making Better Places, Urban Design Now,* (eds. R. Hayward and S. McGlynn), 83–94, Butterworth Architecture, Oxford.

Newman, O. (1973) *Defensible Space: People and Design in the Violent City,* Architectural Press, London.

Punter, J. (1990) The privatisation of the public realm. *Planning Practice and Research,* **3**, 9–13.

Punter, J. (1996) Developments in urban design review: the lessons of West Coast cities of the United States for British practice. *Journal of Urban Design,* **1** (1), 23–46.

Punter, J., Carmona, M. and Platts, A. (1994a) The design content of development plans, *Planning Practice and Research,* **9** (3), 199–220.

Punter, J., Carmona, M.and Platts, A. (1994b) Design policies in development plans. *Urban Design Quarterly,* **51**, 11–15.

Ravetz, A. (1980) *Remaking Cities: Contradictions of the Recent Urban Environment,* Croom Helm, London.

Roberts, M. (1991) *Living in a Man-Made World,* Routledge, London.

Roberts, M., Lloyd-Jones, T., Erickson, B. and Nice, S. (1995) Networking the city: the new agora. Paper given at European Conference *Urban Utopias: New Tools for the Renaissance of the City in Europe,* Berlin, 16–17 November.

Rowe, C. and Koetter, F. (1984) *Collage City,* MIT Press, Cambridge, MA.

Rowley, A. (1996) Mixed-use development: ambiguous concept, simplistic analysis and wishful thinking? *Planning Practice and Research,* **11** (1), 85–97.

Shaftoe, H. (1997) Planning for crime prevention, in *Introduction to Urban Design: Interventions and Use,* (eds. C. Greed and M. Roberts), Longman, Harlow.

Stimmann, H. (1995) New Berlin offices and commercial buildings, in *Downtown Berlin – Building the Metropolitan Mix,* (ed. A. Burg), 6–23, Borkhauser, Berlin.

Tibbalds, F. (1992) *Making People-Friendly Towns,* Longman, Harlow.

Trench, S, Oc, T. and Tiesdell, S. (1992) Safer cities for women: perceived risks and planning measures. *Town Planning Review,* **63** (3), 279–296.

URBED (1994) *Vitality and Viability of Town Centres: Meeting the Challenge,* HMSO, London.

Wang, V. (1995) Do we need use class orders? *London Architect,* September, 9–10.

Whyte, W.H. (1988) *City: Re-discovering the Centre,* Doubleday, New York.

Zukin, S. (1995) *Cultures of Cities,* Blackwell, Oxford.

# Case Study 6.1

## Gillingham Street, Victoria

This development proposal has a number of similar features to that illustrated in Chapter 5, the Tesco supermarket in Brook Green. The scheme, which at the time of going to press is still having the final details being approved by Westminster's planners, is for a supermarket with flats above. However, the site is much more central than the one in Hammersmith, the density of development is correspondingly greater, and the flats are a mix of rented and for sale.

The project is being organized (unlike the Hammersmith scheme) by the housing association that will rent the flats: Network Housing Association. Network are pursuing other projects with private sector partners, which will see both social rented and private accommodation in the same building, but here they are coordinating the entire project.

The site is the former Victoria Bus Garage (not to be confused with the Coach Station), which occupies a site in Gillingham Street, Guildhouse Street and Wilton Road. Westminster Council were keen to see housing on the site, but when it came up for sale several supermarket operators were competing to buy it. At the time, Network were partnered with Safeway, who were only happy for a small area to be developed with housing, mainly over the loading area. Sainsburys won the bidding, partnered with Regalian Homes, but were unable to come to a final agreement with them; the situation was even more complicated by the need to include some social housing. As a result Network and Sainsburys teamed up. At that point the intention was broadly as in Hammersmith for Sainsburys to build their store and then hand over the upper part to Network to build housing. As detailed negotiations proceeded, a quite different arrangement was arrived at.

*Figure 6.9*
Gillingham Street, Victoria,
London.
A section through the
proposed scheme.

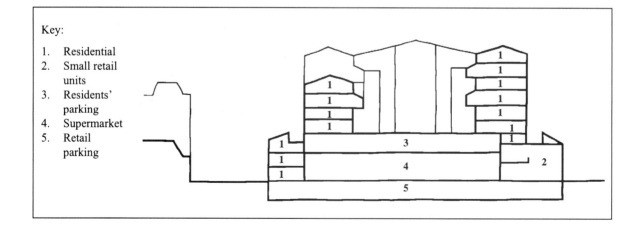

Key:

1.  Residential
2.  Small retail units
3.  Residents' parking
4.  Supermarket
5.  Retail parking

In the end, Sainsburys bought the site then transferred the freehold to Network, who are developing the whole £30 million scheme. The store will be built by a company set up by Network, and Sainsburys will pay the costs of construction of the store. An additional eight shop units are planned, which have a pre-sale lined up to a subsidiary of British Land, who will also take the entire freehold and lease the social housing back on a 250 year lease. The superstore contributes nothing significant to the financial situation. Network will make a profit on the shops, which will help to subsidize the rented element. The housing is planned in two separated back-to-back courtyard arrangements. The housing is split roughly half for sale and half to rent. The private element will be bought by a company who will then market them. Although this company will be paying more than twice the actual construction costs, they can still expect to sell the apartments with around a 15 – 20% profit. The housing association are, as they say, giving up a part of the potential profit in order to lower the risk and guarantee that the necessary finance is available. The net effect should be to allow the units to be let at around £5 a week below the Housing Corporation

*Figure 6.10*
Gillingham Street, Victoria, London.
Architect's impression of the completed scheme when viewed from Guildhouse street with single-aspect flats masking the car parking.
*Levitt Bernstein Associates.*

benchmark. Westminster City Council will be allowed to nominate three quarters of the tenants.

The potential buyer of the shop units was concerned about having housing above, and particularly in relation to social housing. The housing association were equally concerned that, with £250 000 flats above the shops, the nature of the retail lettings was important. As at Hammersmith the possible problem with damage to the supermarket from the flats was an issue. Here it has been solved by inserting an entire floor between the two uses, used for parking for the housing. This in turn creates a design problem, which has been solved by masking the whole car park with single-aspect maisonettes (which will be offered as shared-equity flats).

Network are developing the scheme because they wish to develop social housing. Despite a £3 million subsidy from Westminster City Council, the rents for a straightforward rented scheme here would be exorbitant. The net effect of attempting to get sufficient private housing to keep the social element intact and at reasonable rents is to make the whole scheme a very high-density development. This has proved difficult to negotiate with the planning department, as well as complicating issues of access, means of escape and fire prevention. The supermarket and the two elements of housing each have separate accesses, and in addition Sainsburys insist on being able to get exclusive access at all times to their plant, some of which will be eight or more storeys above the store to avoid noise problems in the residential part of the scheme.

# Chapter 7

# Crime and Mixed Use Development

## Geraldine Pettersson

## Why Focus on Crime?

Surveys have shown consistently that crime, and especially fear of crime, has a very damaging impact on people's peace of mind and happiness. UK residents have identified crime and health care as the two dimensions of urban life that have the greatest influence on their quality of life (Grayson and Young, 1994). In response to people's concerns, putting in place effective ways of tackling and preventing crime is high on the agenda of central and local government.

Over the last 30 years, crime rates have risen for most types of offence, but it is the fear of crime that has gained most ground in people's hearts and minds. Surveys of residents in towns and cities (and to a lesser extent rural areas) show that large majorities are worried that either they or other members of their family will be the victim of crime, especially an incident where their home is burgled, their personal safety is threatened, or their car stolen or damaged. The 1994 British Crime Survey findings on fear of crime (Hough, 1995) reveal that more than a third of people feel unsafe out alone after dark, and this proportion rises to a half for those living in the inner cities. From the same national survey, it appears that large minorities routinely avoid going out alone or avoid certain areas because of fears for personal safety.

Those living in comparatively high crime areas usually express higher than average fears about crime. On single use, inner city housing estates, it is not uncommon for two-thirds of residents to be worried or very worried about being the victim of street robbery and assault, and similar proportions to express serious anxieties in relation to domestic burglary and car crime. Residents of these areas are also most likely to feel unsafe when out alone after dark, with women and older people expressing much higher levels of anxiety than men and younger people.

Not only does fear of crime vary greatly between areas but so also do the level and type of crime and the circumstances in which these incidents take place (Poyner, 1980). Most mixed use developments are located and developed in town and city centres. Thus issues about the relationships between mixed use and the incidence and fear of crime will inevitably be linked to experiences of crime and perceptions of safety in these central districts. However, compared with the plethora of research on inner city estates, studies investigating the dynamics of crime in central business and entertainment districts are few, and there is little empirical evidence on which to quantify fear of crime in these areas. Later in this chapter, findings from our interviews with residents in mixed use developments will describe their experiences and fear of crime, and compare these with the views of those living in single use housing areas.

## Crime and Fear of Crime in City and Town Centres

The limited research that is available on town and city centre crime shows those districts with a concentration of both entertainment and business activities often have the highest frequency of crime and disorder within urban areas.[1] Popular activities such as shopping, tourist magnets, pubs and clubs attract in great numbers both law-abiding clientele and potential offenders. It is also an attractive environment for adventuresome and action-seeking people who are most likely to place themselves in risky situations. The social life is 'predominantly public ... which means a high rate of interactions occur between strangers in streets, squares, public localities and on public transport' (Wikström, 1995). Such interactions can be the catalyst for friction and, often when fuelled by excessive alcohol, may spill over into disorder or assault.

Many of the incidents associated with city and town centre crime are alcohol related. A study of violent crime in Coventry (Poyner, 1980) revealed the highest density of violent incidents in the centre, mostly between strangers, and heavy drinking was a common factor. A study of Newcastle city centre concluded: 'Drinking and disorderliness have traditionally gone hand-in-hand. In modern cities, the city centre or entertainment district has become an arena for both' (Hope, 1985, p. 45). In contrast to these studies, police statistics for Bristol reveal that the frequency of offences against the person is no higher in the central district than in many high-cost residential areas beyond the centre.

However, police statistics for Central London on allegations of crime over a three-month period in 1995 show the concentration in the main shopping and entertainment area of particular types of crime, specifically theft from a person (including pickpocketing and snatches), shop lifting, burglary of commercial premises, assaults and disturbance in a public place or licensed premises. In contrast, allegations of domestic burglary and, to a lesser extent, vehicle crime are low compared with their frequency in areas bordering on the West End, where the opportunity for such crime is much greater.

The type of crime prevalent in many central districts with a concentration of entertainment and business is associated with activity and opportunity. People's anxiety about using these centres mirrors in part their fear of experiencing crime and, in particular, those incidents threatening their personal safety. Home Office research in Coventry revealed high levels of concern about being 'mugged', assaulted or verbally abused in the city centre (Ramsey, 1989). The study also found that nearly two-thirds of respondents sometimes stayed away from that city centre simply as a precaution against crime and disorder. A study in Birmingham revealed that a similar proportion sometimes avoided the city centre specifically for reasons of personal safety (Birmingham Junior Chamber of Commerce, 1987). In part, the dramatic growth in the use of closed-circuit television (CCTV) in town centre streets has been in response to these fears, and is an attempt to match the standards set by shopping centres or malls, where the presence of CCTV cameras is very common (Brown, 1995).

Although initially it may appear paradoxical, people's anxiety about using town and city centres is also fuelled by a vulnerability stemming from a lack of people and a sense of isolation. In a study on changing London, Clout and Burgess (1986) commented:

> Among the striking features of city growth in Britain over the past 150 years have been the increasing distances that separate place of work and place of residence and the greater specialization of land uses in inner city areas. City centres contain very high densities of people during the working day but are virtually depopulated at nights and weekends except for caretakers and cats!

Although late night activities are an increasing feature of some central districts, many can still appear 'a bleak and empty place in the evening after the shoppers and office workers have gone home' (Hope, 1995). In any case, the concentration of late night entertainment, in the absence of other kinds of activities with a wider appeal, is more likely to contribute to fear of crime rather than make a wider populace feel safer. On the basis of the limited evidence available, the key to safer and economically robust central districts would appear to rely on the success of these centres to attract and retain a diversity of people using their district throughout the day and the evening, into the night.

As will be discussed later in this chapter, housing within mixed use developments is seen by many as an important way of generating this activity over the day and night. So also is the development of the '24 hour city', where the centre is primarily an attractive location during the day for the business economy and shopping and, during the evening, for leisure, entertainment, cultural activities, eating and drinking. Cities such as Leeds, Sheffield, Newcastle and Manchester have taken positive steps to encourage diversity in late night uses, including the promotion of a 'club culture', support for longer shop-opening hours, and a more imaginative approach to licensing regulations. For a month in 1993, Manchester extended its pub closing time to 12pm, and for night clubs from 2am to 4am. The longer opening hours were accompanied by an extensive programme of live entertainment. There was a decrease in arrests of 43% over the period and a decrease in alcohol-related incidents of 16% (Lovatt, 1994).

## Reducing Crime and Fear of Crime

Measures to reduce fear of crime and enhance personal safety can have many beneficial effects for the economy and for the quality of life enjoyed by a community of residents and businesses. Many decisions about where to locate a business and buy or rent a home will be based on individual perceptions of safety and security for that locality. Crime prevention measures, if known to be effective and successful, can help to change perceptions of an area and reclaim its popularity.

There are two principal approaches to reducing crime and fear of crime.[2] The first, often known as situational crime prevention, targets the crime-prone situation and aims to make

> Crime more difficult to commit, more risky and less rewarding by putting in place measures such as better security, increased surveillance (including use of CCTV), and property marking (Crime Concern, 1995).

In recent years, evidence on the success of situational intervention has been accumulating (Clarke, 1995), but there are arguments that its effectiveness is sometimes only short-lived or may lead only to the displacement of criminal activity either to other areas or to other types of crime.

The second approach, usually referred to as social crime prevention, aims to prevent criminal behaviour;

> It addresses the underlying social causes of offending and seeks to influence the attitudes and behaviour of those most likely to offend so they are less inclined to do so. It targets the potential offender rather than the crime (Crime Concern, 1995).

Most approaches to crime prevention today would accept the need to combine the most effective elements of both the situational and the social. In relation to mixed use developments, however, most of the pertinent research and theories fall within the scope of situational crime prevention, and it is on this approach that we shall focus.

## Situational Crime Prevention

Most situational crime prevention assumes – to some extent or other – that physical and environmental measures, including design and location, can effectively block out opportunities for crime and enhance personal safety. It assumes that there is a relationship between 'place and behaviour', and that behaviour can be modified or exaggerated through the influence of 'place' (Walmsley, 1988).

One of the earliest recorded examples of managing the design of the environment to deter crime was used in Glasgow in the mid-nineteenth century. M. J. Daunton in his book on working class housing (Daunton, 1986) referred to the central district of Glasgow as 'a maze of narrow closes and wynds'. The Glasgow Improvement Act of 1866 had the objective of opening up the area and would 'it was assumed, lead to both moral and sanitary reform ... it was safe to walk where before there had been murders and robberies'. A contemporary report described the earlier alleys and closes as:

> A series of communicating fortresses, from which the criminal classes sallied forth with comparative impunity at night to ply their nefarious practices, having at hand facilities of escape and refuge (Littlejohn, 1865).

A local magistrate identified that crime had fallen 'largely due to the clearances made, which gave the Police control and supervision over the criminal classes' (Morrison, 1874).

Oscar Newman has been very influential through his work on single use housing estates. His research identified three main factors that made crime easy to commit and difficult to prevent: the impersonal character of areas; the lack of natural surveillance, with poor design and visibility preventing residents from overlooking public areas; and the presence of a myriad of alternative escape routes (Newman, 1972). He advocated four principles for design: to foster a sense of territory and ownership in 'defensible space'; to develop natural surveillance allowing residents to identify and observe strangers within their territory; to create a safe image of an environment where residents knew and cared for each other; and that the neighbourhood should be part of a wider, safer area (or 'moat') protecting it from the dangers of other localities.

It is not easy to assess the effectiveness of Newman's hypothesis, although it has had a strong influence on crime prevention initiatives on housing estates. However, other studies have shown that the effectiveness for crime reduction of design features creating 'defensible space' relies largely on residents not passively viewing their territory but actively challenging strangers who are observed (Merry, 1981). This is a crucial point, applicable to mixed and single use developments. Advocates of the power of natural surveillance to deter crime usually assume that some personal intervention will take place: to question, to challenge, or at least to report. In today's society, much higher fears for personal safety, concerns about possible reprisals, and apprehension that a person approached could be hostile or violent deter many people – including staff responsible for public areas – from personal intervention of any kind.

Any discussion about situational crime prevention, especially in relation to mixed uses, must acknowledge the valuable contribution to the debate of Jane Jacobs and her 1960s analysis of the decline of American cities. In fact, most of the present-day assumptions about the relationship between mixed uses and crime prevention appear to draw heavily on the arguments of Jane Jacobs and little else.

However, the current assumptions on the beneficial value of mixed uses for reducing crime and enhancing personal safety often fail to acknowledge the limitations of her beliefs – more than 35 years on – both for present-day urban society and for the diversity of activities that can now occupy a mixed use development. How we use the urban environment and our expectations of life in the city have changed significantly since 1961. Although Jacobs was writing about the USA, it is still an almost folksy image that she evokes of neighbourhoods where people did not just know or recognize each other but cared about each other and were prepared to be active as the 'eyes on the street' (Jacobs, 1961).

In the much quoted *The Death and Life of Great American Cities* Jacobs proposed that varied land uses and an active street life could hinder opportunities for crime. The most successful city neighbourhoods were those that were:

> close-textured, high-density assemblages of mixed land uses, where many people live within walking distance of many destinations and there is constant coming and going on foot along a dense network of streets.

Jacobs argued that residential monotony – displayed in large housing estates – resulted in inconvenience, with residents located far from services; a lack of public street life; and a fear of the streets after dark. Small scale and the 'exuberant diversity' of uses and activities were promoted as the keys to a lively and safe city scene. Such neighbourhoods not only provided natural surveillance, but helped to establish a stable social structure, where people (including children) knew what was acceptable and unacceptable behaviour.

Jacobs extended the influence of environmental diversity into social crime prevention. She emphasized that the relationship between children and their physical environment is significant for safe neighbourhoods. Jacobs argued that children living in a lively, diverse neighbourhood will learn the kind of behaviour expected of them in public places.

Many theorists and practitioners concerned with personal safety in the urban environment have built on the core principles advocated by Jacobs. Fowler, in his study *Building Cities That Work*, has emphasized the role played by the physical environment in reinforcing attitudes towards public responsibility for the street. He argued that:

> physically diverse neighbourhoods make natural many different kinds of public contacts among street users; these contacts are an important part of a healthy public social life; and a healthy public social life produces fewer criminals as well as fewer chances for crime to occur (Fowler, 1992).

Taking an example of vandalism, Fowler suggests that if adults on a street relate to one another and take responsibility for what goes on, then children will do the same. He comments that:

> if users of an urban space have reason to interact in public, the resulting network of trust and self-confidence puts an automatic dampener on disorderliness and damage to the built environment.

Fowler describes a study in Toronto where residents in a number of physically different areas were asked about their feelings of safety. Those that felt most unsafe lived in neighbourhoods where the buildings were of a similar age, housing was the sole or predominant use, and where there were high-rise developments. Fowler comments further:

> but, just as Jacobs predicted, people living in physically diverse areas, where high density was combined with mixed land use, short blocks, and both old and new buildings were more sanguine about the area's safety.

Alice Coleman's *Utopia on Trial* (1985) is essentially about single use housing developments, and does not explore the relationship between diverse land uses, successful neighbourhoods and crime reduction. However, Coleman acknowledges the importance of both Jacobs and Newman in identifying those principles of design, including the impersonal character of areas and the lack of natural surveillance, that 'made crime easy to commit and difficult to prevent'.

Not everyone agreed, however, with the concepts advanced by Jacobs and her supporters for successful and safe neighbourhoods. In particular, their approach was said to underestimate the power of the social environment, and one of the fiercest counter-arguments came from Lewis Mumford:

> Her [Jacobs'] ideal city is mainly an organization for the prevention of crime. The best way to overcome criminal violence is such a mixture of economic and social activities of every hour of the day that the streets will never be empty of pedestrians, and that each shopkeeper, each householder, compelled to find his main occupations and his recreations on the street, will serve as a watchman and policeman, each knowing who is to be trusted and who is not, who is defiant of the law and who upholds it, who can be taken in for a cup of coffee and who must be kept at bay....

> ...What is responsible for their [the streets'] present emptiness is something Mrs Jacobs disregards – the increasing pathology of the whole mode of life in the great metropolis, a pathology that is directly proportionate to its overgrowth, its purposeless materialism, its congestion, and its insensate disorder – the very conditions she vehemently upholds as marks of urban vitality (quoted in Fowler, 1992).

Despite such criticisms, however, there has been wide acceptance of the concept that lively and diverse neighbourhoods will both hinder opportunities for crime and reduce fear of crime. For example, David Sucher in his book on building urban villages argues that 'the basic technique of urban security is natural surveillance and the human presence ... and eyes on the street promote safety' (Sucher, 1995). He further argues that a diversity of uses creates an urban environment that maximizes the opportunities for natural surveillance – there are more 'eyes on the street'. Sucher does raise the issue, however, of whether people are willing today not only to observe but to act and intervene. He acknowledges that getting people to take action – even if it is only to telephone the police – may be 'easier said than done'. In recognition of an increasingly common practice that people may observe but not react to incidents, even by reporting or providing information as a witness, natural surveillance has been re-termed by some as 'passive surveillance'.

## Natural Surveillance – Is CCTV an Alternative ?

The presence of closed-circuit television cameras has become a familiar sight in private and, increasingly, in public places. Over 40 local authorities already have CCTV systems installed in their town and city centres, and many more systems are planned. When private systems are included, it is estimated that there are over 150 000 professionally installed CCTV cameras in British towns and cities, and 500 more are installed each week (Bulos and Sarno, 1995). Until recently, however, there was little systematic evaluation of their effectiveness, and little information on the ways in which CCTV impacts on crime and fear of crime within public places.

A recent study by the Home Office Police Research Group (Brown, 1995) has examined the use of CCTV in the city centres of Newcastle upon Tyne, Birmingham and King's Lynn; the last of these was the first comprehensive system to be installed, in 1987. All these centres have a low resident population but many venues for entertainment, pubs and clubs.

The main aim of the system installed in Newcastle upon Tyne is to support police operations and to assist in the maintenance of public order. Initially, the cameras were a strong deterrent to crime, but their effect for some offences appeared to fade after a period of time. For burglary and criminal damage, however, the findings from the research suggested that their deterrent effect was more sustained.

As the popularity of Birmingham city centre increased in the 1980s, public safety within the city centre became a major issue. The purpose of installing the CCTV system is not only to assist police operations but also 'to make Birmingham a safer place through tackling the problems of general street crime such as robbery, theft from the person, criminal damage and assault' (Brown, 1995). Although the research findings reveal that the CCTV system has not directly reduced overall crime levels within Birmingham city centre, the cameras have assisted police operations and, notably, have increased the public's perceptions of safety when using the centre after dark. Brown concludes that this increase in feelings of safety 'may be as important for the city centre as an area as any real reduction in crime'.

The main aim of the King's Lynn town centre scheme is to deter criminal activity, including vandalism and criminal damage, which are particularly likely to occur after the closing time of pubs and clubs. The research findings reveal that the use of cameras in King's Lynn has reduced the incidence of various types of offence, particularly burglary and, to a lesser extent, assaults and vehicle crime. In common with the Newcastle findings, the system has also assisted the police to coordinate an appropriate response to incidents.

The findings from the three case studies indicate that CCTV camera systems are effective in reducing the incidence of property crime in central districts; the important factor appears to be that the risk of arrest is increased. However, the research found that the effect on personal crime is less clear, and could be related to the size and complexity of the centre under surveillance. In Newcastle and Birmingham city centres, the presence of the cameras had much less impact on the overall incidence of public order and assault compared with the smaller centre of King's Lynn. In addition, CCTV appeared to have little impact on the overall levels of robbery and theft from a person. Brown concludes from the Birmingham evidence that

> these offences are more easily displaced to town centre areas/streets that are not covered by cameras, but are still routinely used by members of the public.

Another important study examined the impact of CCTV on Sutton town centre (Bulos, 1994), and found that people did feel safer and more at ease with its installation, but this was unlikely to change their shopping or leisure patterns. In common with the Home Office evaluation, the Sutton study emphasized the need for CCTV to be only part of a wider package of measures that actively encourage people to use central districts.

Of particular importance for the issue of natural surveillance is whether people react differently to an incident when a CCTV system is in place. There is very little evidence on the issue of how CCTV influences people's propensity to report incidents or act as 'eyes on the street'. Limited research has shown that members of the public believe the presence of CCTV will have some impact on people's reactions to an incident (Honess and Charman, 1992). It could either encourage them to report, because their information would be substantiated by the CCTV image, or make them less likely to report because they believe the police are aware of the incident anyway. The Home Office research in Birmingham city centre reveals that, of members of the public who either observed or experienced a serious incident and were aware of the CCTV system, none made reference to the presence of the cameras when asked to describe their immediate reaction. As Brown concludes:

> there is no evidence from this data that knowledge of CCTV makes people who witness crimes, or are victims of crime, act differently (Brown, 1995).

From the limited information available, there is no evidence that the existence of CCTV cameras can substitute for the presence of people and activity in contributing to perceptions of safety on the street. CCTV systems are only part of a package of measures available to make city and town centres safer and appear safer, but they are no panacea. One important element, as yet untested through the available research on the use of CCTV cameras, is the extent to which its impact on crime and, especially, fear of crime is influenced by the presence of a greater residential population in town or city centres.

## Expectations for Mixed Use in Reducing Crime

A recurring theme for the government and others advancing the role of mixed use developments, especially in town and city centres, has been the contribution that such developments are said to make as a deterrent to criminal activity and an enhancement of personal safety. Drawing very much on the concept of Jacobs, the protagonists of mixed use development argue that the presence of more people for more hours contributes to crime reduction. They also argue that fear of crime will be reduced, as the centre is no longer deserted in the evening, and people will feel less vulnerable as a consequence.

The Department of the Environment circular entitled *Planning Out Crime* (DoE, 1994) drew together current thinking on the role of planning, architecture and design for crime prevention. The circular referred specifically to the problems of fear for personal safety and security in town centres, and identified this fear as a principal factor influencing why people avoid those centres at night. It commented:

> ...one of the main reasons for that fear is the fact that there are very few people about. Breaking that vicious circle is a key to bringing life back to those city centres. By adopting plan policies that encourage a wide and varied range of land uses, local authorities can help to foster the creation of lively, attractive and welcoming environments.

It was suggested that the development of 'lively, attractive and welcoming environments' may well need to extend beyond land use policies and encompass: public transport policies; the development of so-called 'night economies'; the use of CCTV; the development of recreational and cultural activities 'that bring life to urban areas after dark'. In addition, it advocated developing the potential for establishing residential accommodation in town centres. The circular concluded that:

> all these objectives are conductive to greater activity in the evening and at night, thus increasing the opportunities for members of the public to see what is going on (passive surveillance).

At the local and district level, the potential for increasing safety through the development of mixed uses has been stated explicitly by planners and developers, usually relating to the city or town centre environment. For example, the Leeds City Centre Management Team have developed a proactive approach to improve the local economy and 'create a busier and therefore safer centre', with all participants agreeing that the essential ingredient is more city centre housing to provide a vibrant and safe core. Inspector David Grubb, responsible for policing Leeds city centre, has commented:

> In an area which is vibrant, with lots of people moving about, crime is less prevalent. You no longer get the big turn out at 2am which creates flash points – people drift away gradually during the night (Bevan, 1995).

Andy Lovatt at Manchester Metropolitan University's Institute of Popular

Culture has commented on the wider need to develop busy day to night initiatives:

> If a city evacuates at six every day and the evening economy falls below a certain level, then the bottom falls out of the city and you end up like Los Angeles or Pittsburgh where the busy centre becomes a no-go area after dark. The public realm collapses and the city becomes a nightmare in every way (quoted in Bevan, 1995).

There is strong agreement amongst protagonists for vibrant city centres that housing is the essential ingredient. A proposal by Scottish Homes to build 400 new homes in Aberdeen town centre is part of a wider package aimed to regenerate the area around Union Street through developing a stronger sense of community. Walter Murray, the coordinator for Aberdeen City Centre Partnership (comprising the City Council, Grampian Council and Scottish Homes), has commented:

> Public perception had got to the point where Union Street was regarded as being run-down. One of the things we noticed was how insecure people felt outside normal shopping hours.

Market research undertaken for the Partnership revealed the need to:

*Figure 7.1*
Amhurst Road, Hackney. An example of an inner city conversion to increase housing. New shop fronts have allowed the installation of separate doorways and staircases to allow access to flats on the upper floors. Compare with Figure 7.2 (overleaf).

*Figure 7.2*
Amhurst Road, Hackney.
The 'Living Over the Shop'
initiative has not yet been
universally adopted. Valuable
living space still goes to waste
in many town and city
centres.

enhance the vitality of the centre by broadening its appeal – principally through the creation of residential space and, by the same token, reducing the amount of empty shop space (quoted in *Urban Regeneration*, Autumn 1994).

The Sheffield City Centre Business Plan (Sheffield City Liaison Group, 1996) has also identified the importance of increasing residential accommodation 'in the central area to help create a 24 hour city that sustains shops, supports facilities and *encourages self policing*' (our italics). The Business Plan stressed the importance of diversity in the type of people living in the centre and, in particular, of attracting families with children. Anne Petherick, consultant and influential force for the Department of the Environment's 'Living Over The Shop' initiative, has emphasized the importance of residents with a mix of age ranges for achieving a genuine 'day and night' centre. However, those supporting initiatives for a lively late-night culture and for greater numbers of people to live in the city centre rarely address the possible conflicts that could arise, especially on noise and nuisance.

The role of mixed use development in combating criminal activity and enhancing personal safety has been stated most explicitly by John Gummer, Secretary of State for the Environment. In November 1994, at a CPRE Conference of Towns and Cities, he referred specifically to his belief that mixed use leads to lower crime and vandalism. A subsequent speech to the Association of Town Centre Managers (December 1994) attributed spiralling crime rates to depopulated town centres. The link between mixed use and crime reduction was continued and made more explicit when John Gummer addressed a conference on the role of town centres in urban regeneration (November 1995):

> ...it has also got to be a city centre which is alive 24 hours, and that does mean the creation of mixed development ... people living over shops, people living beside shops, mean that you reduce crime, you make the city centre sufficiently alive to protect it.

## Mixed Use and Crime – Survey Evidence

The University of Westminster, as part of the wider research programme on mixed use development that forms the background to this book, carried out detailed surveys of residents in mixed use developments. The

*Figure 7.3*
Council housing, Hatton Garden, Holborn, London. Multi-storey housing arranged above jewellery workshops and retail premises.

interview surveys, carried out with small numbers of residents in public and privately managed housing developments within mixed use schemes, included questions on their experiences of crime and nuisance and their perceptions of safety. The detailed findings from those surveys are to be published in a separate research paper, but will be drawn on here to provide evidence of how mixed use impacts on crime and safety at the micro level. To date the surveys have been undertaken in central London, Oxford and Glasgow.

The survey findings reveal that for residents in all three city centres, fear of crime is less and perceptions of personal safety out alone after dark are much better when compared with national statistics from the 1994 British Crime Survey and other surveys of residents in predominantly housing areas. In central London (Covent Garden and Holborn), and the city centres of Oxford and Glasgow, the majority of respondents felt fairly or very safe out alone, after dark, in their area. Very few avoided going out in the evening because of fears about personal safety. In contrast, surveys with residents of inner city and suburban estates reveal that up to a third never go out alone after dark, and substantial numbers of those who do go out feel very or fairly unsafe.

The much greater perceptions of personal safety expressed by city centre residents appeared to be specific to that area. When asked whether there were other parts of their city where they would feel safe out alone after dark, less than half of respondents in London could identify such areas. The proportion was higher in Glasgow, but the areas where respondents said they would feel safe were exclusively in the centre or west end of the city. Nearly three-quarters of those living in the Gloucester Green development in central Oxford, however, felt safe in most parts of the city.

For those living in central Oxford, their greater feelings of safety may be, in part, because many of the respondents were young, with an outgoing lifestyle, and familiar with using the city and its attractions in the evening. It may also be because Oxford is generally perceived to be a fairly safe place. This would appear to be borne out by the findings of our survey with residents in a new development at Sandford on Thames, where three-quarters again identified other parts of Oxford where they would feel safe walking alone after dark. In contrast to those living at Gloucester Green, however, the respondents at Sandford on Thames also tended to identify the centre of Oxford as an area where they would not feel safe.

The incidence of victimization was also very low amongst city centre respondents compared with survey findings from many inner city and suburban areas. In common with the national pattern, however, damage to or theft from a vehicle were the most common types of offence. The comparatively low levels of victimization amongst residents in the central districts, for example from domestic burglary, is consistent with police statistics on reported crime and anecdotal information from managers of public sector housing in these areas.

In contrast to the findings from the British Crime Survey and estate surveys, the majority of respondents in the city centre developments are only a bit or not at all worried about either themselves or a member of their household being a victim of crime. In common with national patterns, however, there is evidence from our interviews that women still feel less safe out alone after dark, and are more likely than men to express anxiety about sexual assault. From surveys in predominantly housing areas, it is not uncommon for the majority of residents to express anxiety about being the victim of crime, including burglary, street robbery, assault, and car theft or damage.

From our surveys, the minority who do express anxiety about being

*Figure 7.4*
Council housing, Hatton Garden, Holborn, London. Multi-storey housing arranged above jewellery workshops and retail premises. Many residents complained that the area is deserted outside the rush hour and lunchtimes. This photograph was taken at 4pm on a sunny midweek day.

the victim of crime either tend to be worried about car theft or damage or, as gathered from their responses overall, appear to be people who are generally fearful about most situations. A recent analysis of the 1994 British Crime Survey data has identified a similar feature, with some respondents generally more fearful or anxious than most about a range of potentially risky situations (Hough, 1995).

As well as their experiences of crime and perceptions of safety, respondents in our surveys were asked about their perceptions of noise and nuisance in the immediate locality. It was in response to these questions that the influence of city centre activities and, especially, late-night uses was more prevalent. Those problems identified by a significant number of respondents as serious or quite serious were drunk people causing a nuisance, noise from late-night uses, vagrants or people begging and, to a much lesser extent, noisy neighbours or parties.

The proportions identifying these activities as a problem tended to be highest in central London but, except for problems with noise from late-night uses, these residents were still not in the majority at any of the central London locations sampled. These findings do flag up, however, the present and potential conflict between the encouragement of more late-night pubs, clubs and entertainment activities and those policies for more people to live in the city centre, including families with young children.

What can we conclude from our findings for crime and mixed use developments ? Most of those surveyed, particularly in central London and Glasgow, were not really aware of the mixed use character of their specific building. For most respondents, including those in central Oxford, it was the mixed use character and vitality of their area that the majority liked, and which some linked positively to their perceptions of greater safety and less fear of crime.

The strength of ties within the community does not appear to have a significant influence on people's perceptions of safety in these mixed use areas. On some inner city housing estates, it is not uncommon for between a third and a half of residents to have close friends within easy walking distance, yet this does not appear to make people feel safer or less fearful of crime. From our surveys in mixed use developments, the extent to which respondents had friends or relatives close by or knew the majority of their neighbours did not appear to have an identifiable link with perceptions of safety or anxiety about crime.

The influence of the local community, in the sense advanced by Jacobs, to help informally mould and inform on standards of acceptable behaviour does not really appear to have a role. However, it could well be the case that children and young people growing up in an area with a diversity of uses and users are less bored and more confident in public arenas than their counterparts, especially those living on large-scale housing estates with few activities to engage their interest or divert their energies.

Especially for those owning or renting privately, the scale and design of their building and its relationship to other uses within the locality were positive features for city centre residents. In contrast, those areas that they identified as unsafe were often those characterized by single use housing estates. In mixed use developments, scale and design can be as, if not more, important for creating a safe and secure living environment.

An example of a mixed use development where the housing adheres closely to the design and layout of a typical estate and has experienced similar problems is Wood Green Shopping City in north London. The housing, on a deck built over the shopping and car parking, replicates a ground-level estate, with flats and houses accessed by open walkways and balconies. A survey carried out in 1992 revealed serious concerns for personal safety, graffiti and vandalism, very similar to those expressed by residents on estates in single use developments (Pettersson, 1992).

## Conclusions

The level of crime in any given period can be explained by a whole range of complex factors, including prevailing social attitudes, employment levels, and the distribution of wealth within society. The design of a particular location, or the mix of different uses found there, will almost certainly have little effect on the overall level of criminal activity. However, there will be some effect, as some crimes are opportunist, and the design of an area can affect the opportunity to perpetrate a crime successfully (or the perceptions of potential criminals about the likelihood of getting away with it). In terms of the crime levels in a specific locality, design and mix can have a significant effect. Other factors, such as the style and efficiency of policing, can also make dramatic differences; the murder rate in New York has halved in the early 1990s with new patterns of police activity.

The very mixing of uses may encourage greater criminal activity. In part this is due to the greater levels of activity; more people (especially tourists unfamiliar with the area) increases the potential for street crime. The level of on-street activity is the major factor; burglary levels can be higher in some specific mixed use areas, but often this is where industry and housing are mixed. Some observers claim that the properties least likely to be burgled are those densely packed together with neighbours living nearby, although our evidence (and crime surveys) do not bear this out. Whatever the explanation for different levels of burglary, the idea that enclosed, defensible housing areas keep burglary levels down is supported by the evidence of our surveys.

Our findings suggest that residents of mixed use areas often tend to feel safer and less fearful about crime than those in other urban environments. However, they are also likely to be more concerned by problems of street noise and nuisance. In addition, those currently living in the city centre tend to be either those with close ties to the area, and hence generally more used to and tolerant of its activities, or those attracted to it specifically because of its life and vitality. Either way, these residents are likely to feel safer and less vulnerable by temperament or by familiarity.

The growth of mixed use developments, including housing, in tandem with greater numbers of late-night uses and late-night revellers is likely to generate much higher concerns about nuisance and noise. Such concerns are also likely to fuel worries for personal safety and more general anxieties about crime. For Britain to benefit fully from the vitality and diversity that mixed use areas can provide, the location, design and structure of housing developments and the regulation of late night activities need to positively address this potential for growing tension between uses and users.

*Figure 7.5*
Vogan's Mill, Rotherhithe, London.
A converted rice mill; residents in London Docklands schemes like this enjoy the convenience of living near the City, but many complain about noisy bars and restaurants in the area.

# References

Bevan, R. (1995) 24-hour cities. *The Big Issue,* September.

Birmingham Junior Chamber of Commerce (1987) *The City Pride Survey Report,* Birmingham Junior Chamber of Commerce, Birmingham.

Brown, B. (1995) *CCTV in Town Centres: Three Case Studies,* Crime Detection and Prevention Series Paper 68, Home Office, London.

Bulos, M. (1994) *Towards a Safer Sutton? Impact of Closed Circuit Television on Sutton Town Centre,* London Borough of Sutton.

Bulos, M. and Sarno, C. (1995) *Closed Circuit Television and Local Authority Initiatives: The First Survey,* South Bank University, London.

Clarke, R. (1995) *Situational Crime Prevention,* University of Chicago Press, Chicago, IL.

Clout, H. and Burgess, J. (1986) Central London, in *Changing London,* (ed. H. Clout) London University Tutorial Press, London.

Coleman, A. (1985) *Utopia on Trial,* Hilary Shipman, London.

Department of the Environment (1994) *Planning Out Crime,* Circular 5/94, Department of the Environment, London.

Crime Concern (1995) *The Prevention of Criminality,* Briefing Paper No 2 for the Crime Prevention Partnership, Crime Concern, London.

Daunton, M.J. (1986) *House and Home in the Victorian City: Working Class Housing 1850-1914,* Edward Arnold, London.

Fowler, E. (1992) *Building Cities That Work,* McGill Queens University Press, Toronto.

Grayson and Young (1994) *Quality of Life in Cities,* British Library and London Research Centre, London.

Honess and Charman (1992) *Closed Circuit Television in Public Places: Its Acceptability and Perceived Effectiveness,* Crime Prevention Unit Series Paper 35, Home Office, London.

Hope, T. (1985) *Implementing Crime Prevention Measures,* Home Office Research Study No 86, Home Office, London.

Hough, M. (1995) *Anxiety about Crime: Findings from the 1994 Britsh Crime Survey,* Home Office, London.

Jacobs, J. (1961) *The Death and Life of Great American Cities,* Random House, New York.

Littlejohn, H.D. (1865) *Report on the Sanitary Conditions of the City of Edinburgh.*

Lovatt, A. (1994) *More Hours in the Day,* Manchester Institute for Popular Culture, Manchester Metropolitan University, Manchester.

Merry, S. (1981) Defensible space undefended *Urban Affairs Quarterly* **16** 397–422

Morrison, J. (1874) *A Few Remarks on the High Rate of Mortality in Glasgow.*

Newman, O. (1972) *Defensible Space,* Architecural Press, London.

Newman, S. and Lonsdale, S. (1996) *Human Jungle,* Ebury Press, London.

Pettersson, G. (1992) *Survey of Wood Green Shopping City Residential Tenants* (unpublished), Metropolitan Housing Trust, London.

Poyner, B. (1980) *Development of Local Crime Prevention Programmes,* Tavistock Institute of Human Relations, London.

Ramsey, M. (1989) *Downtown Drinkers; The Perceptions and Fears of the Public in a City Centre,* Home Office Crime Prevention Unit Paper 19, Home Office, London.

Sheffield City Liaison Group (1996) *Sheffield City Centre Business Plan,* Sheffield City Liaison Group, Sheffield.

Sucher, D. (1995) *City Comforts, How to Build an Urban Village,* City Comforts Press, Seattle, WA.

Urban Regeneration (1994) Aberdeen beefs up residential. Autumn.

Walmsley, D.J. (1988) *Urban Living: The Individual in the City,* Longman, London.

Wilkström, P. (1995) *Preventing City-Center Street Crimes,* University of Chicago Press, Chicago, IL.

## Notes

1   Although, given the large numbers of people regularly using these areas, the level of victimization is still likely to be comparatively low.

2   Sometimes, a third though largely negative strand to crime prevention is identified separately and relies on the impact of law enforcement policies and the restraining influence of the criminal justice system. One of the chief problems with relying on punishment to deter crime is the comparatively low detection and conviction rates, particularly for the most common crimes of burglary, car theft and damage.

# Case Study 7.1

# Covent Garden

The schemes surveyed as part of the research for *Reclaiming The City* include a number in Covent Garden. While the case study on the Oxford schemes in Chapter 3 was concerned with comparing locations in the city centre and some way out of the centre, at Covent Garden the comparison was between different tenures within the same geographical location.

The development of Covent Garden took place initially in the 1970s following the transfer of the wholesale fruit and vegetable market to Nine Elms. The area saw tremendous community participation in planning debates about the nature of the area's future, following the Greater London Council (GLC) proposals, which would have seen a huge new conference centre complex developed in the area. By 1978 a new approach had been agreed which saw most of the market buildings retained and many of the warehouses converted to other uses. A number of private sector developers were involved, some adopting a philanthropic approach, which saw the development of mixed uses in areas like Neal Street. Two of the refurbishment projects are described in Chapter 9: Comyn Ching and Thomas Neal's.

## Jubilee Hall

This scheme involved both new-build and refurbishment on the edge of the market area. Jubilee Hall was originally one of the market buildings, and was adjacent to a site for redevelopment. Unlike other market buildings it was not listed, and was earmarked for redevelopment. While negotiations proceeded to agree a scheme (eventually finalized in 1980 with Capital and Counties), the local community association had taken a short lease on the building and were using it as a sports hall, while a market was organized on the ground floor. They threatened to take legal action over the failure to list the building, causing the development deal to be abandoned. A new GLC administration invited the community association and their community architects, Covent Garden Housing Project, to propose a different scheme retaining the building. A consortium of users was put together with the local Soho Housing Association, and a scheme was designed for speculative offices, housing and retention of the market and sports hall. Only then was a potential developer identified: Speyhawk, who were willing to proceed with only 17% of the floorspace for commercial letting. The deal was finally struck in 1984, with the Housing Project as architects. The 125 year lease cost Speyhawk £1.3 million, and they leased the housing association the housing site for only £5 000 and leased the sports hall and other facilities to the Covent Garden Community Association for £20 000. The market traders contributed £3 million, which covered the cost of a two-storey reconstructed structure that formed the base for the housing. This was paid for by each of the 124 stall holders contributing £3 500; some of them raised this through a mortgage from a local bank.

The discovery of poorly filled seventeenth-century basements over important Saxon remains added unforeseen costs and created delays. Despite the low costs of construction for the housing, they still exceeded the indicative limits operated by the Housing Corporation. Speyhawk paid the additional £23 000 costs themselves. The out-turn prices for the flats (1987) were £26 600 for a one-person flat and £46 000 for a two-bedroom four-person flat.

## Odham's Walk

This is another scheme from the 1980s, which followed the redevelopment of the market. Here, however, it was the GLC who, as planners for the area, provided the development. Odham's Walk is a local authority housing complex, which has been described as being modelled on an Italian hill village. The outer parts of the site are in public use, mostly as retailing. A number of pedestrian entrances lead into the centre of the site, where different floors of residential accommodation are served by lifts and balconies, and access can be gained to the health centre, which operates from the site. The outer face of the building is vertical; the inner parts are terraced to form a series of small courtyards and spaces. Following the demise

*Figure 7.6*
Jubilee Hall, Covent Garden, London.
The Speyhawk/Community Consortium development which shows the market beneath offices on the corner and housing association flats to the right. The sports hall can be seen on the far left of the picture.

*Figure 7.7*
Odham's Walk, Covent Garden, London.
The former ITEC, now French Connection, with flats above. The pedestrian entrance to the health centre is just beyond the shop.

of the GLC there have been a number of changes in use: the former training centre for youth, the ITEC, has become another retail unit, and a number of flats have been acquired under the 'right-to-buy' legislation in what is a very sought-after and valuable location.

The survey of residents who occupy these two developments was compared with those who live in Comyn Ching and Thomas Neil's, both schemes incorporating private flats. The public tenants in Odham's Walk, like the housing association tenants in Jubilee Hall, had all lived in the area for a number of years, although the Jubilee Hall residents had been there longer. The private owners and renters, however, had generally been only a year or two in the area, if that. Over half the private owners had another home, and these were widely scattered from Bristol and Sussex to France, New York and Hong Kong. What the residents did also showed tenure differences. A majority of the housing association residents interviewed were not working – most of them were pensioners. At Odham's Walk a similar ratio of those still in the public sector were pensioners, but a number of flats are now in private ownership. While the employment of the private residents included bankers, writers and artists, those living in the public rented properties tended to be employed in service jobs, typically in the Opera House, as a taxi driver, or as a theatre technician.

Most people interviewed had chosen to live in the area: most of the public (and housing association) residents because they had always done so; the private occupiers because of the convenience of the location. However, none gained any direct benefit from the mix of uses in the building they lived in, and over half found noise from the other uses or the immediate vicinity disturbing. Although most of the public routes through Odham's Walk are now kept closed, residents still complained about people passing through (which may therefore be a more historic than contemporary concern). The really difficult balance of living in a busy city centre is shown in response to questions about the benefits and problems of living in the area. A majority liked the location, its convenience for activities and facilities, and 'the bustle of the centre'. Equally they disliked the noise, pollution and overcrowding. Often the same person listed the bustle and the noise as good and bad factors.

The housing association tenants knew all their neighbours, and several had relatives nearby. The private owners knew few or none of their neighbours, although more had friends nearby (except where they had purchased their rented flat, when they also knew all their neighbours). The public tenants knew most of their neighbours, and several had relatives nearby, although few had friends in the same category. Car ownership was low generally, but higher among the private owners, who all relied on on-street parking spaces. A few private owners had given up owning a car as not being needed following moving to the area. Most people used public transport; a few owned bikes, but there was a problem in finding satisfactory secure storage space. (This is true across all tenures.)

There are several local shops, including a fairly new Tesco Metro. Almost all respondents walked to do their shopping, although one car owner travelled to Vauxhall. All respondents who work either walked or used public transport (except the taxi driver!). In terms of safety, a majority felt safe walking at night in their own area, but some were wary of other areas, and similarly thought others would not feel safe in their area. Actual experience of crime was variable: some Jubilee Hall tenants had suffered break-ins; otherwise experience of crime in the previous 12 months was of car crime, mostly vandalism.

# Chapter 8

# Local Policy and Mixed Uses

## Andy Coupland

### Developing Government Policy

As has been noted in the introduction and in Chapter 3, government policy on mixed uses has been developing through advice issued in Planning Policy Guidance notes. However, these are only part of the policy framework that determines the basis on which planning decisions are made. Local authority planning policies are certainly as important, as they often influence decisions more directly. They will also affect the attitude of developers and landowners considering the development of particular sites.

Like government policy, local authority plans have also changed in recent years. Our concern in this publication is with urban developments, in larger towns and cities. The emerging local plans and unitary development plans (UDPs) have, in a number of cases, started to reflect the need for a greater mix of uses, and in a few cases go further and require such a mix. This chapter looks at some of those policies, and how the property market is responding to this changing policy situation.

In particular situations, local authorities have sought a mix of different uses in certain schemes for many years. There are also many examples of site-specific planning briefs that identify a number of different uses that may be appropriate, without necessarily selecting which should be developed, or what mix of different uses should be sought. What is notably different is that some authorities now have policies that seek a mix on a universal basis, across the entire authority. Unlike other parts of this book, this chapter incorporates a number of case-study examples as part of the main body of the text.

### Local Authority Policies: Camden

The emerging plans of a number of local authorities require a mix of uses in all or part of their plan areas. Notable in this regard are several London boroughs, including Westminster, Camden and Tower Hamlets.

Each took a slightly different approach, and had different justifications for the policy, but each had a general preference for a mix of uses in all or part of the borough.

Camden's policies are perhaps the most stringent, and therefore bear closer examination. The Camden UDP has been in preparation for much of the 1990s, and was examined at a public inquiry in 1995. The main policies for mixed uses evolved as the plan proceeded towards the public inquiry. The policies presented at the inquiry were RE5 and REx. They are worded:

> (Policy RE5) The Council will encourage proposals to incorporate a mix of land uses appropriate to the scale and location of development. In appropriate circumstances the Council will seek a planning obligation under s.106 of the Town and Country Planning Act 1990 (as amended by the Planning and Compensation Act 1991) to secure a satisfactory balance of uses.

> (Policy REx) The Council will normally expect proposals involving redevelopment of over 500 m² floorspace and proposals for a net increase of business or commercial floorspace of over 500 m² (through redevelopment, extension or change of use) to incorporate a mix of land uses. Commercial and business uses to which this policy relates include B1, retail, tourism uses, leisure and cultural uses and commercial sui generis uses. In assessing the appropriate proportion of secondary uses to be incorporated, the Council will have regard not only to the detailed nature, scale and location of the development, but also to the predominant scale, character and mix of land uses in the surrounding area. The appropriate mix of uses will vary (London Borough of Camden, 1995).

The policy then lists the possible uses that may be appropriate in different parts of the borough. The justification for the policy in part relates to the requirements of PPG13, which specifically encourages both mixed use developments and the creation of more housing in central locations. It develops this idea by stating:

> The mix of development in a locality – be it urban or rural – determines its attractiveness and vitality. For example, planning for a variety of uses – shops and restaurants – on the ground floor of developments will help keep streets lively. Attention to preserving or enhancing continuous pavement level streetscapes and the avoidance of blank frontages such as 'dead' shop or office frontages, can be a major contribution to retaining pedestrian activity, retaining the commercial life of an area, and to crime prevention ... By providing a wide range of facilities at the local neighbourhood level, the need for people to use cars to meet their day-to-day need will be reduced. Local planning authorities should actively encourage through their own actions and their plans, a wide range of facilities at the local level.

Camden Council in particular noted the reference to the plan-making element of this statement. The Council also referred to other government statements including *Quality in Town and Country – a discussion document* and *Planning out Crime* to support their policies. In relation to sustainability they noted the statements in PPG12 on the provision of local facilities to minimize car use.

The Council's case in creating these policies was summarized in the evidence presented to the public inquiry. The intention was to protect and develop existing residential communities and to achieve greater energy efficiency, amenity and sustainability of the built environment.

> By definition, mixed use areas comprise a number of different uses in close proximity. A single trip to or within the area can serve a number of different uses for residents, workers and visitors, thereby reducing the need to travel, promoting greater flexibility and energy efficiency savings (and significant economic benefits) and advantages for some groups, for example, disabled people (particularly if a variety of uses exist at street level) and others who may be 'travel disadvantaged'. In addition, areas which combine a mix of activities with a high quality and character of environment are likely to prove attractive to residents and visitors and become successful as locations for small businesses and services. In some cases a mixed use approach may also assist in securing the implementation of plan policies, for example to secure the provision of additional housing (including affordable housing) or small business units.

There was opposition to the Council's proposed policies from a number of objectors: over 30 to each policy. These objectors were predominantly land-owners and developers with interests in the borough. In preparing evidence to counter their objections Camden prepared maps showing the average number of uses in the central area of the borough, which illustrated the diverse nature of the land uses throughout the central area.

The Council's evidence explained the need to adopt policies such as this; the demand for land was high, supply limited, and the operations of the market therefore raised prices to effectively exclude certain uses. They also pointed out that it was not practical to leave it to the developer to determine whether or not to include other uses in a scheme:

> At its extreme this could mean relying on the last developer in a street to provide alternative uses contributing towards an area's mix and vitality.

The adoption of the 500 m$^2$ threshold for the operation of the policy was clearly potentially contentious. Camden argued that by providing a specific measurement they enabled developers to be clear whether or not the policy applied to them. The flexibility allowed by the wording of policy REx nevertheless allows exceptions to be made in appropriate circumstances. Camden made reference to the inspector's report from the public inquiry into the Westminster UDP, where a threshold had been supported as the most effective approach. The size of threshold selected was justified by the need to keep a mix at an appropriately local scale (as with flats over shops) and because analysis of the existing mix and size of units showed that significant parts of the borough, in Clerkenwell, Fitzrovia and Covent Garden, were characterized by small-scale properties. The Council's report noted that in Westminster the inspector had recommended a threshold of only 200 m².

It is interesting to note that Camden's policy allows considerable flexibility in how much the other uses should consist of in a mixed use scheme, and what the uses should be. This in part reflects a perceived difficulty in being more rigid, and therefore potentially being seen as unreasonable. The council do not wish to frighten developers off, but rather to ensure that major uses (most probably high-value commercial projects) should not overwhelm an area.

The objectors' argument was essentially that the Council were being too prescriptive and not sufficiently flexible by applying a policy across the whole borough; single use schemes should not be refused unless they cause demonstrable harm. Many argued that the policy went beyond reasonable policies and was a back-door method of trying to obtain planning gain. An objection made by four of the UK's largest property developers argued that the policy ignored the market and placed undue restrictions on development. In a slightly differently worded objection several other objectors argued that the mix of uses should be a matter for the market, and that a mixed use requirement often makes developments unfundable or not viable.

The Council answered all these points by stressing that the policy is fundamentally flexible where necessary, but that the market, left to its own devices, would almost certainly not be willing to create the mix of uses (and in particular meet wider plan objectives such as meeting housing need) without such an approach.

The objections by the British Land Company can be seen as an example of the views of a number of the larger development companies. British Land employed a planning consultancy to object to the mixed use policies on their behalf. The consultants stated that British Land considered that the Council's mixed use policies undermined the potential of the area defined by the Council as the Central Activity Zone (CAZ – that part of the borough with the greatest existing density of commercial uses) for 'travel-intensive uses such as offices'. The argument was put that central London's office and business activities were of national importance, and that they were too important to be diluted by other uses. An argument was advanced that the mixed use policies required other uses, such as residential uses, which are less travel-intensive and therefore undermine what was, in the developer's view, 'the potential for expanding office development in these areas'.

As is common in such planning disagreements, each side of the case selected quotations from different parts of the same policy documents to justify their position. Camden identified those parts of PPG13 that refer to mixed uses. British Land referred to those sections that address the need to locate travel-intensive uses close to good travel facilities. In many ways each addresses separate arguments, coming to the discussion from quite a different viewpoint and with little apparent acknowledgement that the other view may have any validity.

In practice the British Land case was weakened somewhat by their acknowledgement that several of the policy documents on which they were relying express a preference for mixed uses, particularly the more recent policy statements.

Concern was expressed that the supply of new space is limited, while demand (despite the recession and its effects on property) is rising. Therefore, the developers argued, there should be encouragement for the redevelopment of new office space; the mixed use policies would work against this. In listing examples of contemporary office development activity it is ironic that a scheme in Marylebone by Bank Parisbas should be referred to; this includes a significant residential element, included to meet the mixed use requirements of Westminster City Council!

British Land's consultants made the suggestion that the policy should allow the possibility of what they described as 'swaps', where requirements for mixed uses are provided off-site. This, they argued, would create the opportunity to provide 'mixed use areas rather than necessarily requiring a mixed use building in every case'.

The case presented by British Land against Camden's mixed use policy shows very clearly the difficulties in getting agreement to a broader approach to development. It illustrates many of the points made in Chapter 5. Property developers and investors specialize in one part of the market – in this case, offices. They develop office buildings, and as owners of major office property in Camden (in particular the Regent's Place office complex, formerly known as the Euston Centre) they wish to redevelop their buildings as new offices. They know (as well as anyone knows) the market for offices, believe that they are a valuable element of the economy (and for their company), and do not wish to have to build other types of development, or to dilute schemes with other uses.

Yet Camden's policy is far less rigid than the objectors suggest. In part it is based on the observation (as also noted in Chapter 5) that large parts of the borough are now empty, with little sign of demand for new commercial uses. British Land would seem to see the problem in terms of their land holdings and, as is often the case, prefer to believe that their developments are unquestionably lettable even if rival developers have problems with letting or developing space. But for Camden the policy would allow a case to be made (for example) that Euston Road is not an appropriate location for housing, so offices should predominate. However, further along the Euston Road where it becomes Marylebone Road (and traffic flows are identical) there are several very large residential buildings (some with other uses incorporated), where flats cost over £200 000. This suggests that there is no such thing as an inappropriate location for housing – just poorer or better sites.

## Tower Hamlets

The UDP in Tower Hamlets also identifies policies to encourage a mix of uses. The borough is on the fringe of the City of London, to the east, and has seen significant change over the past 20 years as the City has expanded. Whole streets have been redeveloped, with a complex mix of housing, clothing manufacturing and wholesaling and local shopping all being cleared away for new office developments, many occupied by companies in the insurance sector, and very few with any other use incorporated into the building.

In the borough's UDP proposals, policy on mixed use development is developed in relation to the CAZ (as in Camden, the main commercial area, which in Tower Hamlets now also includes the Isle of Dogs former Enterprise Zone including Canary Wharf). The policy applies to schemes providing over 3 000 m² of retail or business floorspace: a much higher threshold than in Camden. The policy in Tower Hamlets makes specific reference to the provision of housing: an aspect of the policy that generated a number of objections.

Tower Hamlets policy on mixed use was amended as a result of the objections, and in its final version, ( London Borough of Tower Hamlets, 1995), read:

(Policy CAZ3) Within the central area zones, development for business (B1) and retail (A1, A2, A3) uses providing gross additional floorspace of 3 000 m² or more, will normally be required to be composed of an integrated mixed use scheme (using negotiated agreements where appropriate), subject to the following considerations:

1. The character and function of the surrounding area;

2. The scale and nature of the development;

3. The physical constraints of the site;

4. The other policies and proposals of this plan.

It might be thought that this policy, which is rather less onerous than that in Camden, would be generally acceptable. The policy itself makes no reference to the provision of housing (although the supporting text indicates a preference where these can be achieved). But there were significant objections to the policy, of a similar nature to those in Camden. For example, Taylor Woodrow Property Co, with significant property interests including the St Katharines Dock, objected to the policy on the basis (among several other reasons) that it represented a requirement for planning gain, contrary to government guidance. (A similar case was put by British Land, among other objectors, at the Camden inquiry.) Tower Hamlets were able to point to RPG3 (*Strategic Planning Advice for London*, 1989), which made it clear that promoting a mix of uses is distinct from seeking planning gain. As at the Camden inquiry, Tower Hamlets were able to quote circulars on *Planning and Crime Prevention* and Planning Policy Guidance notes in support of their approach to mixed use development: notably PPG12 and PPG4.

As with Camden, therefore, it is clear that new planning policies that reflect government support for mixed uses are still being seen by parts of the development industry as (at least potentially) too restrictive. The policies would appear to have inherent flexibility and lack detailed requirements for a particular mix. This might at other times be criticized for allowing developers too much freedom to provide token additional uses, or the chance to argue the inappropriate nature of their particular site for mixed uses. Yet clearly the development industry – or significant parts of it – has yet to accept the idea of mixed uses as being anything but an unacceptable imposition.

## Bedfordshire

Planning policies are being developed for mixed uses outside city centre locations. The 1995 Deposit Draft of Bedfordshire's Structure Plan is one of the first to make specific reference to mixed use development. One of the strategic aims of the plan is:

> to promote mixed uses and the concept of 'urban villages' within urban areas and specific sites within the strategic corridors.

The plan examines the concept of sustainable development, referring specifically to mixed uses in this context. Policy 20, on sustainable design and energy conservation, encourages local planning authorities to apply clear urban design principles, and in particular  to promote:

> urban vitality and public security by encouraging mixed uses and higher densities in areas well served by public transport.

*Figure 8.1*
Globe Court, Bethnal Green, London.
An example of a mixed use scheme in Tower Hamlets; the developers, Hampstead Homes, have developed a housing scheme behind this roadside block of offices over shops (so far unlet) with a health centre. The scheme received government City Grant support.

The county's policy on the release of employment land stresses that where new releases of land are necessary these should be as part of a mixed development scheme that includes new housing.

Policy 33 identifies the ways in which local authorities can help to promote 'urban villages' by mixing house types and tenures, incorporating social facilities including shopping and educational facilities, providing local and accessible employment opportunities, and also providing public space, provision for walking, cycling and public transport on a human scale designed around 'pedestrian priority access and movement'.

## Problems in Practice: London Docklands

While these emerging plans include policies that go as far as the local authorities feel is reasonable in requiring mixed uses, there are a number of implemented projects that illustrate that the universal application of such a policy could run into difficulties. The opposition of developers to mixed use developments is not wholly blind prejudice; examples can be found where mixed uses have not worked. Equally it is worth considering some other examples that illustrate the limitations of a policy in creating the required mix of uses.

The area of London's Docklands offers a number of examples. Since 1981 parts of the London boroughs of Southwark, Newham and Tower Hamlets have been controlled, for planning application purposes, by a government-appointed body, the London Docklands Development Corporation (LDDC). The operation of this organization has been examined in considerable detail elsewhere (Brownill, 1993; Coupland, 1994). For the purposes of this chapter it is necessary only to point out that the LDDC is almost universally seen as being supportive of development, to a degree far beyond that which would be true of the elected local authorities. The LDDC holds neither a wide nor a long-term remit; its main concern is to encourage the creation of development within its area. The main measure of success is the value of development created or invested, not specifically of broader social or employment goals.

Although plan-making powers remain with the elected local authorities, a complex relationship exists between them and the LDDC, who are designated as local planning authority (thus determining planning applications, but not responsible for the drawing up of plans). Despite the local authority plan-making powers, there has been little change in policy direction by the LDDC as a result of local authority intervention. LDDC planning policy is hard to find in documentary form; a number of development frameworks have been published over the years, but in only a few cases has development followed the pattern identified in the framework. Most of the developable land in the London Docklands area has gone through the ownership of the LDDC, and it is through its powers as land-owner when disposing of sites that the organization has often influenced design or land-use issues. However, the planning process in terms of decision making on planning applications submitted once a site has been disposed of can be followed, particularly in the last few years when the public have been able to attend LDDC Planning Committee meetings.

In certain areas the LDDC policy has been very supportive of mixed use development. In Greenland Dock, in Southwark, a developer called Skillion created an unusual looking scheme named Baltic Quay. The development, designed by Marshall, Haines and Barrow, consisted of a residential element of 96 apartments together with 11 shop units and 50 000 ft$^2$ of office space. The development is located in a area of former working dock surrounding retained water areas. Most development in the area has been housing, although there is a water-sports centre and a large retail development nearby. Other sites were identified as suitable for a mix of uses, but no other developer felt confident about including any uses other than housing, except a couple of local shops and a water-side public house.

Although the housing sold or leased successfully, the offices did not let, and eventually the company owning the scheme was placed in receivership. The new owner received permission to convert the offices to residential units. Some two years later a further application was submitted to change the shops into residential use, as none of them had been leased.

The LDDC's flexibility and willingness to encompass mixed uses was tested by an application in the Wapping area of Tower Hamlets.

*Figure 8.2*
Baltic Wharf, Greenland Dock, London.
Developed as a mix of offices, flats and shops. Now housing with vacant shops beneath (see Figure 8.3).

Here an application was submitted for residential units to be constructed on top of existing industrial workshops. The location was far from ideal (particularly, one would have thought, from a marketing point of view) as one side faced the Highway, a heavily-trafficked through route, while the other would have faced the News International printing works. Despite the general presumption in favour of development, the LDDC refused the proposals on grounds of lack of amenity (particularly in relation to the industrial units underneath). The developers appealed to the Secretary of State, who, despite the policies in favour of mixed uses, agreed with the LDDC and turned the scheme down.

*Figure 8.3*
Baltic Wharf, Greenland Dock, London.
Vacant shops beneath housing, now proposed for conversion to further flats.

## Butler's Wharf

Another Docklands scheme illustrates how mixing uses can create unexpected problems. Butler's Wharf was first identified for redevelopment by Town and City Properties, who acquired the site in the 1970s. The complex of warehouses stretched back from the riverside next to Tower Bridge, and had been identified for decades with the importation and processing of spices. Eventually the site was sold on, to a consortium of businessmen fronted by Terence Conran, at that time still involved with the Habitat furnishing chain as well as with his other design-related companies. Initial elements of redevelopment involved external cleaning and internal redevelopment of both the huge riverside warehouses and some of the later concrete-framed buildings: one for residential purposes, one for the charitable Conran Foundation's Design Museum. The riverside warehouse was at first marketed as the 'next Covent Garden', with upper floor flats over a variety of retail and catering units. However, despite superb views of the river and a convenient location for the City, the flats sold very slowly. A planning application for permission to use the space for office use was approved, but the recession ensured that there was no serious letting interest for this use. The retail units were among a number created in the Bermondsey dockside area, with others in major residential projects in the vicinity, including Tower Bridge Plaza and The Circle. The nature of the residential occupants, who seem to have been either occupying company-let units

*Figure 8.4*
Butler's Wharf, London. A new mixed use area with the public realm reclaimed from private warehouse wharves.

or *pieds-à-terre* accommodation, meant that demand for any services in the area was very limited; almost nobody can be found during the day or at weekends in the entire area, despite its consisting of over 1 000 residential units.

Conran, who had resumed a career as a restaurateur elsewhere in London, created the Gastrodome from several of the riverside retail units, providing three separate restaurants with a number of specialist retail food outlets. This was very successful (although it did not prevent the entire project from being put into receivership). As a result, a number of other restaurant operators were attracted to the vicinity and applied to

*Figure 8.5*
The Circle, Bermondsey, London.
A predominantly residential scheme whose original mix included shops, unlet after five years.

open in retail units. A significant change has occurred, with most of the Shad Thames street frontage in restaurant use, and very few other shops or services. This led to a much livelier area, particularly at night, so that a planning application in 1995 for a further restaurant attracted over 50 objections from local residents. They claimed that they had expected to see far fewer people around late at night, and that the noise from people leaving the different premises, often then taking a taxi home, was very much more of a disturbance than they had expected.

## Bradford: Forster Square

In West Yorkshire the development of a significant site at Forster Square in Bradford illustrates that policy statements alone may not be enough to ensure that mixed use development takes place.

Bradford can in some respects be seen to be overshadowed by its near neighbour Leeds, whose population, and therefore city centre, is larger. However, Bradford is still competing successfully to attract new investment in a broad range of jobs, including tourism and electronics. Property investment, although difficult to achieve, is still being attracted to the city.

Planning policy is reasonably clear; the Deposit UDP was approved in September 1993. This is the main planning framework for the whole district – the city and surrounding area – and identifies several sites where 'central area uses' are appropriate. On these sites, retail, commercial and residential uses are all acceptable, although the plan does not require a mix of uses. However, in a number of locations development briefs exist for specific sites.

As well as the UDP, the City Council planners have produced a number of other policy statements and documents. Amongst these is *The Heart of the Matter* – a document subtitled *A Strategy for Bradford City Centre*, written in 1992 to inform the debate concerning the future of the city centre. This document was approved by the Community and Environment Committee of the City Council, but in planning terms has no formal status. It examined a range of problems, and identified some possible solutions, including the opportunity to adapt older property to other uses, including residential, under the heading 'mixed uses'. The Forster Square development site was promoted with a development brief that strongly supported mixed development. The brief was developed after earlier proposals fell through for a large shopping centre, which would have extended the city centre shopping area. Burton Property Trust's proposals kept the site from being developed for a number of years. The recession of the late 1980s led the company to steadily revise their proposals, and eventually to abandon them.

The site is located on the edge of the city centre, within the ring road (although a small part of the site is cut off by a recently completed part of the ring road, known as Hammstrasse). It was formerly a railway marshalling yard, and following reconstruction of a small passenger station, BR offered the remainder of the site for sale, with an invited development competition, meeting a brief provided by the planning department of the City Council. This brief specifically referred to the Council's wish to see:

> A variety in terms of uses within each building and within the development generally. Each uses (sic) must be compatible and give mutual trading support to the other and together provide for a lively ambience at ground floor level.

The brief also stated that:

> Retailing, operating from low-rise metal-clad buildings with significant areas of surface level car parking will not be acceptable on any part of the site.

The initial attempt by developers to meet this brief produced a preferred developer, St James Securities. A locally based company, with experience of developing in both Bradford and Leeds, their scheme attempted to meet the brief, albeit with little or no mixing of uses between the different elements proposed in the scheme. The developer explains that, for the scheme to be funded, different areas of use may be funded by different agencies.

The scheme that was initially proposed consisted of a shopping mall, single storey in construction, through the area currently used for car parking behind the Midland Hotel. This linked to the station forecourt, with an office element then filling the remainder of the site to Hammstrasse of around 15 000 m². The further part of the site, cut off by the road, was initially identified for housing (this proposal was rejected by the planners, although in part it met their requirement for a mix of uses). This was then superceded with a proposal for a stand-alone leisure centre, now changed again to more retailing. For a variety of reasons the scheme has been altered as the plans have progressed. The servicing of the single-storey mall proved to be almost impossible to design satisfactorily, and potential operators of the retail element (mostly discount operators) were unwilling to commit themselves to a location that remained fairly invisible, behind the listed Midland Hotel and the bulk of the 1960s office block that wraps round the front of the site. At the same time it bcame necessary for the office to be more centrally located within the site, next to the station.

*Figure 8.6*
Forster Square, Bradford.
Artist's impression of the
front of the office to be let to
the Inland Revenue.
*David Lyons and Associates.*

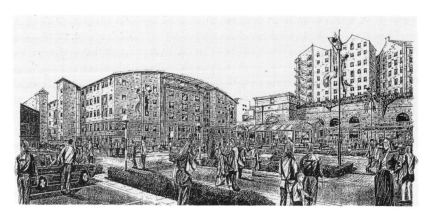

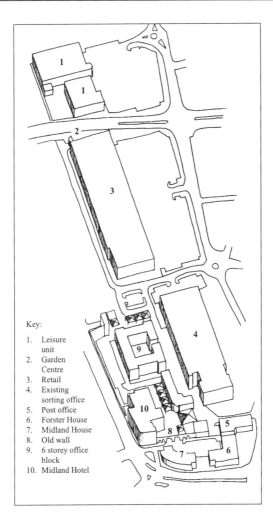

Key:
1. Leisure unit
2. Garden Centre
3. Retail
4. Existing sorting office
5. Post office
6. Forster House
7. Midland House
8. Old wall
9. 6 storey office block
10. Midland Hotel

*Figure 8.7*
Forster Square, Bradford.
An early plan of the scheme, showing the arrangement of uses on the site. The scheme has now been revised to replace the leisure use with more retail units.

The idea for the retailing element seems to reflect earlier aspirations for the major retailing project developed by Burton Property Trust. While *The Heart of the Matter* identified the continued contraction of city centre retailing, and the increased threat from out-of-town shopping, it can be argued that this did not filter through to realistic expectations for the Forster Square site in the development climate of the early 1990s.

Elsewhere in Bradford the Aldermanbury site, part of the West End development initiative, although more centrally located and closer to the shopping centre, was nevertheless accepted as a site for purely office uses. No retail, restaurant or other activity was proposed, in part because there was a long-term commitment to purely office use of the site.

Bradford is viewed by many of the potential funders for development as fairly peripheral. Leeds takes most of the investment, as it is the regional centre and only 10 miles away, and has a much more significant office development area. While a few speculative office developments have been developed in Leeds in the past few years, this has not been generally the case in Bradford. In the economic climate of the 1990s, it is almost certainly necessary to have a pre-let for any substantial new-build office development. (Although the city centre Aldermanbury site saw construction start in 1994 without a pre-let, work halted at foundation level.) The only other speculative office scheme of any size was a refurbishment of a listed warehouse into offices in the Little Germany area, which proceeded with a financial contribution from City Grant.

St James were vying with a number of other developers for any potential users of their office buildings. The one known possible letting was to the Inland Revenue, which has a significant operation in Bradford, and which was seeking a new location to concentrate activities currently spread over a number of sites. It became clear that if Forster Square was to be their preferred choice, the preference of the Inland Revenue was for there to be no incidental uses in the building. St James are in no position to argue with this – the rival Aldermanbury building was one of several that could be used by the Revenue, where this would not be an issue. While there is some confusion about who had the idea of making the building office use only, (with the developer and the Inland Revenue stating that it was the other's idea) the end result is a building which has a restaurant, creche and possibly a kiosk shop, but only for the staff working there, and with the entire site, (car park included), behind a 1.8 m security fence.

For the Forster Square scheme to be built, it had to have wholly office uses, located where originally the shopping element was proposed, with the shopping moved to the rear of the site. Strictly speaking, provided the design of the shopping units is sufficiently prestigious with (for example) brick facades and a curved roof, the proposal could be argued to meet the brief – i.e. not metal-clad sheds.

In almost every other respect, however, the scheme fails to meet the Council's aspirations in the brief. It is not an integrated mix of uses, it is low rise, and it does have extensive surface-level parking. It remains true that this is almost certainly the only form of retailing that could be funded, or for which demand exists to fill it. It has some benefit in creating a series of retailing units on the edge of the existing city centre, which might otherwise seek to locate further away. However, the scheme will meet almost none of the City Council's original intentions, and this brings the planning brief, and its context, into question. Because available city centre sites could be developed for single (office) use, the Council planners were in no position to force their preference for mixed uses on a less centrally located and poorly serviced site. The Council's Estates Department favoured single office use on the Aldermanbury site, which the City Council owned, as it would generate a greater return to the Council, although this also undermined the Planning Department's preference for mixed use elsewhere in the city, such as Forster Square.

The economics of developing in Bradford are also unlikely to allow complex or expensive solutions, such as underground servicing, or to encourage the more expensive construction costs that mixed uses can entail. While the Council could reject the proposal, it might be hard to sustain at appeal, but more to the point would most likely lose the possible development of the site for several, possibly many, years.

If the Forster Square site were owned by the City Council, an entirely different picture might emerge. Requirements on developers imposed other than through the planning system could offer the opportunity to ensure a mix of uses as originally intended. However, the harsh realities of development finance would make the creation of a more integrated mixed scheme a very difficult undertaking.

The problems in developing mixed uses on the Forster Square site show quite clearly how difficult it is to achieve mixed uses in some locations. Policy would have to be 'fireproof' to insist on the mix of uses indicated in the planning brief. Despite ministerial comments and speeches, the government has yet to show itself willing to support the imposition of mixed uses – they are keen to see it, and oppose any more rigid zoning that might prevent it. The government view on policies which require a mix of uses may become clearer once reports are received on plans like the Camden UDP, but none of the recent ministerial statements have indicated a policy shift to require all local authorities to do any more than encourage a greater mix of uses.

## Ensuring a Mix of Uses

Examples can be found that show other difficulties with the limitations of the planning system in creating or retaining a mix of uses. In the London Borough of Islington, construction of a major banking headquarters known as Regent's House was approved in 1980 at The Angel, an area of both commercial offices and retailing. The building included a ground-floor arcade intended to be used for retailing, linking the specialist antique market at Camden Passage (immediately to the north of the building) with a small parade of shops attached to the Underground station to the south. By 1988 the owners of the building, The Royal Bank of Scotland, had made it clear that they had no intention

*Figure 8.8*
Regent's House, The Angel, Islington.
A 1980s office block intended to have shopping beneath (see Figure 8.9).

of letting the retail units, citing security as the reason. After several years of leaving the units boarded up they applied for planning permission for the shops to be used as office space, integrated into the use of the remainder of the building. Islington Council refused planning permission for this change, arguing that the loss of retail floorspace would undermine the economic viability of the area and would:

> Prejudice the overall aims proposed for the development as a whole, which was to create a lively activity area adjoining a landscaped public square with immediate access to public transport facilities.

The bank appealed to the Secretary of State for the Environment, and in 1989 an Inspector recommended approval of the alteration, thus effectively closing a significant street frontage to public use. The inspector noted Islington Council's concerns about vitality, but pointed out that the main shopping area was on the other side of the High Street, and that the Borough Plan did not specifically protect shopping uses on the site. He agreed that the shops 'could be let without difficulty for a wide variety of shop or related town centre uses'. He continued:

> I agree that such uses would be the optimum kind of use at this location close to the point of entry to the centre of large numbers of people from public transport facilities. However I have to say that, in

*Figure 8.9*
Regent's House, The Angel, Islington.
The pavement and colonnaded arcade beneath the office block, intended as shops but now used as offices.

the absence of any harm to the vitality of the town centre as a whole or any clear policy objection, this hardly amounts to a sound reason for refusal of planning permission.

Although this decision might be made differently today in the light of emerging government guidance, it is interesting to note that the inspector really did not address the issue of creating a lively area with a mix of uses at all. Much more recently, in Glasgow in 1995, the owners of the St Enoch Shopping Centre have applied to replace the leisure use of an ice rink with 40 000 ft² of further shops. The Secretary of State for

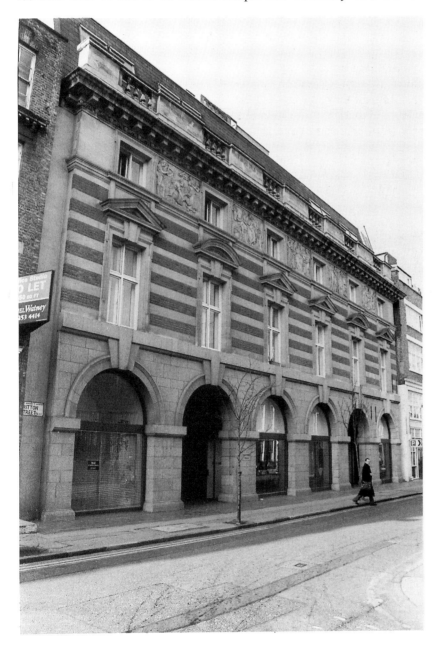

*Figure 8.10*
Britton Street, Clerkenwell, London.
The reconstructed former gin distillery facade, which now fronts flats provided as part of the redevelopment by YRM for their own offices.

Scotland has indicated that he agrees that this change can occur.

An earlier planning decision in Islington illustrates how much both planning policy and the housing market in Central London have changed in a relatively short time. In 1972 an application was made by the architects YRM to develop a new building for their own occupation in Clerkenwell. The site in Britton Street had already had some construction work undertaken to create the foundations for a warehouse. Islington Council refused the application because they were opposed to office development and the loss of general industry (which still operated in the area at that time). The scheme was approved on appeal, with 18 'craftsmen's studios' (later amended to 20) to be developed behind a re-built listed facade from a gin distillery originally located nearby in Turnmill Street. Three shop units were also included, as well as workshop space. This mix of uses proved difficult to fill, and Islington agreed a change from craft workshops to housing in 1976. However, the freeholder went into liquidation, and the housing was completed only to a shell finish. No housing associations were able to take the scheme over as it would cost much more than the cost limits imposed by the Housing Corporation at that time. Islington Council were unable to acquire the block for key workers for the same reason.

The policies of Islington Council are now very similar to those of other councils, which seek to ensure a mix of uses. Wherever possible the council encourage the incorporation of non-B1 (office) uses, including, in some cases, residential uses. However, the economic realities of the property market (as explained in Chapter 5) have started to change the nature of planning applications in the borough. This has led to a rather ironic situation, where the mix of uses is actually becoming less in some parts of the borough. In the Nags Head area near Archway, for example, two large building complexes have received consent for change of use to residential. One, the former headquarters of the Post Office

*Figure 8.11*
Royal Northern Hospital, Archway, London. Residential conversion is planned for the former hospital site.

Bank, built in the 1920s, is now being marketed as the Beaux Arts Building. The other, immediately opposite, is the former hospital, which it also intended will be redeveloped as housing. The net result is that two large employment uses having gone, the area becomes almost entirely residential in character.

The degree of change in planning policy – particularly in terms of implementation – should not be underestimated. The Secretary of State for the Environment, John Gummer, has said that during the 1960s centres suffered 'planning apartheid' through zoning. While this is political

*Figure 8.12*
The Beaux Arts Building, Archway, London. Residential conversion to 'lofts' of the former post office bank headquarters building.

rather than academic language, it is undoubtedly true that segregating and removing non-conforming uses were a feature of planning policies in the 1960s and 1970s. An example can be seen in Coventry, where in 1973 the City Council produced the first of a new style of plan, the Structure Plan. This was based on a more corporate management style of organization, and saw a switch in emphasis from the massive rede-velopment of the 1960s comprehensive development areas. Instead, 24 'action areas' were proposed, each based on renewal and repair of exist-ing housing areas. While the planning legislation of that time did not require the removal of what were termed 'non-conforming uses', it did include powers to allow local authorities to deal with such uses.

Coventry chose to concentrate on using these powers in the action areas to remove industries that were seen as incompatible with housing. As Chapter 2 explained, Coventry, as many other cities that expanded as a result of industrialization, ended up with a complex mix of rapidly (and not necessarily well) built housing in amongst industrial uses. The scale of this can be seen from Coventry's programme, which identified over 500 companies to be moved and allocated a budget of over £1 million. Hobbs (1991)shows how this policy changed over the next few years. Coventry suffered from the recession of 1974, losing thousands of jobs and having to reduce council budgets drastically. The relocation of industries relied on sufficient funding, and public expectation of action (after an extensive public consultation exercise) was high. As a result the council changed the term 'non-conforming use' to 'bad neighbour industries', reducing the range which required attention.

The 1973 £1 million budget became just £220 000 in 1975/76, con-centrated in just two action areas. By 1979 plans were advanced in one of these areas, Red Lane. The proposals to remove industry were lim-ited; areas of industrial activity were now to be tolerated, with grants to try to improve environmental aspects of the sites. In the same year the allocated funds to implement relocations under the action area plan for Red Lane were halved, a process repeated in 1980. As jobs in the city became ever more precious, policy changed, and a number of firms were assured that no compulsory relocations would be pursued.

> The bad neighbour programme continued to be reduced after 1983. A number of proposals for relocation passed through the legal and administrative procedures and a number of firms moved voluntarily. But the ability of the City Council to acquire such sites for residen-tial development or public open space was undermined by the lack of finance (Hobbs, 1991).

The proposals to relocate industries were undoubtedly popular with local residents. Many such industrial premises are still operating in cities today, and from time to time some of them feature in news reports when harmful effects on the health of the resident community come to light. But as the example above explains, planning has really been unable to provide a solution to these problems, and has certainly not been as dramatic or as rigid in reality as the Minister's comment might suggest.

## Conclusions

Government policy now favours mixed use development. In particular in recent years Planning Policy Guidance notes have increasingly stressed the importance of mixing uses, and evolving versions of PPGs are increasingly stressing this aspect of policy. The Secretary of State for the Environment has stated that:

> Too much emphasis has been placed on zoning and segregation of land uses. It derives from the determined neatness of planners and it has nothing to do with the proper growth of community.

He has also said:

> The high water mark of zoning frenzy is past, the development community, both the planners and the builders, will need to review afresh their attitude to properly mixed development.

Nevertheless, local authorities are now being encouraged to zone sites in their local plans – but for mixed uses.

Continuing his advocacy of mixed uses, the minister has called for more positive and flexible development plans and the inclusion in them of sites for mixed use. This concern with zoning is not immediately clear; many local authorities have few if any sites with specific 'zoning' – rather, they have a set of policies that apply across a borough or specific parts of their area. The concern would seem to be connected more with the attempt by some boroughs to retain particular uses by refusing permission for change of use (from industrial to residential for example). In practice, such policies are relatively unusual, and it would be surprising for the Secretary of State to uphold an appeal unless, as was noted in the Wapping example, there are good amenity related reasons for doing so. Clearly there are environmental factors that have to be considered, perhaps even more carefully where residential and other uses are in close proximity, especially where the other uses might create nuisance, as was seen in the example of Butlers Wharf.

Some local authorities are now attempting to create policies that ensure that mixed uses are developed throughout their cities or boroughs, but most are recent plans, and so relatively untested. Existing plans that have such policies (for example in Westminster) are successfully obtaining a broader mix of uses, but the local development economy in these locations allows mixed use developments to be economically successful without the difficulties found in areas with lower land and development values. A survey of over 30 local plans and UDPs shows that comparatively few have explicit city-wide policies to encourage mixed uses, but many more have specific sites allocated for a mix of uses. The survey shows that more recent plans have stronger policies, although to date all the policies either 'seek' or 'encourage' mixed uses. Policies requiring such uses have been included only where, for example, a threshold in size of development is included.

The zoning of sites for mixed uses is clearly being taken seriously by government-appointed inspectors of planning inquiries. One of the first refusals of planning permission because the scheme failed to identify sufficient mixed uses occured in Wimbledon in 1995. A proposal to redevelop the Plough Lane football stadium for a Safeway supermarket weas rejected by the Secretary of State, supporting his inspector. The UDP, which had been through a public inquiry, allocated the site for a mix of leisure, community, retail and B1 uses. The scheme's rejection was on the basis of conflict with the emerging plan.

In some locations it may be the limitations of the local property market that prevent the development of truly integrated mixed uses, and it may not be realistic for local authorities to try to insist on them. In Bradford's Forster Square it could be argued that the creation of offices and retailing on the site amounts to a mixed use scheme. It would have been difficult for the local authority to refuse the application for development, as the developer would almost certainly make this case if they chose to appeal against a refusal.

The greatest difficulty remains with potential funders and occupiers. There is a certain irony that it should be a government department who have created a highly secure private office development in the the Bradford scheme. This can also be seen in the design for the new Inland Revenue offices in Nottingham, where the restaurant for staff and other non-office functions are grouped into a separate building within the complex, and are also not available for use by the general public.

The practical design and financial difficulties in creating (for example) housing over retail units, or integrated into office units, are almost certainly much too great to overcome for the time being in places where the economics of development are tight. However, as the next chapter shows, mixed use developments have been undertaken in a wide range of locations, and in circumstances that may be replicated with increasing frequency in the future.

## References

Bedfordshire County Council (1995) *Structure Plan 2011* (deposit draft).

Bradford City Council (1992) *The Heart of the Matter – a Strategy for Bradford City Centre.*

Brownill, S. (1990) *Developing London's Docklands: Another Great Planning Disaster?,* Paul Chapman, London.

Coupland, A. (1992) Docklands, dream or disaster? in *The Crisis of London* (ed. A. Thornley), Routledge, London.

Hobbs, P. (1991) 'The response of local planning activity to economic change: the case of the City of Coventry' in *Town Planning Responses to City Change,* (eds V. Nadin, and J. Doak), Gower, Aldershot.

London Borough of Camden, (1995) *Camden Urban Development Plan,* (revised from 1993 deposit draft).

London Borough of Tower Hamlets (1995) *Unitary Development Plan Inquiry Evidence.*

# Chapter 9

# Why Developers Build Mixed Use Schemes

## Andy Coupland

## Introduction

This chapter examines a number of examples of mixed use schemes that, despite the prevailing views noted in earlier chapters, have been undertaken by developers. There are, as was noted in Chapter 1, a range of reasons why mixed use developments might be the preferred option for development. The case study on Gloucester Green in Oxford shows one of those situations: where the land owner (in that case, Oxford City Council) expressed a preference for a mix of uses developed in an integrated manner. In the last chapter, examples were noted in London Docklands, where the landowner, the LDDC, expressed a preference for mixed uses. Other examples, such as Bradford's Forster Square development, were developed in the context of a planning brief that expressed a preference for a mix of uses. (The success or otherwise in that example is examined in greater detail in Chapter 8.) However, these are examples where the policy or landowning context established the principle of mixed use development, and the schemes followed. But in some circumstances the preference of the developer is to create a mixed use scheme.

This chapter examines what these circumstances might be, and considers a number of examples of projects that have been undertaken in the past few years.

## Listed Buildings and Conservation Areas

One factor that has influenced developers is where they wish to undertake redevelopment involving listed buildings, or in conservation areas where groups of buildings are protected for their collective design qualities. In these sorts of situation developers may be unable to create a cleared site; they may have to retain all or some of the buildings on the site. These may not be easy to use for a single purpose, or may have a greater value if used in a variety of different uses. Examples in London's Covent

Garden area like Thomas Neal's or Comyn Ching show how large commercial developers were willing to take on complex design solutions involving the redevelopment of sites with existing buildings in place. The uses to which the redeveloped sites were then put include housing, offices, retailing and restaurants and, in the case of Thomas Neal's, a theatre as well. Thomas Neal's was developed in the late 1980s on a half-acre site north of the Covent Garden Market complex, in an area where retailing was starting to take off as it became known for fashion shopping. The scheme consists of 16 residential units (ten flats, five maisonettes and a penthouse), 29 shops, three restaurants, four office

*Figure 9.1*
Thomas Neal's, Covent Garden, London.
The shopping centre entrance showing elements of the former use as a warehouse.

suites (in total 1 800 m²) and the Donmar Warehouse Theatre. The scheme was designed by RHWL. The shops are arranged in two tiers around a triangular top-lit glazed courtyard, with the offices on two sides above the shops and the theatre on the third side. The residential elements occupy the upper floors above the shops at the 'wedge' end of the triangle, facing the Seven Dials junction.

The buildings dated back to the mid-nineteenth century, when the market had expanded to replace the fashionable housing and shops that had been developed in the eighteenth century, although some Georgian buildings formed part of the complex. These created particular problems as their floor levels did not match the Victorian buildings, which the plans proposed to link together for the residential element of the project. The developer, Langbourn, appeared initially to have misjudged the market. While the residential element of the project was fully taken up by 1993, some of the retail units remained empty over a year later. Originally the scheme was to have included more housing and less retailing; ironically the plans were changed, as retailing was expected to bring a greater return.

The Comyn Ching block is also triangular, with one point facing the Seven Dials Monument. The unusual name for the scheme comes from the name of the landowner of the site, an architectural ironmongery company who first acquired property on the site in 1723. The scheme, designed by Terry Farrell, required more new development than Thomas Neal's, although the problems of retaining poorly constructed historic

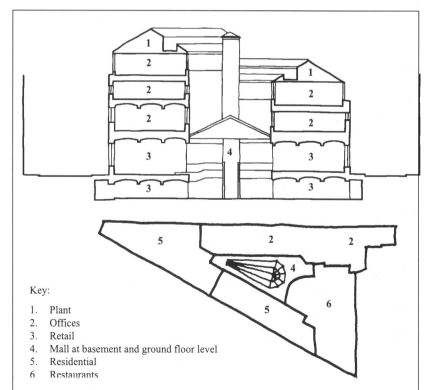

Key:

1. Plant
2. Offices
3. Retail
4. Mall at basement and ground floor level
5. Residential
6. Restaurants

Figure 9.2
Thomas Neal's, Covent Garden, London.
Floor layout and section through the scheme.

buildings were very similar. Some of the original early eighteenth century buildings remained, and these were retained (albeit with considerable refurbishment) while some Victorian buildings, notably on the site's corners, were cleared away. The mix of uses in the completed scheme is more simply arranged than at Thomas Neal's; the Seven Dials corner was redeveloped with an office block, while the Shelton/Mercer Street corner saw the construction of a new residential building. Work commenced in June 1983, and the demolition of the Seven Dials corner (including the removal, storage and subsequent re-use of 270-year-old

*Figure 9.3*
Thomas Neal's, Covent Garden, London.
Housing and offices above retailing, with a theatre too, in a converted warehouse.

*Figure 9.4 (opposite)*
Comyn Ching, Covent Garden, London
The entrance to Ching Court, the public courtyard at the heart of the refurbished development of housing, offices and shops.

panelling and a staircase) allowed the clearance of outbuildings in the centre of the site, which has become a public space, Ching Court. The earlier phases of development were carried out by Comyn Ching; in the mid 1980s they sold on the development sites at Seven Dials and Shelton Street to Taylor Woodrow (as Taylor Woodrow Capital Developments), who then acted as developer for the whole site. The whole scheme was tied up in a complex legal planning agreement to ensure that the 'easy' offices were not developed at the expense of the 'difficult' housing. (This shows as well as any example how markets and developers' attitudes

*Figure 9.5*
Comyn Ching, Covent Garden, London.
The new-build corner of Shelton Street with refurbished housing, offices and shops beyond.

change over relatively short periods – these days the offices would be hard to shift; the residential would be the 'easy' element. The scheme was highly regarded in architectural terms, and commercially successful, with all elements of the scheme being occupied fairly quickly.

## Glasgow

A similar example can be found in Glasgow with the Merchant City scheme which came to be known as the Italian Centre. This too saw a mix of retail, restaurant, residential and offices, as did the larger (and more residentially focused) scheme in the same area of the city at Ingram Square.

The Italian Centre was developed by a local developer, Classical House, creating a mix of housing and offices over restaurants and shops. The scheme is located in the Merchant City, the early trading heart to the east of Glasgow's city centre, which, from the late 1970s, has seen a series of redevelopment and refurbishment projects leading to the creation of flats from former warehouses. Retailing was a new element to the restructuring of the area, and the developer's idea was to focus on high fashion rather than a more 'normal' retailing project. The site was owned by Glasgow City Council, who invited four developers to compete with ideas, and then selected the most expensive of the four. The council also

*Figure 9.6*
The Italian Centre, Merchant City, Glasgow.
The inner courtyard showing the public art at the heart of the redevelopment of shops, offices and flats.

became shareholders in the project in exchange for a profit share, and put up bank guarantees for the developer to be able to raise commercial funding. In both these cases the planning policy encouraged the mix of uses, and some public money from the Scottish Development Agency was also forthcoming to support the initial refurbishment of the buildings.

The developers created a project that broke a number of market 'rules'. The scheme created high-value retailing in an off-pitch location. The design allowed for slots to create windows into the basements, reducing the zone A (prime) space (although enhancing the potential use and rent for the basements). The scheme also included a high visual profile, with the inclusion of a significant element of public art (as can also be seen in Covent Garden Thomas Neal's scheme).

*Figure 9.7*
The Italian Centre, Merchant City, Glasgow.
The retained facade with the Versace shop below flats.

*Figure 9.8 (opposite)*
Ingram Square, Merchant City, Glasgow.
The new-build corner block with shops beneath housing.

In total there are 32 apartments, some 7 400 m² of office space, and shops and restaurants created from remodelled buildings around a court-yard enlarged from the existing Victorian warehouse buildings. The space is incorporated into the overall design (although not covered as in Thomas Neal's). The scheme has been surprisingly successful, attracting both Armani and Versace as well as Italian restaurants.

Ingram Square is an altogether bigger project, covering a whole street block in the Merchant City and consisting of over 240 flats (both new-build and conversion) with 20 shops. Developed by Edinburgh-based Kantel developments, a firm started by two architects, the detailed designs

*Figure 9.9*
Ingram Square, Merchant City, Glasgow.
Inside one of the courtyards in the centre of the housing.

were by Elder and Cannon, a firm of highly respected Glasgow architects. Kantel initially looked in 1984 at the Houndsditch building, a large warehouse building (listed Grade B) covering a third of a sizeable street block. Built in 1854, the building had been added to in such a way that housing conversion was almost impossible without tackling the entire street block. Glasgow City Council owned much of the remaining property, and a joint feasibility study led to a tri-partite company, Yarmadillo, between Kantel, the City Council and the SDA.

The conversion of the warehouse building proved problematic; the internal spaces had very high ceilings, but total reconstruction behind retained facades would have been too expensive. The compromise solution of inserted mezzanine gallery bedrooms was a precursor of a much repeated marketing approach to this design problem: the 'loft' apartment. One of the blocks was redeveloped as student accommodation for Strathclyde University (mirroring the LSE halls of residence created by Terence Conran at Butler's Wharf). Interestingly, in terms of the debate over security (Chapter 7), the city planners ruled out the developer's idea for the courtyard to have cafes and small shops, preferring to see it as a private space for residential amenity.

Within the block as a whole a wider range of uses exist as, in addition to the shops developed by Yarmadillo, the City Council retained ownership of a block housing small manufacturing businesses.

Jim Johnson, in appraising the scheme for *Architects Journal*, praised the project as a model for urban redevelopment:

> Hopefully the lessons will be absorbed in other cities but most of all by the blinkered property development industry, which still appears to hanker after the large scale, single use developments believed to be the only guarantee of a secure return on investment (Johnson, 1987).

Another more recently announced scheme illustrates that Glasgow developers are still considering mixed use projects. The former Bremner's department store, abandoned for many years, was recently identified for a project that would see the creation of a new shopping use with flats being constructed on the upper floors.

## Bristol

In Bristol an early example of mixed development arose on a city centre site at Queen Street. After complex negotiations over several years, the Policy Section of the City Council produced a brief in 1980 for 50/50 offices and housing. The final outcome was the 1986 Sun Alliance building, and smaller housing development by Lovell Urban Renewal. The two schemes were initially to be developed and designed as a whole, but the site was then split and the housing developed separately, although in design terms in relation to the offices.

Throughout Bristol's recent history it has been community based amenity groups who have been in the vanguard of demands for mixed use development. By the early 1960s the central area was still in ruins.

Most of the 1960s was taken up with developing office space, completing the shopping centre, and accommodating ever larger road projects, including an inner and outer circuit road. Mixed uses were to be achieved through traffic segregation on different levels, quite closely following the sorts of ideas developed in the Buchanan Report. While the most important individual historical buildings were saved, the mass of high-quality Georgian and seventeenth-century architecture was considered expendable. One beacon in an otherwise dark period was a film called *Dead Centre*, produced in 1960 by a group centred on the School of Architecture. This warned of the problems of allowing office development in the former heart of the city, around Wine Street, describing Broadmead as the archetypal 'dead centre' – dead after 6pm.

Despite this, throughout the early 1970s important historic or architecturally valuable building continued to be cleared to make way, predominantly, for the road programme. Once the docks were closed and proposals drawn up for their development it became clear that community pressure was necessary if the docks were not to be 'partially reclaimed' (filled in). From 1973 onwards the Bristol City Docks Group produced an important series of reports – described by John Punter as 'quite outstanding' in their quality: 'their analysis and prognosis will remain relevant for the foreseeable future'. They called for 'an explicit Jane Jacobs' type vision of dense mixed use in physical and social terms

*Figure 9.10*
Sun Alliance, Bristol.
The housing (by Lovell) to the right and Sun Alliance offices on the harbour quayside in the centre of Bristol.

with diverse districts, short blocks, vital street life and watersides'. The move in 1974 by the Arnolfini Gallery to the waterside nineteenth-century warehouse, Bush House, with three floors of offices on upper floors cross-subsidizing the arts venue, illustrated perfectly the Docks Group's vision. By 1977 the City Council had produced an Opportunities Report in which the need for more city centre housing was strongly supported, as well as the draft Local Plan. Significant new housing – some housing association, although mostly for sale – has been provided close to the city centre on Baltic Wharf (opposite Hotwells, beyond the SS *Great Britain*), where 200 units were built, and on the opposite side of the Floating Harbour at Rownham Mead (formerly Merchant's Dock).

Closer to the city centre, housing was provided at Bathurst Basin and on Redcliff Backs, where old warehouses were converted to provide both private and rented accommodation. In 1996 the dire warnings of the 1960s have started to come true as the offices built at that time are now redundant. But, as in parts of London, more and more of these are now being considered for conversion to housing, a process actively supported by the City Council.

The creation of mixed use areas – if not necessarily with buildings with an integral mix of uses – has occurred extensively in former industrial areas, and often where the buildings are important for historical, urban design or financial reasons. Often the costs of conversion in a marginal location may be lower than the costs of clearing away and starting again. Housing Associations have been responsible for innovative conversions of former industrial mills or warehouses in Wapping, Bermondsey, Bradford, Bristol and Manchester among many other examples. The private sector has undertaken many similar projects in location throughout London (including Docklands and Clerkenwell), as well as many waterside locations like Gloucester and Leeds, and other city centres as in Birmingham's Jewellery Quarter.

## Saltaire

Outside Bradford's city centre two developments can be found that illustrate a further development of mixed use development. Some of the mill complexes used by the wool industry were particularly magnificent, and the two most important that remain are at Listers Mill in the Manningham area of the city and at Salt's Mill in Saltaire, some 5 miles from the city centre.

Both complexes of buildings are massive – each over 100 000 m². Each remained in use until relatively recently, although not for its original use. Salts Mill, once a mohair-spinning plant, was later used for carpet yarn. Lister's Mill was once a worsted-spinning mill producing yarn for fabric woven to make suits, but more recently has been used for weaving heavy furnishing fabrics.

Both properties have been sold to new owners: Salts Mill in 1989 to Jonathan Silver, a local entrepreneur, and Listers Mill in 1995 to a Merseyside-based property development company.

Salts Mill forms the centrepiece of the model village of Saltaire, designed for the mill owner, Sir Titus Salt. Although structurally the mill was in good condition when sold, it had limited road access. Jonathan Silver had some previous experience of taking a large building and developing new uses, having been a co-owner of a similar complex of buildings in another Pennine town – Dean Clough Mills in Halifax. Here a variety of commercial and artistic uses were developed in the former mill buildings. Having sold his interest, following a couple of years' travelling, Silver bought the Salts Mill complex to try something similar on his own.

Initial development of the ground floor of one of the mill buildings took the form of an art gallery, the 1853 Gallery. This was created by acid cleaning the walls and floors, and then hanging paintings and prints from the heating pipes that ran the length of the room. The gallery exhibited and sold the work of David Hockney, a Bradford native and personal friend of Silver. While negotiating to improve road access by putting a new bridge over the river from a nearby commercial development, Silver next leased a small part of another set of the mill buildings to a small locally based electronics company, Pace, involved in the manufacture of satellite receiver dishes and processing equipment.

A further gallery was developed for visiting exhibitions on the floor above the 1853 Gallery, while various other artistic activities were welcomed, including performances of opera. A proposal was put forward by the Victoria and Albert Museum in London to set up a new centre to display their Indian collection, and both Salts Mill and Listers Mill were considered for the use. Although Jonathan Silver made an offer to house the collection, Listers was chosen in preference.

However, other developments proceeded, including a letting for a shop for Edinburgh Woollen Mills and a further retail use by Silver himself selling suits manufactured using cloth from his father's weaving company (a business that Silver himself had been in through the 1970s, when he owned a chain of retail clothing stores). Pace expanded rapidly, and occupied significantly larger areas of space.

Other high-tech electronics companies joined them. By 1993 Silver reckoned that the combination of workers at Pace (and the needs of their marketing team) combined with the visitors visiting the Gallery and shops were sufficient to justify opening a restaurant, Salt's Diner, an American-style dining room on a further floor of the block that houses the gallery. This too has been a considerable success.

Salts Mill represents one man's vision of creating a mixed use development in a superb range of historic buildings. While some luck has obviously played a part in its success (particularly in the growth and success of Pace Electronics) much of the credit must go to Jonathan Silver for both recognizing and seizing opportunities when they presented themselves, and for a breadth of vision that has allowed a series of unlikely but mutually supportive uses to be developed into a mixed use scheme unlike any other.

Other developers have been attracted to the success of the project and have converted the New Mill (in different ownership) on the other side of the river into expensive private apartments, again creating a new form of development for this part of the country, and paving the way for other developers to consider similar schemes for the city centre.

Meanwhile the new owners of Listers Mill have announced their proposals for the equally massive mill complex. Initially a specialist shopping centre was proposed: a 'factory shopping' complex. There are already a range of factory and mill shops which operate successfully throughout Bradford, related to the continued activity of the textile and wool trades. Elsewhere in the buildings both private housing developments and subsidized housing association units were proposed, as well as commercial space and a nursing home. As the funding could not be found, the proposal to create a museum has now been dropped. In the summer of 1996 the developer announced that the scheme was not proceeding, and a new development proposal is now being sought.

Both these developments illustrate how the existing historic fabric of the city is being adapted and developed to meet new opportunities for activity. In the process they show how a range of complementary activities can be developed in buildings that once represented an industrial mono-culture. In the case of Salts Mill it is already possible to see how a deserted set of buildings has become a thriving and increasingly popular development.

All of these examples are of buildings or schemes where existing buildings have, to a greater or lesser extent, determined that a mix of uses will be the most convenient way to develop a scheme. However, this is not intended to suggest that the schemes selected are in some way an 'easy option' – in almost every case they are not. In several of these examples the developer has chosen to carry out the selected project despite the difficulties, because they believe in creating a better, more mixed environment. This is unquestionably the case in the next example, Oxo Tower Wharf. Here the organization responsible for developing the scheme, Coin Street Community Builders, undertook a mixed use conversion of a building as part of a wider vision of a large-scale redevelopment project specifically intended to have a mix of uses.

## Coin Street and Oxo Tower Wharf

One of the most consistent sources of pressure for increasing the amount of housing in London has been the community sector, particularly under the auspices of CHiCL (Communities and Homes in Central London). Throughout the 1970s and early 1980s the arguments developed by the voluntary sector were taken up by local politicians, culminating in the community areas policy of the Greater London Council. One outcome was the development of certain sites in Central London to meet local aspirations, in one important case by a development organization, Coin Street Community Builders. This is a community-based organization who were formed both to oppose massive office schemes proposed for the site, and to develop an alternative strategy. Their members had been influential in the creation of the community areas policy, which in turn led to the unique opportunity to develop their site.

The Coin Street development consists of a number of important redevelopment sites on the Thames riverbank. The total site area is 13 acres (5.2 ha), and the site was covered with various cold-stores and related industrial warehousing structures. However, the potential value of the site was obvious, situated as it was next to the National Theatre and with superb views of St Paul's up-river. In the 1970s the site was owned by the meat-processing interests held by the Vestey family, who had been involved with the site for many years. In the early 1970s the expansion of the city started to offer opportunities for redevelopment, and with the Kings Reach hotel under construction (later converted to offices following the receivership of the developer) major development proposals were drawn up. At the same time, however, community groups were formulating their ideas for what should be done to revitalize an area where thousands of industrial jobs were closing and thousands of residents moving out (the population halved to around 5 000 between 1961 and 1981).

A complex series of political and planning policy about-turns through the 1970s (Brindley *et al.*, 1989) saw local residents designing their own proposals for the eight development plots. An arduous planning

*Figure 9.11*
Oxo Tower Wharf, London. Section through the reconstructed building showing the complex range of uses in the completed building.

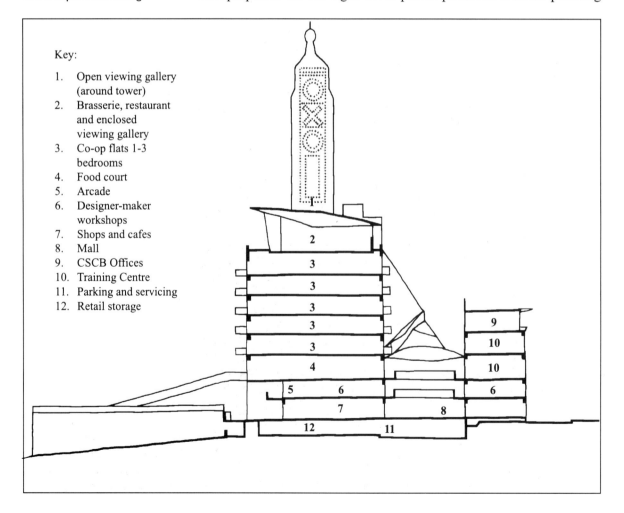

Key:

1. Open viewing gallery (around tower)
2. Brasserie, restaurant and enclosed viewing gallery
3. Co-op flats 1-3 bedrooms
4. Food court
5. Arcade
6. Designer-maker workshops
7. Shops and cafes
8. Mall
9. CSCB Offices
10. Training Centre
11. Parking and servicing
12. Retail storage

inquiry in 1979 saw the locally prepared scheme competing for permission with plans for over a million square feet of offices prepared by developers Greycoat. The level of community involvement in preparing their scheme and in producing detailed evidence against the commercial project was remarkable. The decision of the new Secretary of State for the Environment, Michael Heseltine, was not expected. He refused both schemes: the commercial for being 'massive and over-dominant' and the community scheme because housing failed to exploit

*Figure 9.12*
Oxo Tower Wharf, London. The newly completed exterior of the riverside block. The riverside walkway runs through the colonnade underneath the building.

the employment potential of the site. He challenged the two sides to come up with a mixed scheme for the site. Greycoat (now linked with another part of the landholding in the area, Commercial Properties) came back with a Richard Rogers designed string of blocks of varying heights linked by a glazed pedestrian mall along the riverside. Although it was mainly offices – a million square feet – there was also some housing, shopping and light industrial units. The Association of Waterloo Groups submitted their scheme for 400 homes, light industry, shopping and public open space in 1980. Protest from local residents forced a head-to-head public inquiry between the two schemes, which eventually ended in March 1988. In the meantime the outgoing Conservative GLC administration had agreed to dispose of the public land involved to Greycoat, provided they obtained all the necessary approvals within three years. The incoming Labour administration backed the AWG scheme and made funding available to support the community scheme. Michael Heseltine announced that planning permission would be granted for both schemes, but after a series of delaying legal battles Greycoat failed to obtain all the necessary legal road closures to enforce the land sale. Instead, in 1984, with no prospective tenant for the office scheme, they sold their land to the GLC. This allowed the possibility of the community scheme proceeding.

In June 1984 the newly created Coin Street Community Builders, using mortgage funds from the GLC itself and the Greater London Enterprise Board, acquired the site for £750 000, and before the year-end started demolishing the Eldorado cold store to make way for the open space running down to the river. The next phase of development consisted of three-storey family housing, operated as a co-op. Construction commenced in June 1986, and the new riverside walkway (forward-funded by the axed GLC) opened in 1987.

One important aspect of the development from the earliest days of its conception has been the intention of the group that the development should consist of a range of different uses. The reason the group sought this mix was because of the range of needs in the area. There was little public open space, and very little new housing for local people. On the other hand, office jobs (if locals could obtain them) were available in their thousands within a ten-minute walk. The planning consent, while concentrating on housing as the predominant use, also required other activities to be developed. The mix of uses is found not only within the site as a whole, but within individual buildings, particularly the Oxo Tower Wharf Building.

Formerly known as Stamford Wharf, the Oxo Tower Building is a landmark on the riverside (designed as it was in the 1920s to avoid restrictions on advertising). Here a range of different uses have been developed inside the reconstructed shell of the warehouse.

There were always likely to be difficulties in developing a mix of uses in a building whose origins were industrial, having been designed as a cold-store in use for many years in connection with the meat trade, which used the wharves on the site. It is worth considering these in more detail. As noted elsewhere (and confirmed by the Coin Street developers) funders are wary of refurbishment, and even more so where a mix of uses is intended to be the outcome. Again, mixed uses were not a principal aim of development, but retention of the building and meeting different requirements led to the approach. The Coin Street Community Builders wanted public access on the riverside and, if possible, the rooftop. They wanted to offer a range of shopping and eating opportunities, and to maximize the amount of co-op housing that could be created. They rejected a range of other proposals to use the space for rehearsal space or recording studios because the public access would be limited. This meant that, reluctantly, they became developers for the whole project to refurbish and reconstruct the building. This in turn meant selling the idea to commercial lenders to raise the capital. This proved difficult in the extreme, but eventually a two-stage deal was established, whereby the risk for the lender was offset against the income stream from the other uses on the site (including the valuable temporary car parking). This allowed the first-stage investigation and repair of the frame to go ahead. As well as removing asbestos, this revealed the state of the structure. This was a huge gamble; a 10% repair was within budget, 30% would be a problem, and anything more would bankrupt the entire Coin Street operation. Fortunately the necessary repairs came in within budget.

The building now consists of 88 rented flats (through a housing co-op) with the ground floor of retail workshops for craftspeople and a second floor food court. Again, Coin Street is unique; the developers could not find an operator willing to cover the wide range from basic, inexpensive food to more luxurious offerings that the developers wanted. So they decided to employ a manager and lease the different serveries separately, coordinating both the design and running of the whole operation. The rooftop restaurant has been let commercially to Harvey Nichols, who have never operated outside their Knightsbridge base before.

## Conclusions

There are a number of reasons why developers undertake mixed use schemes. Sometimes it is because the planning system requires it. On other occasions it is because the preservation of all or part of the development site restricts the possibility of major change, and makes a mix of uses the most viable option. In some examples the land-owners (usually public bodies) control the choices for development, and want to see a particular mix of activities. In a few (rare) cases the developers (as in Coin Street) believe so strongly in obtaining a mix of uses that they will wait until the means to create that mix can be found. And, as the case study on Brindleyplace shows, sometimes it makes economic sense to do so – although that might not be quite so apparent when funding decisions are being made.

## References

Brindley, T., Rydin, Y. and Stoker, G. (1989) *Remaking Planning*, Routledge, London.

Johnson, J. (1987) Bringing it all back home: Ingram Square, Glasgow' *Architects Journal* 6 May, 39-51.

## Further reading

*Coin Street Community News* (1993) Coin Street Community Builders, London

Gardner, C. (1993) English elegance, Dutch treat. *RIBA Journal*, February, 45–48.

Ibbotson, S. (1985) Historic precedent. *Architects Journal* 6 March,47–58.

Weatherhead, P. (1991) Piazza pizzazz. *Building* 22 March, 39–42.

# Case Study 9.1

# Brindleyplace, Birmingham

Brindleyplace is the name for a 17 acre mixed use development on a site assembled by Birmingham City Council in the 1980s. The strategy for developing the city centre as a pedestrian-friendly area developed through the 1980s, linked to an economic development strategy that saw the creation of the National Arena and an International Convention Centre. Both of these were located on a large area of land previously used for industry, but largely deserted, close to the city centre. A development brief prepared in 1987 identified the area for a 'people attracting' development to complement the Arena and Convention Centre. Initial development proposals were made by Merlin, who later teamed up with developers Shearwater, before pulling out of the scheme to be replaced by Rosehaugh, who paid £26 million for the site in 1990. Merlin were interested in retailing; Rosehaugh revised the scheme to include more office space and also introduced a housing element. By 1992 a detailed set of

*Figure 9.13*
Brindleyplace, Birmingham.
The development scheme
viewed from the city centre

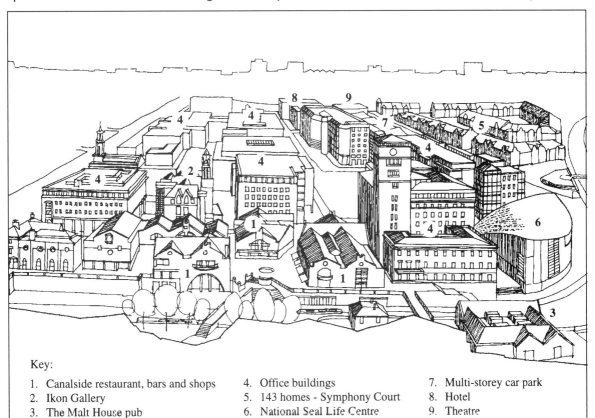

Key:
1. Canalside restaurant, bars and shops
2. Ikon Gallery
3. The Malt House pub
4. Office buildings
5. 143 homes - Symphony Court
6. National Seal Life Centre
7. Multi-storey car park
8. Hotel
9. Theatre

proposals had been agreed, with a pedestrian-oriented central square, retailing and restaurants (some incorporating listed elements) along the canalside, and a further leisure attraction nearby. At the end of that year Rosehaugh were in receivership, and Argent took over the project, paying just £3 million to the receivers. The detailed plans were only slightly amended, with the housing element separated off and the retailing/restaurant area (the Water's Edge) started first, along with the infrastructure and the first office building.

By 1995, when Argent refinanced the scheme, the land value was back to over £25 million, the Water's Edge was trading successfully, the housing was selling well (at over £200 000 for a family house), and potential office occupiers were queuing to take buildings. Four of the next five office buildings are now under construction, two of them let to British Telecom and Lloyds Bank. The first office building to be completed is under offer, the National Sea Life Centre is open, and a multi-storey car park is being built. Over £100 million has been committed, with short-term finance supplied by Hypobank. The company have made it clear that the success in arranging that finance was when the mix of uses did not extend beyond separate buildings (as in Bradford at Forster Square). The project would also not be as successful today if it was still carrying the initial land purchase debt, which was written off when the first developer went into receivership.

*Figure 9.14*
Brindleyplace, Birmingham. The Water's Edge to the left, new canal bridge to the city centre, and National Arena in the background

# Chapter 10

# Mixed Use and Exclusion in the International City

## Peter Newman

### Conviviality and Distance

Writing about his home in Greenwich Village, Richard Sennett (1994) reflects that the images of variegated city life strongly represented by Jane Jacobs 'work like a charm' on 'ageing, bourgeois bohemians' like himself. But the picture of conviviality, bustle, neighbourly interaction and harmony that Jacobs wrote about contrasts with the new reality of the Village. Jacobs saw a neighbourhood fused together by diversity and difference. Sennett sees indifference between the various inhabitants. There are strong social differences between tourist and resident, homeless person and drug dealer. Each group seems to let the other alone. The drug culture has converted buildings into 'shooting galleries'; homeless people have arrived on the streets, but keep clear of the drug routes. The homosexual community in the west Village has become more politically engaged in the struggle against AIDS, and this is the concern of most of the art produced in the area. Sennett argues that these different groups tolerate each other, in what is now only a visually mixed community. There is no common political action or civic culture.

This image of Greenwich Village is depressing, and portrays a microcosm of profound urban problems. In the nightmare city of drugs, homelessness and poverty, different groups live in proximity but steer clear of each other and of the police. The image frightens many Americans, and has done for years. Film makers reproduce the image, often using Detroit as the film set. The fear may not be as great for Europeans, but global communications mean that, dubbed into whatever language, we have all seen the nightmare city. These images give us a picture of the 'wild zones'. In the USA such fears have provoked flight to the suburbs, and the enclosure and fortification of the 'tame zones'. The division between the 'wild' and the 'tame' can be seen, Lash and Urry (1994) argue, both at global scale and within local areas.

The tame zones are:

> ... areas of political, economic and cultural security often with strong boundaries separating them off from the wild zones of disorganized capitalism (Lash and Urry, 1994).

This chapter is concerned with the creation of new 'tame zones', and responses to diversity and difference that promote enclosure and segregation within the city. The focus is on large urban development projects. There are international trends in the large-scale reconstruction of cities. Important features of the new landscapes created are their separation from the rest of the city and their internal distinctions catering for different customers. Most large – mega or meso – projects have a mix of uses. They also have distinctive markets, and differentiate themselves through complex imagery, but are exclusive rather than inclusive. Many of the images of difference and conviviality strongly portrayed by Jane Jacobs reappear in the marketing of exclusive spaces and 'work like a charm' on investors, city managers and customers alike. In contemporary urban projects there may well be juxtaposition of different uses and differing groups, but the dominant message of large new projects is segregation and exclusion. Before we look at some examples of large development projects we need to take a closer look at the language of enclosure and the persuasive images of 'tame zones'.

## Enclosure – Market Place, Community and Quarter

Judd (1995), argues that 'The enclosure of commercial and residential space is becoming a defining and ubiquitous feature of American cities'. Christopherson (1994) agrees that 'gated' housing developments have been the fastest-growing form of residential living. Control over these new urban spaces is exercised by the companies that own and manage them. The public realm is therefore disappearing, and new forms of private control require new images to sell them to residents, tenants, occupiers and to citizens in general. The marketing and promotional image of the large enclosed development has become important. Judd criticises two images in particular – the 'market place' and the 'community'.

In commercial developments the dominant image is of a clean 'market place' from which the homeless are excluded and which offers protection from the weather and from crime. The enclosed shopping centre is of course not new. Birmingham's New Street station centre proclaimed in the 1970s:'Welcome to New Street. No Loitering'. The centres of the 1990s offer a range of urban experiences – Cité Europe outside Calais has a collection of *'places'* imitating Bruges and Lisbon. for example. The imitations are better than reality, being centrally placed in a catchment for international shoppers. The *places* are clean, there are no cars or beggars, and it never rains. They are, however, closed at night, monitored by security cameras with guards to control access. The new management of older commercial centres such as the Milton Keynes centre also favour early closing.

Judd uses the Peachtree Centre in Atlanta to exemplify processes of exclusion in US cities. There is a mix of commerce, shops and hotels connected by glass tubes with few secure entrances from the old streets. The separation is both physical and also social, between rich and poor residents of the city. Inside the centre is the realm of office workers, tourists and commuters. Such megastructures are described as 'fortified cells of affluence' (Davis, 1992, quoted in Judd). The image of the fortress expresses the relationship to the world outside. Inside, space is private. The squares and market places of the advertising images are not public but private space: space controlled by agreement between owner and tenant about the activities of selling that are permitted. All enclosed centres are exclusive, some more than others. Haila (1995) describes the careful imaging of the Palais Renaissance centre in Singapore, which subtly lets you know that you can't afford to be there.

Outside the fortresses, urban space has been enclosed by less apparent means. Christopherson argues that the success of the mega-mall encouraged the owners and managers of buildings in central business districts to seek ways of controlling the street environment. The spread of 'Business Improvement Districts', (BIDs), has been the response. In BIDs many formerly public functions and services – cleaning, parks, policing – are privately managed, giving business more direct control over their environment and private control of public space. In the UK town centre, management has brought the private sector into street management, and the initiative in designing transport, environmental and security improvements has passed to a range of quasi-public bodies armed with public money. For example, an allocation from the Single Regeneration Budget was made to a local employers association in Waterloo in order for them to plan and carry out environmental improvements. Lessons from the USA in the private management of the city are being applied in the UK.

The enclosure of some residential developments in the USA appears even more dramatic than the downtown fortress. Gated compounds, borrowing ideas from foreign embassies and diplomatic compounds, have proliferated. Suburban America has grown used to a politics of exclusion. Davis, for example, refers to 'The White Wall' in his analysis of Los Angeles. The expansion of residential associations and 'Common Interest Developments', (CIDs), develops the techniques of exclusion. The CID idea has also been transferred from suburbia to secure urban developments. Exclusion is not only achieved through low-density suburban development but in high-density urban towers. Developers talk of 'positive ghettoism'. CIDs also govern their residents. CIDs select like and like-minded residents.

> The rules and regulations that govern the residents of CIDs are designed to specifically prevent the complex voluntary interactions, the change and flux, that compose the symbols of urban community and lay the foundation for democratic processes (Judd, 1995).

The marketing of fortified residential compounds stresses images of community. But any meaningful civic life is excluded by the lack of mix. The politics of the CID does not integrate into the wider city. The CID shuts itself off, and 'community' politics is localized and fragmented.

In residential developments the image of 'community' is deployed in ways that deny communal and civic values, and which isolate rather than integrate groups of residents. In the commercial centres the image of the market place covers the reality of privatized space, where the bustle and debate of the market are strictly controlled. Christopherson (1994) argues that the regulation of urban life is not new. However, what is distinctive about the contemporary city, she argues, is the degree and form of regulation. Policing is less visible. To most citizens, forms of regulation are obscure. The tenancy agreement and CID rules regulate privately and invisibly. High prices exclude the poor from many parts of the city, and the homeless know that they are not welcome in the new market places. What the tame zones of housing and commerce seek to achieve is distance and security from the terrors of the wild. The 'walled', 'gated' and 'fortress' city recalls a medieval landscape, or perhaps more accurately the mythical landscape of Tolkein's 'perilous realms', where the only safe place is within the city walls.

Enclosure can be achieved by sharp physical division or by less visible means. An important marketing image for the tame zone is that of the city 'quarter'. This larger scale is important to city planners in their search for new identities to attract investors and build confidence. Many cities have become more concerned with aesthetics and image than with other traditional aspects of town planning. For example, Hubbard (1995) describes the processes of reorganizing the centre of Birmingham, where images of the city's industrial past were deployed to repackage a series of new 'quarters'. The new quartering of the centre created opportunities for new investments in reorganized real estate markets to provide specialist services to visitors. New signs and environmental improvements guide tourists, business visitors and residents through the re-imagined city. The conscious linkage of the new quarters to Birmingham's industrial past was useful in making the transformation of the centre for international markets more palatable to the locals. Successful urban design gives the new quarters clear boundaries, marking the reoccupation of commercial tame zones.

The image of the 'market place' appeals to firstly shoppers, the 'community' to residents, and the 'quarter' to a range of other consumers including voluntary visitors. The separation into zones may be sharper in the US city, but the social forces behind these new patterns of exclusion and segregation are global, and their impacts appear world wide.

## Exclusion and Segregation – Global Trends

Christopherson (1994) admits that the US city is more threatening than its UK counterpart and hence there is a more urgent concern to construct the secure fortress. But segregation and exclusion are worldwide social trends, which have spatial presence everywhere. The US dystopias represent a growing reality in an urban system that is increasingly global.

We can summarize many of the debates on globalization in a few sentences. Sites of production have become dispersed but, with the assistance of technological changes, services, in particular financial services, have concentrated in a few command and control centres (Sassen, 1991). Alongside the so-called producer services – banking, insurance – other urban services have also grown in importance as manufacturing has declined. Cities have been restructured as centres of consumption. At the top of the urban hierarchy, shopping centres, hotels, tourist attractions, and high-value residential developments are all evidence of consumption-dominated economies. What is new is the extent to which these new markets have become internationalized. At the same time the provision of services – business, therapeutic, expressive – has become much more specialized. Globalization creates differences and new segmented markets. In these consumption and service economies information has become supremely important. Providers shape new products while customers, individuals and communities recreate their identities. However, difference and diversity are not always to be celebrated. For example, ethnic diversities have been commodified into a limitless choice of restaurants (Christopherson, 1994).

As a result of these processes, urban space has been re-invented and re-imagined, as cities position themselves in global flows of information, about finance, or products or services. The global economy values commercial, residential, leisure and communication uses and the combinations they offer. For example, Canary Wharf attracts flows of business and financial information but also coaches full of tourists. The restructuring of space has involved the replacing of socially structured space reflecting former social orders with spaces reflecting and creating new divisions. Globalization is reconfiguring urban areas. Within cities old senses of place, both physical and social, have disappeared, and new spatial images have been put in their place.

Globalization creates diversity; it also creates social divisions. Sociologists talk of the 'one third – two thirds' society, where a substantial proportion of people are excluded from work, political life and the flows of information that are the reality of the contemporary world (Lash and Urry, 1994). Outside the urban new spaces, the flagships of a global economy, are, as we have seen, the 'wild zones', beyond information flows and insecure.

Globalization has of course impacted on the property industry. Some companies operate worldwide. The creation of new urban spaces, tame zones in large projects, becomes the skill of a few professionals, who may move from one city to another. A limited number of companies, such as Kumagai Gumi and Ove Arup, and a limited number of engineers and architects will be associated with large developments. This group constitutes what Lash and Urry refer to as one of the 'small worlds' of globalization around which information and intelligence on global projects flow. The city planners in most cases also have an active role in promoting their part in the process. Paris has a permanent exhibition of city building and large projects in the Pavillon de l'Arsenal; Tokyo plans a permanent 'world urban research centre'.

Property finance has also been globalized. Davis (1992) describes the scale of Japanese investment in Los Angeles. Mitsubishi bought the Rockefeller Centre, a symbol of the power of the dollar. Shirayama bought part of London's County Hall. Direct foreign investment has helped to fuel property booms in European cities. Hong Kong and Singapore investors have invested heavily in development projects in China. Flows of private capital make many large projects possible. Private capital may, however, be more important in financing development in China, where the state has traditionally taken the risk out of capital projects, rather than in Europe.

To summarize, globalization has divided cities between those areas of dense information flow and excluded zones. New development, promoted by public or private capital and an internationalized development industry, creates new spaces for consumption or production for new invented communities and internationalized markets. Globalization has also engendered fierce competition between cities. There is competition for prestige developments, for grants for new infrastructure, roads, railways and telecommunications, or grants for festivals and cultural investments that will give a city a better position in this competitive market. Almost all large European cities are in competition for international business, and this involves providing exhibition centres, world trade centres, and hotels, and the remodelling of downtown areas. Only a handful of cities are not pursuing such international ambitions. The question arises as to how far cities have a choice about whether or not to compete. If they do engage in international competition then new quarters and market places are inevitably required, which orient themselves to international markets and not to local need.

## The Large Project

This next section looks at some examples of large-scale city replanning, who new projects are for and the images they create. Large projects exemplify the trends of segregation and exclusion discussed above. They mark sharp boundaries with the rest of the city, and the process of urban redevelopment helps to shape new spatial and social divisions.

Olds (1995) analyses several large projects around the Pacific Rim. He argues that all such projects tend to offer a single vision of global urban utopia – a vision of international development serving global markets. High-profile buildings aid the creation of such images. One significant difference he notes, bearing in mind the above discussion, is that projects may be primarily oriented either to consumption or to production. Vancouver's Pacific Place is an example of a consumption-oriented project. The scheme covers 80 ha, including offices and hotels but also accommodating a large new resident population (Olds, 1995). Mullins (1991) describes residential schemes like this as 'consumption compounds'. They are built for a specific international market separated from domestic property markets, and physically distinct and impressive.

Examples of projects aimed at capturing production activities include those in Yokohama and Shanghai. Yokohama's Minato Mirai 21 extends over 110 ha costing $20 billion, and offering office and convention centres. The competition in Shanghai is the 90 ha Pudong project. In both cases, as well as building communication centres, business meeting places and business tourist centres, the projects seek to attract publicity through arts festivals and international events. The festival 'market place' is an important part of the large project. In addition to cultural activity, buildings also have to have strong aesthetic appeal if they are to compete successfully in global competition.

The small world of architects and planners is very important in the global positioning of development products. And some planning ideas have a global currency and 'work like a charm'. For example, Richard Rogers' proposals for the Pudong development in Shanghai claim a direct inheritance from Jane Jacobs, creating a 24 hour balanced development. What is forgotten is that Jacobs favoured the small scale rather than the mega project (Olds, 1995).

## Euralille

In 1994 the architect Rem Koolhaas said that 'At the moment (Lille) is an unimportant city'. However, the arrival of the TGV brings a 'virtual community' of 50 to 70 million within an 90 minutes of the city. According to the project's designer: 'It has been quite difficult to identify, for ourselves and for our client, whether this was a project for Lille or for this virtual community'. The development is ... 'a new wave of

*Figure 10.1*
Euralille, France.
The entrance to the shopping mall.

modernization which has to coexist with the historical decor, but which has nothing to do with it' (quoted in Popham, 1994). The existing city is reduced to 'historical decor'; the locals are offered the spectacle of watching trains go by.

The Euralille project was conceived at the end of the 1980s. The city of Lille promoted itself as a European city; the new Euralille commercial centre targeted international business visitors, financial services and international and regional shoppers. At the end of 1995 the city joined another international competition for the 2004 Olympic Games.

Having secured the TGV interchange in 1987, the conurbation-wide Urban Community (CUDL) developed ideas for a large commercial centre to be built over the station. The Euralille project was one of a number of development projects across the conurbation aimed at developing economic potential (Newman and Thornley, 1995). The development aimed to exploit its cross-roads location and to capture international conference and exhibition business. One office tower offered accommodation to international business, and another provided headquarters accommodation for a national bank. Attached to the offices, a large commercial centre provided a regional shopping centre, but also hoped to attract a large number of international shoppers from Belgium and England. Some of the original ideas for Euralille were scaled down in response to the views of the local 'greens', and some open space was included as part of the development project. Euralille makes a significant contribution to the office and commercial centre of the conurbation. Its significance also lies in its marketing, and in the contribution the development itself has made to the international promotion of the conurbation.

Publicity and promotion were integrated into the project in a number of ways. An internationally recognized architect was appointed to the project; French development and architectural experts were co-opted onto a consultative committee; and foreign banks were included as nominal partners in the development company formed to oversee the project (Newman and Thornley, 1995). The TGV station and the exhibition centre were completed ahead of the main development, and potential tenants of the commercial space could thus be drawn to Lille. Promotion was a vital part of a largely speculative development in which most of the risk rested on the public sector. The largely publicly owned Euralille development company acquired the land, and public money funded transport interconnections and other infrastructure. The bank, Credit Lyonnais, built their own office tower, but the remainder of the commercial space was speculative. The World Trade Centre competes for the same international business as Birmingham or Stuttgart. The shopping centre is in competition with other regional and international centres such as Cité Europe outside Calais. Marketing and promotion were clearly important to the commercial success of the project. The Euralille project also focused international attention on the conurbation. The change of image from one of industrial dereliction to a centre of service sector growth and modern communications has enabled the conurbation to compete in other international competitions.

The project stands adjacent to the centre of the old city, but in style separates itself from it. For Koolhass it is 'a piece of Japan set down in Lille'. The international business part of the project has little to offer the old city. The hypermarket is well located on public transport, but local traffic is underground. The TGVs run on the surface as a visible sign of the international status of the city. The commercial centre, like all such developments, is clean, secure and policed. Out of sight are the large housing estates typical of French city planning, with high levels of unemployment and giving rise to periodic riots. The new 'market place' needs its security. After the regional shopping centre opened at La

*Figure 10.2*
Euralille, France.
The office tower for Credit Lyonnais.

Défense, rival gangs from the suburbs used it as a meeting place. There is no chance of unwanted visitors in modern shopping centres.

The project turns away from the old city to the flows of trains and financial and commercial information. The marketing of the project had a local as well as an international audience. The mayor spoke of a *turbine tertiare*, associating images of the industrial past with a dynamic new city. The legitimacy of the project rests on the popularity of the mayor. He has considerable influence and reputation, being a former prime minister, a senator, president of the conurbation planning authority, and president of the development company that built the centre. Local and party loyalties ensure his continuing support. However, political support depends on successful projects, and maintenance of the dynamic images of modernization and success. The Olympic candidature of the city helps to sustain the political regime by looking forward to new horizons, new jobs and services trickling down to the local population.

## Seine Rive Gauche

Seine Rive Gauche is the last of a series of mega projects in Paris. During the 1980s the city considered many alternatives for the sites along the river in eastern Paris, including grounds for an Olympic Games. The decisive factor influencing the decision to build a large office complex was concern about the competitive position of the city in relation to its European rivals (Technopolis International, 1993). European and international competition became a dominant theme in city policy at the end of the 1980s. The comprehensive development plan (PAZ) for Seine Rive Gauche was approved by the city council in 1991, and included 900 000 m² of offices, making a substantial contribution to the office stock and the capacity of the city to attract international business. The city set up a development agency to manage the project and guaranteed loans amounting to Fr. 1.2bn to undertake expensive engineering works. However, potential investors (including Société Générale, the regional council, the University, and the Ministry of the Interior) subsequently withdrew their original interest in taking office space in Seine Rive Gauche. The bank, Société Générale, are developing two office towers at La Défense rather than locate in Paris. The property crisis has had damaging effects on the development. The detailed planning was undertaken during the late 1980s property boom. Since then the market has slumped. Seine Rive Gauche is on the other side of the city from the prime office locations in the golden triangle, and other suburban centres at La Défense and Roissy have large rival supplies of office space.

However, the project was not to be all offices, and APUR (Atelier Parisien d'Urbanisme, the city planning agency) proposed mixing the large office element with other uses to create a better balanced new 'quarter' of the city. The idea of the quarter was deployed to avoid political hostility to another vast office centre, and to help in its marketing. The new quarter would, according to its publicity, have the mix of uses and the liveliness and character of other parts of the city already firmly imprinted in the international imagination. The plan proposed 520 000 m² of housing, two-thirds of which would attract state housing subsidies (SEMAPA, 1993). The new population was estimated to reach 15 000; 50 000 jobs were to be created, and a large student population was to be generated by location of new university buildings on the site. The new quarter was to be serviced by a new public transport interchange linking metro and RER services, and these projects are programmed in the expenditure plans of both state and regional government. The development company (SEMAPA) commissioned numerous urban design studies of the possibilities for revitalizing the area around Austerlitz station, which was to remain in its location close to the city centre, with the greater part of the railway track and rail yards outside the station being decked over to make the bulk of the large development site.

At the centre of the site is the new national library. The library was a late addition to the planning of the quarter, and was planned independently by advisors to the President. Other locations, including some in suburban Paris, had been examined, but the city council eventually persuaded the President to accept a site within the project for redeveloping the south-east sector. The benefits for the city's plans for Seine Rive Gauche were that the new library would bring an early start to development activity, and secure the new transport links and developer confidence in the possibility of a new quarter of the city developing among the vast railway lands to the south east of the city. The PAZ therefore set out a mixture of land uses, with office development concentrated along a central boulevard – Avenue de France – running the length of the site.

The opening of the library in 1997 provides the opportunity to start the first phase of development and attach it to the library development. A social housing scheme for 350 subsidized flats was started in 1994. Nine hundred and fifty units are planned. A small office development will also be built in this location, together with open spaces and other facilities. The new Météor underground railway connection is due to be complete by 1998.

The idea of the 'quarter', with a mix of cultural activity and a university as well as a small resident population, appeals to international investors. However, for the resident population living immediately to the west of the project, the scheme failed to take the opportunities to meet local and city-wide needs. Local organizations argued for more social housing and more open space. They were relatively successful in delaying the project while the courts considered the argument about open space. A further crucial objection was to the central boulevard. While development of the railway lands would offer the potential of access to the river, the boulevard effectively cut it off. The new international population would have that access and views, but the population of the 13th arrondissement behind the project would gain little. A further concern was that new public transport links would stop at the new development, giving it good service into central Paris but denying that to the neighbouring communities.

The city overcame the bulk of these objections and survived various legal challenges. The city of Paris is a rich and, in many respects, autonomous local government organization. The strategy of the Chirac regime since 1977 involved a gradual remodelling of the eastern part of the city, with the effect of decreasing working class jobs and working class residents. For over a decade this strategy was successful in political terms in that the regime gathered more and more council seats at the periodic elections. The regime also built up the international prestige of the city and of its mayor as an international political figure (Haegel, 1994). The governing regime also had influential connections to national government. Following the 1993 national election the mayor of the 13th arrondissement became minister of culture, and thus responsible for the library project. He was also a close ally of Chirac and president of SEMAPA. However, the regime has come under attack, and its ability to carry through the Seine Rive Gauche project is less certain. The city lost its mayor in 1995, and Chirac's political successors were unable to continue previous electoral successes in the local elections that year. Many seats in eastern Paris were taken by opposition parties. One of the election issues was the redevelopment policy of the regime. Since that election, Seine Rive Gauche has been challenged by the new city council opposition. Concessions have been made, and the project director and the new mayor now favour a less commercial, more flexible approach to development. The market has also continued to undermine the original plans. The large loans have to be renegotiated. Office development is not so lucrative. One sale of office development to a pension fund in 1995 was made at Fr 10 500 per m$^2$ less than the target for office space set by SEMAPA in 1991. Such a reduction in price could not be borne on 900 000 m$^2$. The opposition parties on the city council want to see more cultural uses on the sites – university extensions, workshops, development related to the library. But such a mix of uses will not produce the revenue that the engineering works for the mega project require.

## King's Cross

In London, by contrast, under Thatcherism large development projects had to be privately financed (at least in rhetoric). However, it was the same pressures of competition and the desire to capture international flows of business information that drove land-owners and developers to bring forward a large commercial project for King's Cross railway land at the end of the 1980s. The London case is geographically similar to Seine Rive Gauche – vast areas of railway land and underused warehousing – but in every other way the stories are different. Edwards (1992) describes the development consortium's proposals and Newman (1990) the privatized planning process. The developer's international architect led the way. Public planning was weak strategically following abolition of the GLC and locally because of the inability of the borough council to produce strong planning guidelines. In the event, the large office-led project failed, largely because of the collapse of the commercial property market in London in the early 1990s. Uncertainty about the government's plans for the international station at King's Cross also weakened the viability of the project.

At various moments, opposition groups representing local community interests put forward alternative proposals, but the significant change came about as a result of changes in government policy towards urban regeneration. Political opposition in the London boroughs had been effectively eliminated in the 1980s. By the early 1990s the boroughs could be brought back in to play some role in regeneration. The market was weak, and needed encouragement. Community groups could also be brought back in. However, this new inclusive style of planning was on the government's terms. There had first to be adherence to the fundamental principle of developing and promoting London as a world city (Coopers and Lybrand Deloitte 1991; DoE, 1993; London Pride Partnership, 1995). Secondly, any government funding would be available only to projects that achieved the government targets. These ranged from economic targets concerned with training to changing or balancing housing tenure. The new government urban policy initiatives from 1991 onwards were tightly controlled. The Single Regeneration Budget programme is managed through detailed contracts.

In this context new plans for King's Cross railway lands emerged. The project 'King's Cross. A New Quarter for London' won £37.5 million of funding in 1995. The project proposed safeguarding or creating 2 700 jobs, training opportunities for 5 300 residents, and 1.4 million m$^2$ of new commercial development. The project had a new geographical shape. The previous plan was concerned only with exploiting the potential of the railway land. The 'new quarter' proposal is concerned with the surrounding area of hotels and council estates, and we should expect a better integration of social objectives than in the restricted physical boundaries of the earlier proposals. There is also a much broader-based consortium behind the project, including local community interests. But given the government's overriding international objectives, key elements have not changed. The project aims to create a 'gateway' for international visitors. Hotels are to be created, and existing hotels that house homeless families turned back to tourist accommodation. A new centre for community facilities and a hostel for homeless young people is located at the back of the area out of sight of the international traffic. Some community projects are existing commitments repackaged in the plan for the new 'quarter'. There is to be a 27 camera CCTV system. What is being created is a new tame zone, which will 'enhance London's role as a world city' and in which people will be 'better trained and more prosperous, better housed, healthier and more secure'. A large part of the former office project area is excluded, waiting for the market to pick up.

## Conclusions

The European response to globalization has been to create new international projects, but with perhaps more public control and public finance than in other parts of the globe. But the desire everywhere is to create new secure tame zones. The mega projects have, however, run into market and political difficulties. The weakness of the office market

where offices were underneath flats led to these being rejected, as they prove unpopular with potential residential occupants. Vertical segregation was favoured, as this also allowed some flats to be sold on the private market.

The final mix sees 40% of the space for flats and 60% for office/industry and services. Play areas and a kindergarten are included, and housing includes 185 student apartments and a 120 bed hotel, as well as a restaurant, bars and a hall for parties and concerts.

*Figure 10.9*
Pelikan-Viertel, Hanover. The market place at the centre of the scheme, with Harry's bar underneath offices in converted buildings

# Chapter 11

# Mixed Use Development: Some Conclusions

The patterns of how we live our lives affect the patterns of physical development. Changes in the physical arrangement of buildings and infrastructure are relatively slow – it takes time and money to remove existing structures and replace them, or to add new ones to the existing volume of development. Changing the use to which existing structures are put can also take time. We have planning rules to control many of these changes, and there is inertia in the system, created by the hope that the previous use may still be viable in the future – a hope held sometimes by the planners, and sometimes by the buildings' owners.

It is clear that major change has taken place in recent decades, which affects the physical disposition and uses of buildings, and further change is likely to continue for several more decades. Technology, family and social arrangements, and employment patterns as well as many other aspects of our lives are radically different today from 20 or 30 years ago. Some changes have been sudden, as new technologies introduce new opportunities instantly available to all. Others take greater time to permeate society, but may, over time, have just as significant an effect.

As Chapter 2 shows, the pattern of the way we mix land uses has changed over centuries in significant ways. The reasons why systems of control were introduced to remove certain uses related to a period when many industrial activities were potentially or actually dangerous for the residential population who lived in close proximity to these activities. The development of commerce and clerical jobs around the same time that the railways developed led to cities' expanding dramatically into the open land around them. The same period of technological development saw a greater move from rural to urban areas as agriculture needed fewer and fewer workers, while industries continued to develop and expand. Wholly residential areas were built and, as industry developed, so too did industrial estates. In the centre of many of the larger cities residential populations were displaced by increasing densities of commercial activity.

However, as Chapter 4 explains, these city economies have continued to change. Employment in manufacturing industry has continued to fall over the past two decades. The location of much of the remaining manufacturing activity is no longer where it once was in the city – either in the centre or on the fringe. Instead of relating to rail networks and local markets, industry relies on fast road connections with warehousing, airports and ports. This favours edge-of-city or greenfield locations with good motorway links. The workforce can reach these locations because car ownership is now so high and still economically viable. They are also favoured by many commercial office users, relocating or developing on business parks located next to motorway connections. In the Netherlands these locations are strategically planned by being linked to public transport infrastructure, allowing the workforce easy access by other means than the private car (Faludi in Breheny, 1992). In Britain this is seldom if ever the case, so most staff use private cars.

The reasons why different land uses are not mixed together, even today, are in part the same that they have been for many years. Some activities still demand physical isolation – or at least separation – from others; particularly residential uses. However, this is generally less true than once was the case; the industries that remain in the UK, or which are developing currently, are often cleaner and quieter than those that have gone, and many are perfectly capable of being located close to residential areas.

Chapter 5 shows that the development and investment industry often prefers a fragmented approach. Developers usually build one type of structure: housing, offices or shops. They are advised by companies with expertise in a particular part of the market, with little knowledge or interest in the other parts. The funding investors prefer a 'clean' invest-ment, preferably with a single tenant: certainly with a majority use. Many tenants also prefer to occupy an identifiably separate building, with no contact or interference from other users.

However, there is less justification for some of these reasons than has been the case in the past, and, as the sustainability and crime chap-ters have shown, there are good reasons for moving in a different direction in future. In fact, as many of our examples and case studies illustrate, there have been many moves in a different direction. Many city centres have a greater residential population than only a few years ago. Con-cerns have been expressed and policy initiatives taken to address many of the issues of viability and vitality of town and city centres.

Many of these changes are not having a dramatic effect. The exist-ence of the out-of-town and edge-of-town shopping centres and superstores has been considerable, and will continue to affect existing centres. The expansion of car use has been significant, and projections all point to its continuing. However, there are trends that suggest that this may not be a permanent situation. Throughout North America and Europe attempts are being made to limit car use. In the UK too this is being attempted by a few local authorities, although the opportunity to use public investment for such projects is very limited. However, car-free centres are being expanded (as in Cambridge), and park-and-ride schemes are becoming more carefully developed, expanded and targeted at long-stay parking requirements.

In Europe as a whole there are car-sharing schemes – 230 cities have some 15,000 subscribers. In the UK no scheme has yet been established, although it is under consideration in Edinburgh. Our research has shown, contrary to our initial expectations, that car ownership and use by city centre residents is significantly less than the national average. This contrasts with locations that in other ways offer very similar residential accommodation, but which are not close to the city centre. Here car use is greater than the national average.

Small but significant technological changes will continue to have an impact on the vitality debate. As an example, technology in banking has had a significant effect on patterns of activity that has yet to be fully appreciated. The advantage of encouraging town centre shopping trips is that they are linked trips (Safeway, 1995). This means that only one journey can serve a number of purposes, thus reducing car use and

*Figure 11.1*
Little Britain, the City of London.
Soon to be converted to housing, these old commercial premises would have been swept away for office development until very recently.

sequent emissions. One of the frequently cited reasons for going to a town or city centre is to go to a bank (or building society, which is in effect a bank). However, banks are introducing automatic telling machines, which can do a great deal more than just issue cash: they can receive payments, transfer funds between accounts, and issue information about account balances. Increasingly these telling machines are being sited in out-of-town and edge-of-town stores.

Tele-banking is also developing fast. This allows the financial institution to be located anywhere in the country, at a location convenient for recruiting the staff needed to operate the service at as low a cost to the bank as possible. Telecommunications developments allow that to be almost anywhere, so many of these new operations are located in the business parks mentioned above, or in towns where land is cheap and unemployment high, often therefore in the north of England. Similar developments can be observed in the retail insurance business, where car, house and life assurance policies are increasingly issued by tele-insurance companies (frequently owned by larger companies), like the tele-banking companies, in unexpected locations.

Both these developments mean that the need to go into town either to transact business connected with personal accounts or to visit an insurance broker has reduced considerably. As building societies have merged, so the number of branch offices has reduced. These changes are beyond the scope of 'control' by town planning – and it is hard to see why or how they should be controlled, offering as they do significant benefits for users. They are typical of many small but important ways in which patterns of activity alter, and of how these in turn impact on the need for facilities in different locations.

Urban sociology can show us much about the ways in which our patterns of activity have changed over recent years. As Chapter 6 noted, the ideas put forward by Jane Jacobs are one of the most enduring influences on the debate about mixed use development. Her view of the world – or how it could and should be – finds resonances in many political comments in the years since then. Her description of a community, where there is a mix of uses and complex relationships between the individuals who occupy those uses, has been very influential. She listed a number of 'generators of diversity', all of which she says must be fulfilled to ensure 'exuberant diversity in a city's streets and districts':

- The district, and indeed as many of its internal parts as possible, must serve more than one primary function; preferably more than two. These must ensure the presence of people who go outdoors on different schedules and are in the place for different purposes, but who are able to use many facilities in common.

- Most blocks must be short; that is, streets and opportunities to turn corners must be frequent.

- The district must mingle buildings that vary in age and condition, including a good proportion of old ones, so that the economic yield they produce varies. This mingling must be fairly close-grained.

- There must be a sufficiently dense concentration of people, for whatever purpose they may be there. This includes dense concentration in the case of people who are there because of residence.

Often, by implication if not by direct statement, commentators have noted that 'community isn't what it was'. This is a particularly common view in newspapers – the view that crime is now everywhere and only a few years ago doors were left open and anyone could call on everyone else in the street. This is more myth than reality. However, there are important social changes that in part have led to, or at least relate to, the changing mix of land uses.

Mobility is one key constituent of this change. Mobility by individuals over time around the country (or even around the world) has a significant effect. Mobility by individuals between home, work, leisure and other activities is equally important.

The idea of 'community' is an important one, which bears closer investigation. Many politicians believe that by encouraging the creation of mixed use developments they are creating new communities. John Gummer described the proposed mixed use project that will replace the Department of the Environment's Marsham Street headquarters as 'a new community for London'. But the term 'community' for many commentators implies involvement and responsibility, a mix of young and old, rich and poor. Most developments in the UK, whether they are

*Figure 11.2*
Clerkenwell, London.
A developer has acquired
7 acres of former commercial
property, and is converting it
to a mix of uses, including
residential use.

mixed use or single use, do not reflect this, and most developers are actively hostile to the idea that they should do so.

The recent concern of politicians to promote or support community is in many ways in contrast to the direction of other policies. Walmsley (1988) notes that community, when used as an ideology to mean what should be, rather than what is, is linked to notions of utopia. This came to prominence during the Industrial Revolution, when notions of communty were contrasted with individualism and with the atomization and alienation that went with an emphasis on private property and profit.

The belief that some idyllic village life is preferable to the alienation and degradation of urban life was noted in the introduction to this book. Many of those who call for mixed use development suggest that this will lead to a more village-like development, with inherent (although usually undefined) benefits. A government minister for planning, Robert Jones, speaking at the AGM of the Urban Villages Forum at the end of 1995, was quoted to say that

> One of the biggest modern problems ... is concern about the quality of urban living – the sense of anonymity and facelessness that many people have in all too many areas of our cities. In a society where people do not know their neighbours and where ties of the family have been weakened, the role of development was not just one of creating bricks and mortar, it was also about helping to recreate a sense of place and community

The Urban Villages Forum exists to sponsor the idea of mixed use urban development, and has received sponsorship from the government and English Partnerships. Ian Colquhoun, in his book on urban regeneration projects, summarizes the Urban Villages Forum's principles of development for urban villages (a phrase that, like mixed use development, is used by different people to mean different things, especially in the USA):

- Multi-use development in 40 ha (100 acre) neighbourhoods with a resident population of between 3 000 – 5 000.

- There should be mixed uses within each street block as well as within the village.

- Houses and flats should balance workspace so as to achieve a theoretical 1:1 ratio between jobs and residents able and willing to work.

- The development should cater for changing social trends, including increasing numbers of retired people and people working from home.

- The mixture of uses should be accommodated with a variety of sizes and types of building. In the more densely built-up heart of the urban village, preference should be given on ground floors to shops, restaurants, pubs, workshops, studios and other active uses which bring life to the buildings and the spaces in front of them.

- There should be a mixture of tenure for both housing and employment uses.

- The motor car should be accommodated, but not allowed to dominate the environment.

- Ecologically sound forms of development and energy generation should be an integral part of the design to produce a sustainable environment.

- Full public involvement needs to be positive, genuine and credible.

(Colquhoun, 1995)

*Figure 11.3*
Soho Mills, Bradford.
A housing association
conversion to provide
student flats in the city centre
from a former textile mill

This approach is not a wholly new one. After World War II the new towns were created with many similar aims. The chairman of the Stevenage Development Corporation made a speech in 1947 quoted in a local paper: 'We want to revive that social structure which existed in the old English village, where the rich lived next door to the not so rich and everyone knew everybody' (quoted in Pahl, 1970).

One of the main justifications offered by Michael Heseltine, as Secretary of State for the Environment, for the creation of the Urban Development Corporations in London and Merseyside was that they would 'balance' otherwise unbalanced communities. This was on the basis that the area at the time consisted predominantly of local authority housing, and that introducing professional and managerial workers into the area in owner-occupied housing would balance the community. Observers have noted that, far from balancing the community in any sense other than the purely statistical, the creation of significant up-market housing in the area has divided it socially and economically, creating no obvious benefits for the community who were already resident.

For over 50 years urban sociologists have been saying that these physical developments may not create the benefits that their supporters would wish. Ruth Glass made this point as long ago as 1948 in her book on Middlesbrough:

> It is not clear... why the resuscitation of village life within urban communities should be regarded as being so delightful and so progressive nor how it is to be accomplished....The mere shortening of the physical distance between different social groups can hardly bring them together unless, at the same time, the social distance between them is also reduced (Glass, 1948, quoted in Pahl, 1970, p.119).

The basic differences that were thought to exist between rural and urban residents are still implied in current government policies. Little difference can be found between Britain and the USA in this context. Redfield (1955), for example, sees rural society consisting of relatively small groups of people who know each other well, and who share exclusive, face-to-face interactions. They limit the number of contacts with people from outside their area; they are an inward-looking society, based on and bound up with a particular locality. Clearly it is still possible to find places where this description would fit, but many will have a parallel group of residents who have moved from other, usually urban, areas, who have little or no direct interaction with this group.

Urban life has been seen as intrinsically inferior by many, like Wirth (outlined in Gans, 1968), who describes a series of superficial relationships based on work, housing or a shared interest. This leads to superficiality and anonymity in urban living, with social or ethnic groups carving out their own geographical areas, breaking down the overall sense of society characterized by rural areas.

However, since the 1960s, rural areas have become far more reliant on the car, far less self-contained, and far more likely to have former urban residents moving in to share in their perceived benefits.

The development of many technological devices, and their widespread ownership, has led to significant changes in people's lifestyles. With dramatically increasing levels of home ownership, sociologists have observed and developed the concept of privatism. This can be seen to be true in both urban and rural locations. Kumar comments:

> We are rapidly becoming a home-centred society to an extent that must surprise even the sociologists of the 1950s and early 1960s (Kumar, 1986, quoted in Saunders, 1990).

Areas change, but our expectations and images of the areas may relate to an earlier version of reality. Young and Wilmott (1957) defined many people's idea of 'community' in their late 1950s study of Bethnal Green. The picture then was of a tight-knit group of people, who knew everyone else in their neighbourhood, were often related to them, and who could exchange favours and responsibilities as and when needed. Privacy, it was implied, would be hard to find in the area, but there would be little difficulty in borrowing the ubiquitous cup of sugar from a neighbour.

However, their study of Woodford, carried out soon after the Bethnal Green study, showed a very different picture. Their study of a newly settled council estate on the outskirts of London had already suggested that Bethnal Green might be different from other areas. Here they found:

> people cut off from relatives, suspicious of their neighbours, lonely; the atmosphere was very different from the warmth and friendliness of Bethnal Green (Wilmott and Young, 1960).

But Woodford was different again. Here they found a friendliness and support networks that were in some ways similar to those in Bethnal Green. But while in Bethnal Green that supporting, almost enveloping community spirit was universal, in Woodford it was far more selective. It was related to groups of friends with common interests or activities: clubs and activities related to child rearing or religion. And the findings in Woodford can be said to reflect the way in which most parts of Britain have moved:

> Higher incomes mean that class divisions are no longer so securely based upon the structure of the workplace; the new divisions are based more upon consumption standards... All classes in Woodford are more and more striving to earn more and spend it on the same things, in and around the home and the little car that goes with it (Wilmott and Young, 1960, p.115).

Anthea Holme's re-survey of Bethnal Green in the 1980s showed that here, too, significant changes had taken place. She comments on how home-centred people had by then become:

> The corollary in Bethnal Green to this new home-centredness was the emptiness of the streets and corridors and staircases in the housing estates ... no longer could it be said that people in Bethnal Green were (in Young and Wilmott's words) 'vigorously at home in the street' (Holme, 1985, quoted in Saunders, (1990).

What has occurred in terms of changed residential patterns in the past few years is complex. In the USA the gentrification of city centres and the return of a residential population is actively encouraged in many cases as a way of privatizing inner-city renewal (Williams, 1984, quoted in Walmsley, 1988, p.122). In the UK it would be hard to identify any such explicit policy until very recently, except perhaps in the case of London Docklands. But clearly the re-use and conversion of buildings for residential use on the fringes of the central business districts of several UK cities is significant.

Our research shows that some of these new inner city residents are

*Figure 11.4*
Mezzo, Soho, London.
A converted warehouse (later used as the Marquee club) now has London's biggest restaurant underneath luxury flats in the heart of Soho.

creating new communities. They vary considerably in style; some know their neighbours, share their responsibilities for property, and interact on more than a cursory level. These are entirely within housing rented either from the local authority or a housing association.

Other groups of residents are no more than that. Many are temporary or part-time occupants of the housing. They do not, for the most part, know each other, so they do not take responsibility for any collective aspect of their housing. They fit in with Webber's idea of 'community without propinquity'. The residents of this housing do have friends, contacts, a complex social life, but one unrelated to the location of their housing. Toffler has noted this trend, pointing to the fact that, in the USA, from 1948, in every year at least 20% of the population changed their address (Toffler, 1970, p.78).

The development of communication technology has already been noted as a crucial component in the changes and choices now available to employers and employees in a wide range of service jobs. While the development of tele-banking and other services in hitherto unthinkable locations is one part of the story, the opportunity for individuals to use tele-cottaging is equally important.

Many writers have noted the possible effects of the new technologies, and how employment patterns will change. Jenkins and Sherman (1979) initiated a debate on the future volume of work, and correctly predicted the likely impact in many areas. They failed, however, to predict the spatial effect of the dramatic increase in computing power, and the flexibility which that would offer employees.

Throughout the 1980s the idea of the city 'yuppy' was displaced by the concept of the 'telecottager', working from home on a powerful microcomputer, linked to others working in a similar way through fax, modem and perhaps video. The raw information which such workers would manipulate (accounts, facts, material for editing) would be available through the internet, from information libraries or on CD-Rom. Home could therefore be anywhere, and the image developed of the executive, working from home, living in the depths of the Welsh, Cornish or Scottish countryside.

However, there is a different and perhaps more likely scenario. Why should such a development not occur in a similar manner, but in the city? The advantages of the technological links are identical, but with the additional benefits of easily reached facilities, other similar workers to share experiences with in close proximity, easy access to any repairs to equipment, potential for eating out, seeing a film, viewing an exhibition. For some the benefits associated with the countryside will still be a powerful draw, but for many others, (particularly, it could be argued, the younger, childless individuals or couples), the city offers a much more attractive range of opportunities. The Henley Centre report confirms this:

> In the 1980s growth in the number of 16–24 year olds, who are more attracted to cities, helped to slow the rate of de-urbanization. Data from the Henley Centre Planning for Social Change survey showed

that young people want to live near facilities that are most commonly found in the urban environment – entertainment and sporting facilities for example. Accordingly it is not surprising that the same survey showed that young people have a more positive attitude to city life in general (Henley Centre, 1994).

This occupation of parts of our cities by younger people is not as new a phenomenon as we may think. Pahl (1970) observes that the 1951 census showed that the centre and West End of Greater London showed:

> a very high proportion of young people aged 20–24 – between 30 and 40 percent above the Greater London average – and a very low proportion of young children – in the case of Westminster 40 percent less than the Greater London average.

Our research shows that this is as true as it was 40 years ago – and really this should not be a surprise. The proportion of the population who are not involved in child rearing is more than those who are. These people are the ones who are most likely to be attracted to the new, vibrant, mixed use areas in our cities. They will not necessarily be young people; a proportion of the 'empty nesters' whose children have left home (or those who never had children) will also find positive aspects in living in a location that allows access to a wide variety of activities and facilities.

Changes to existing town and cities that result in unwanted offices or shops should not be seen as necessarily wholly a bad thing. Change is inevitable, and no pattern of development is immutable. Abandoned areas of cities and towns are a wasted asset, but flexible and positive planning policies, which acknowledge that other uses will have to be identified, can turn a perceived negative situation into an opportunity. Areas that were once residential were developed and incorporated into shopping streets. Now, as shopping patterns alter and demand for space reduces (at least in these locations), there is no reason why these should not once again become residential locations.

The trick is to return these areas to a useful function which offers more than just one use. It is difficult, but by no means impossible to design housing, employment facilities, places to shop and to eat, to en oy culture, films, music, nightclubs and other facilities in ways which do not affect each other in negative ways, but which offer the greatest ange of opportunities to as many residents and visitors in as enjoyable and sustainable a way as possible.

In 1970 the American Institute of Architects commissioned a report on the future of cities. It concluded that government-stimulated rebuilding investment was crucial:

> Without such new stimulus, downtown cannot be restored to middle-class economic viability of any kind remotely approaching a natural order. Its residential populations will be wealthy (especially in apartments as second homes), childless, or poor; and its business populations will be limited to the servicing of a constantly narrowing arc of commercial activity (McCue and Ewald, 1970).

Our research shows that much the same could be said of many of the UK's cities today. Residents are reclaiming the city, but they are predominantly wealthy (and often occupying second or company-owned homes), childless, or poor. The flight of the middle-income family with children to the lower-density suburbs continues *en masse*. Communities of mutual interest replace geographical communities. Rising standards of living continue a preference of private over public transport, so that the hopes of reducing emissions may be forlorn without introducing policies that result in a radical change in travelling patterns. Creating

*Figure 11.5*
County Hall, London. One of the largest office-to-residential conversion undertaken to date: the inland block of County Hall, the former offices of the GLC , is now 411 luxury flats.

more, or higher-density mixed use development may do little to change this situation. A more radical approach will be needed to intensify the densities of existing suburban and rural towns, as well as mixing more uses where currently monopoly uses exist. These will be harder to achieve, and politically even more contentious than the policies introduced so far.

New government policies can help: the Planning Policy Guidance Note 6 on *Town Centres and Retail Development* was revised in June 1996. It goes further than any previous statrement: not only is diversity of use encouraged, but so too is the idea of creting planning briefs for mixed use areas and encouraging occupation of flats over shops. Planners are told to take:

> a pro-active role with owners to try to identify new uses for vacant buiildings, especially vacant office buildings in town centres that may be suitable for cenversion to other uses, such as flats or hostels (DoE, 1996a).

They are also encouraged to promote mixed use developments that provide additional housing and create lively street frontages.

This degree of support for mixed use development is unprecedented. It is supported by the draft revisions to PPG1, the guidance on the *General Policy and Principles* of planning, published in July 1996. This dramatically changes the basis for planning that has been published before, by putting sustainability as the basis for the UK planning system, and mixed use as a way of delivering this:

> Local planning authorities should include policies in their develop-ment plans to promote mixed uses in appropriate places, particularly in town centres and other areas well served by public transport as well as in areas of major new development (DoE, 1996b).

The guidance goes on to suggest how local authorities might include these policies, and to encourage the creation of urban villages where they can be established. It also supports the use of detailed planning briefs.

As earlier chapters have explained, this may not be easy. Developers are unable or unwilling to proceed with mixed uses in many circumstances. But their protest may be contradicted by their actions. Chapter 8 explained how Camden Council's planning policies on mixed use were objected to by a range of developers as being too rigid and unreasonable. Among those objectors were British Land, Sun Alliance and the Property arm of the National Westminster Bank. But British Land have been willing to negotiate the purchase of the freehold and shops in the Gillingham Street scheme (Chapter 6). The Sun Alliance were recorded as paying a remarkable rent of over £700 per square metre for their new offices above a new Marks and Spencer store in the City of London, and the National Westminster Bank are completing a new building in Covent Garden which complies with Westminster Council's policies by providing a mix of retailing and residential accommodation as well.

Getting a horizontal mix may not be as easy as getting uses in separate blocks. This is the arrangement that even historic mixed use estates like Howard deWalden are trying to achieve, to minimize the disturbance between users. But properly designed (and with new-build schemes there are no good reasons to do anything badly), even horizontal mixes can be created.

Our examination of German practice suggests that mixing uses may be neither as widespread nor as universally popular as we might imagine. There is some evidence to suggest that for a variety of reasons mainland European attitudes may be moving more towards UK views. But again,

*Figure 11.6*
64 Buckingham Gate, Victoria, London.
Very occasionally UK developers have mixed uses horizontally. Here is a tower with the Rolls Royce showroom on the ground floor, seven floors of offices with its plant above, then seven floors of apartments above that.

there are examples of projects that continue to attract developers and finance where they are required to create a mix of uses, just as there are even larger and more impressive US schemes.

Cities are about interaction between people. The bigger cities offer greater choice of interaction, and an increased liklihood of meeting people who share interests or activities: the bigger the city, the more esoteric the interest that can be sustained. The convenience of having those choices – the choice of 23 different cruisines in the same street – can only be provided where there is a critical mass of people who can choose between what is on offer.

By mixing land uses choice can be increased: the opportunity to live, work, recreate, all within a short (and ideally walking) distance is something that has not been available in many cities in the recent past, but which is once again on offer in an increasing number. Mixing uses can also increase the convenience with which these choices can be experienced: more shops and restaurants are starting to make city centres, even the centre of the City of London, more civilized and interesting places to visit, and to spend more time in. Better cultural and entertainment facilities can make the experience of the city even more rewarding. The property market is starting to appreciate this; the planning system can encourage the market in the right direction. Mixed use development is no panacea, but its contribution to continuing to improve towns and cities should not be underestimated.

*Figure 11.7*
Quartier 205, Friedrichstadt Passagen, Berlin.
A new major development in the city centre, US funded by Tishman Speyer Properties, with three floors of shops and restaurants, offices over that and 40 luxury apartments on the top three floors.

## References

Breheny, M. (1992) *Sustainable Development and Urban Form*, Pion, London.

Colquhoun, I. (1995) *Urban Regeneration*, Batsford, London.

Department of the Environment (1996a) *Planning Policy Guidance Note 6: Town Centres and Retail Developments,* HMSO, London.

Department of the Environment (1996b) *Consultation Draft on Planning Policy Guidance Note 1: General Policy and Principles.*

Gans, H.J. (1970) *People and Plans,* Penguin, Harmondsworth

Gummer, J. (1996) at *London in the 21st Century*, Central Hall Westminster, 17 January.

Henley Centre for Forecasting (1994) *Local Futures 94: Prospects for Local Markets After the Recession.*

Jacobs. J. (1961) *The Death and Life of Great American Cities*, Penguin, Harmondsworth.

Jenkins, C. and Sherman, B. (1979) *The Collapse of Work,* Eyre Methuen, London.

Jones, R.(1996) in *Estates Gazette*, 20 January, p70.

McCue, G.M. and Ewald, W. (1970) *Creating The Human Environment,* University of Illinois Press, Chicago, IL.

Pahl, R.E. (1970) *Patterns of Urban Life*, Longman, London.

Redfield, R. (1955) *Peasant Society and Culture,* University of Chicago Press, Chicago IL.

Safeway (1995) *Traffic & Parking at Food Retailing*, TRICS/JMP Consultants, London.

Saunders, P. (1990) *A Nation of Home Owners*, Unwin Hyman, London

Toffler, A. (1970) *Future Shock*, Pan Books, London.

Walmsley, D.J. (1988) *Urban Living; The Individual In The City*, Longman, London.

Young, P. and Willmott, D. (1957) *Family and Kinship in East London*, Routledge & Kegan Paul, London.

Willmott, D. and Young, P. (1960) *Family and Class in a London Suburb*, Routledge & Kegan Paul, London.

# Index

Illustrations numbered in bold
Tables numbered in italics